COLLECTED WHEEL PUBLICATIONS

VOLUME 7

NUMBERS 90 – 100

BPE

BPS Pariyatti Editions

BPS Pariyatti Editions
An imprint of Pariyatti Publishing
www.pariyatti.org

Although this is an American edition, we have left any British spelling of words unchanged.

First BPS Pariyatti Edition, 2020
ISBN: 978-1-68172-148-4 (Print)
ISBN: 978-1-68172-149-1 (PDF)
ISBN: 978-1-68172-150-7 (ePub)
ISBN: 978-1-68172-151-4 (Mobi)
LCCN: 2018940050

Contents

WH 90 to 92 The Life of Sāriputta
Nyanaponika Thera 1

WH 93 The Eight Marvellous and Wonderful Truths
Bhikkhu Khantipālo 79

WH 94 The Truth of Anattā
Dr. G. P. Malalasekera 105

WH 95 to 97 Sixty Songs of Milarepa
Garma C.C. Chang 129

WH 98 & 99 Apaṇṇaka Sutta, Cūla Māluṅkya Sutta, Upāli Sutta
Nārada Thera, Mahinda Thera 217

WH 100 Buddhism in Sri Lanka
H. R. Perera 271

Key to Abbreviations

A	Aṅguttara Nikāya	Paṭis	Paṭisambhidamagga
Ap	Apadāna	Peṭ	Peṭakopadesa
Bv	Buddhavaṃsa	S	Saṃyutta Nikāya
Cp	Cariyāpiṭaka	Sn	Suttanipāta
D	Dīgha Nikāya	Th	Theragātha
Dhp	Dhammapada	Thī	Therigātha
Dhs	Dhammasaṅgaṇī	Ud	Udāna
It	Itivuttaka	Vibh	Vibhaṅga
Ja	Jātaka verses and commentary	Vin	Vinaya-piṭaka
Khp	Khuddakapāṭha	Vism	Visuddhimagga
M	Majjhima Nikāya	Vism-mhṭ	Visuddhimagga Sub-commentary
Mil	Milindapañha	Vv	Vimānavatthu
Nett	Nettipakaraṇa	Nidd	Niddesa

The above is the abbreviation scheme of the Pali Text Society (PTS) as given in the *Dictionary of Pali* by Margaret Cone.

The commentaries, *aṭṭhakathā*, are abbreviated by using a hyphen and an "a" ("-a") following the abbreviation of the text, e.g., *Dīgha Nikāya Aṭṭhakathā* = D-a. Likewise the sub-commentaries are abbreviated by a "ṭ" ("-ṭ") following the abbreviation of the text.

The sutta reference abbreviation system for the four Nikāyas, as is used in Bhikkhu Bodhi's translations is:

AN	Aṅguttara Nikāya	DN	Dīgha Nikāya
MN	Majjhima Nikāya	Sn	Saṃyutta Nikāya
J	Jātaka story	Mv	Mahāvagga (Vinaya Piṭaka)
Cv	Cullavagga (Vinaya Piṭaka)	SVibh	Suttavibhaṅga (Vinaya Piṭaka)

The Life of Sāriputta

Compiled and translated from the Pāli texts by

Nyanaponika Thera

WHEEL PUBLICATION NO. 90/91/92

Prologue

In many temples of Sri Lanka you will find on either side of the Buddha image the statues of two monks. Their robes are draped over one shoulder and they stand in the attitude of reverence, with joined palms. Quite often there are a few flowers at their feet, laid there by some pious devotee.

If you ask who they are, you will be told that they are the Enlightened One's two chief disciples, the arahats Sāriputta and Mahā Moggallāna. They stand in the positions they occupied in life, Sāriputta on the Buddha's right, Mahā Moggallāna on his left. When the great stupa at Sāñchī was opened up in the middle of the 19th century, the relic chamber was found to contain two stone receptacles; the one to the north held the body relics of Mahā Moggallāna, while that on the south enclosed those of Sāriputta. Thus they had lain while the centuries rolled past and the history of two thousand years and more played out the drama of impermanence in human life. The Roman Empire rose and fell; the glories of ancient Greece became a distant memory; new religions wrote their names, often with blood and fire, on the changing face of the earth, only to mingle at last with legends of Thebes and Babylon; and gradually the tides of commerce shifted the great centres of civilisation from East to West, while generations that had never heard the Teaching of the Buddha arose and passed away. But all the time that the ashes of the saints lay undisturbed, forgotten in the land that gave them birth, their memory was held dear wherever the Buddha's message spread, and the record of their lives was passed down from one generation to another, first by word of mouth, then in the written pages of the Buddhist Tipiṭaka, the most voluminous and detailed scripture of any religion. Next to the Enlightened One himself, it is these two disciples of his who stand highest in the veneration of Buddhists in the Theravada lands. Their names are as inseparable from the annals of Buddhism as that of the Buddha himself. If it has come about that in the course of time many legends have been woven into the tradition of their lives, this is but the natural outcome of the devotion that has always been felt for them.

And that high esteem was fully justified. Few religious teachers have been so well served by their immediate disciples as was the Buddha. This you will see as you read these pages, for they tell the story of one of the two greatest of them, Sāriputta, who was second only to the Buddha in the depth and range of his understanding, and his ability to teach the Doctrine of Deliverance. In the Tipiṭaka there is no connected account of his life, but it can be pieced together from the various incidents, scattered throughout the canonical texts and commentaries, in which he figures. Some of them are more than incidents, for his life is so closely interwoven with the life and ministry of the Buddha that he plays an essential part in it, and on a number of occasions it is Sāriputta himself who takes the leading role—as skilled preceptor and exemplar, as kind and considerate friend, as guardian of the welfare of the bhikkhus under his charge, as faithful repository of his Master's doctrine, the function which earned him the title of *Dhammasenāpati,* Marshal of the Dhamma, and always as himself, a man unique in his patience and steadfastness, modest and upright in thought, word and deed, a man to whom one act of kindness was a thing to be remembered with gratitude so long as life endured. Even among the arahats, saints freed from all defilements of passion and delusion, he shone like the full moon in a starry sky.

This then is the man, of profound intellect and sublime nature, a true disciple of the Great Teacher, whose story we have set down, to the best of our ability, in the pages that follow. If you, the reader, can gather from this imperfect record something of the qualities of man perfected, of man fully liberated and raised to the highest level of his being; of how such a man acts and speaks and comports himself towards his fellows; and if the reading of it gives you strength and faith in the assurance of *what man may become,* then our work has been worthwhile, and is fully rewarded.

Part I

From Birth to the Attainment of Arahatship

The story begins at two brahminical villages in India, called Upatissa and Kolita, which lay not far from the city Rājagaha. Before our Buddha had appeared in the world, a brahmin lady named Sāri, living in Upatissa village, conceived; and also, on the same day at Kolita village, did another brahmin lady whose name was Moggallī. The two families were closely connected, having been friends with one another for seven generations. From the first day of their pregnancy the families gave due care to the mothers-to-be, and after ten months both women gave birth to boys, on the same day. On the name-giving day the child of the brahmin lady Sāri received the name Upatissa, as he was a son of the foremost family of that village; and for the same reason Moggallī's son was named Kolita.

When the boys grew up they were educated, and acquired mastery of all the sciences. Each of them had a following of five hundred brahmin youths, and when they went to the river or park for sport and recreation, Upatissa used to go with five hundred palanquins, and Kolita with five hundred carriages.

Now at Rājagaha there was an annual event called the Hilltop Festival. Seats were arranged for both youths and they sat together to witness the celebrations. When there was occasion for laughter, they laughed; when the spectacles were exciting, they became excited; and they paid their fees for the extra shows. In this manner they enjoyed the festival for a second day; but on the third day their understanding was awakened and they could no longer laugh or get excited, nor did they feel inclined to pay for extra shows as they had done on the first days. Each of them had the same thought, "What is there to look at here? Before these people have reached a hundred years they will all have come to death. What we ought to do is to seek for a teaching of deliverance."

It was with such thoughts in mind that they took their seats at the festival. Then Kolita said to Upatissa, "How is this, my dear Upatissa? You are not as happy and joyous as you were on the other days. You seem now to be in a discontented mood; what is on your mind?"

"My dear Kolita, to look at these things here is of no benefit at all. It is utterly worthless! I ought to seek a teaching of deliverance for myself. That, my Kolita, is what I was thinking, seated here. But you, Kolita, seem to be discontented, too."

And Kolita replied, "Just as you have said, I also feel." When he knew that his friend had the same inclinations, Upatissa said, "That was a good thought of ours. But for those who seek a teaching of deliverance there is only one thing to do: to leave home and become ascetics. But under whom shall we live the ascetic life?"

At that time, there lived at Rājagaha an ascetic of the sect of the Wanderers (*paribbājaka*) called Sañjaya, who had a great following of pupils. Deciding to get ordination under him, Upatissa and Kolita went there, each with his own following of five hundred brahmin youths and all of them received ordination from Sañjaya. And from the time of their ordination under him, Sañjaya's reputation and support increased abundantly.

Within a short time the two friends had learned Sañjaya's entire doctrine and they asked him, "Master, does your doctrine go so far only, or is there something beyond?"

Sañjaya replied, "So far only it goes. You know all."

Hearing this, they thought to themselves, "If that is the case, it is useless to continue the Holy Life under him. We have gone forth from home to seek a teaching of deliverance. Under him we cannot find it. India is vast, if we wander through villages, towns and cities we shall certainly find a master who can show us the teaching of deliverance." And after that, whenever they heard that there were wise ascetics or brahmins at this or that place, they went and discussed with them. But there was none who was able to answer their questions, while they were able to reply to those who questioned them.

Having thus travelled through the whole of India they turned back, and arriving at their old place, they agreed between them that he who should attain to the Deathless state first, should inform the other. It was a pact of brotherhood, born of the deep friendship between the two young men.

Some time after they had made that agreement, the Blessed One, the Buddha, came to Rājagaha. It was when he had delivered the Fire Sermon at Gāyā Peak that he remembered his promise, given before his Enlightenment to King Bimbisāra, that he would come to Rājagaha again when he had attained his goal. So in stages the Blessed One journeyed from Gāyā to Rājagaha, and having received from King Bimbisāra the Bamboo Grove Monastery (Veluvana), he resided there.

Among the sixty-one arahats (saints) whom the Master had sent forth to proclaim to the world the virtues of the Triple Gem, there was the Elder Assaji, who belonged to the group of five ascetics, the Buddha's erstwhile companions before his Enlightenment, and afterwards his first disciples. The Elder Assaji had returned to Rājagaha from his wanderings, when one morning, while he was going for alms in the city, he was seen by Upatissa, who was on his way to the Paribbājaka ascetics' monastery. Struck by Assaji's dignified and serene appearance, Upatissa thought, "Never before have I seen such a monk. He must be one of those who are arahats, or on the way to arahatship. Should I not approach him and ask, 'Under whom have you been ordained? Who is your teacher and whose teaching do you profess?'" But then he thought, "It is not the proper time now for putting questions to this monk, as he is going for alms through the streets. I had better follow behind him after the manner of supplicants." And he did so.

Then, when the Elder had gathered his alms food, and Upatissa saw him going to another place intending to sit down and take his meal, he prepared for him his own ascetic's seat that he carried with him and offered it to the Elder. The Elder Assaji took his meal, after which Upatissa served him with water from his own water-container, and in that way performed towards Assaji the duties of a pupil to a teacher.

After they had exchanged the usual courteous greetings, Upatissa said, "Serene are your features, friend. Pure and bright is your complexion. Under whom, friend, have you gone forth as an ascetic? Who is your teacher and whose doctrine do you profess?"

Assaji replied, "There is, O friend, the Great Recluse, the scion of the Sākyas, who has gone forth from the Sākya clan. Under that Blessed One I have gone forth. That Blessed One is my teacher and it is his Dhamma that I profess."

"What does the venerable one's master teach; what does he proclaim?"

Questioned thus, the Elder Assaji thought to himself, "These wandering ascetics are opposed to the Buddha's dispensation. I shall show him how profound this dispensation is." So he said, "I am but new to the training, friend. It is not long since I went forth from home, and I came but recently to this teaching and discipline. I cannot explain the Dhamma in detail to you."

The wanderer replied, "I am called Upatissa, friend. Please tell me according to your ability, be it much or little. It will be my task to penetrate its meaning by way of a hundred or a thousand methods." And he added:

"Be it little or much that you can tell,
The meaning only, please proclaim to me!
To know the meaning is my sole desire;
Of no avail to me are many words."

In response, the Elder Assaji uttered this stanza:

"Of all those things that from a cause arise,
Tathāgata the cause thereof has told;
And also how they cease to be:
This is the doctrine of the Great Recluse." [1]

Upon hearing the first two lines, Upatissa became established in the Path of stream-entry, and to the ending of the last two lines he already listened as a stream-winner. When he became a stream-winner, and before he had achieved the higher attainments, he thought, "Here will the means of deliverance be found!" and he said to the Elder, "Do not enlarge upon this exposition of the Dhamma, venerable sir. This will suffice. But where does our Master live?"

---

1. "*Ye dhammā hetuppabhavā tesaṃ hetuṃ tathāgato āha, tesañca yo nirodho, evamvādi mahāsamaṇo 'ti.*" This gāthā was later to become one of the best-known and most widely-disseminated stanzas of Buddhism, standing for all time as a reminder of Sāriputta's first contact with the Dhamma and also as a worthy memorial to Assaji, his great arahat teacher. Spoken at a time when the principle of causality was not accorded the prominence it enjoys today in philosophical thought, its impact on the minds of the early Buddhists must have been revolutionary.

"In the Bamboo Grove Monastery, wanderer."

"Then please go on ahead, venerable sir. I have a friend with whom I agreed that he who should reach the Deathless State first should tell the other. I shall inform him, and together we shall follow on the road you went and shall come into the Master's presence." Upatissa then prostrated himself at the Elder's feet, saluted him and, taking the Elder's leave, went back to the park of the Wandering Ascetics.

Kolita saw him approaching and thought, "Today my friend's appearance is quite changed. Surely, he must have found the Deathless State!" And when he asked him about it, Upatissa replied, "Yes, friend, the Deathless State has been found!" and he recited to him the stanza he had heard. At the end of the verse, Kolita was established in the Fruition of stream-entry and he asked, "Where, my dear, does the Master live?"

"I learned from our teacher, the Elder Assaji, that he lives at the Bamboo Grove Monastery."

"Then let us go, Upatissa, and see the Master," said Kolita.

But Sāriputta was one who always respected his teacher, and therefore he said to his friend, "First, my dear, we shall go to our teacher, the Wanderer Sañjaya, and tell him that we have found the Deathless. If he can grasp it, he will penetrate to the Truth. And even if he does not he may, out of confidence in us, come with us to see the Master; and hearing the Buddha's teaching, he will attain to the penetration of the Path and Fruition."

So both of them went to Sañjaya and said, "Oh our teacher! What are you doing? A Buddha has appeared in the world! Well proclaimed is his Teaching and in right conduct lives his community of monks. Let us go and see the Master of the Ten Powers!"

"What are you saying, my dear?" Sañjaya exclaimed. And refusing to go with them, he spoke to them of the gain and fame they would enjoy if they would share his—the teacher's—place. But they said, "Oh, we should not mind always remaining in the state of pupils! But you, O teacher, you must know whether to go or not!"

Then Sañjaya thought, "If they know so much, they will not listen to what I say." And realising that, he replied, "You may go, then, but I cannot."

"Why not, O teacher?"

"I am a teacher of many. If I were to revert to the state of a disciple, it would be as if a huge water tank were to change into a small pitcher. I cannot live the life of a pupil now."

"Do not think like that, O teacher!" they urged.

"Let it be, my dear. You may go, but I cannot."

"O teacher! When a Buddha has appeared in the world, people flock to him in large crowds and pay homage to him, carrying incense and flowers. We too shall go there. And then what will happen to you?"

To which Sañjaya replied, "What do you think, my pupils, are there more fools in this world, or more wise people?"

"Fools there are many, O teacher, and the wise are few."

"If that is so, my friends, then the wise ones will go to the wise recluse Gotama, and the fools will come to me, the fool. You may go now, but I shall not."

So the two friends left, saying, "You will come to understand your mistake, O teacher!" And after they had gone there was a split among Sañjaya's pupils, and his monastery became almost empty. Seeing his place empty, Sañjaya vomited hot blood. Five hundred of his disciples had left along with Upatissa and Kolita, out of whom two hundred and fifty returned to Sañjaya. With the remaining two hundred and fifty, and their own following, the two friends arrived at the Bamboo Grove Monastery.

There the Master, seated among the fourfold assembly,[2] was preaching the Dhamma, and when the Blessed One saw the two coming he addressed the monks, "These two friends, Upatissa and Kolita, who are now coming, will be two excellent disciples to me, a blessed pair."

Having approached, the friends saluted the Blessed One reverentially and sat down at one side. When they were seated they spoke to the Blessed One, saying, "May we obtain, O Lord, the ordination of the Going Forth under the Blessed One, may we obtain the Higher Ordination!"

And the Blessed One said, "Come, O bhikkhus! Well proclaimed is the Dhamma. Now live the Life of Purity, to make an end of suffering!" This alone served as the ordination of these venerable ones.

2. That is, monks, nuns, and male and female lay followers.

Then the Master continued his sermon, taking the individual temperaments[3] of the listeners into consideration; and with the exception of the two chief disciples all of them attained to arahatship. But the two chief disciples had not yet completed the task of attaining to the three higher paths of sanctity. The reason for this was the greatness of the "knowledge pertaining to the perfection of a disciple" (*sāvakapārami-ñāṇa*), which they had still to reach.

Upatissa received the name of Sāriputta on becoming a disciple of the Buddha, while Kolita became known as Mahā Moggallāna. Now the Venerable Mahā Moggallāna went to live at a village in Magadha called Kallavāla, on which he depended for alms food. On the seventh day after his ordination, when he was doing the recluse's work (of meditation), fatigue and torpor fell upon him. But spurred on by the Master,[4] he dispelled his fatigue, and while listening to the Master expounding to him the meditation subject of the elements (*dhātu-kammaṭṭhāna*), he completed the task of winning to the three higher paths and reached the acme of a disciple's perfections (*sāvaka-pāramī*).

But the Venerable Sāriputta continued to stay near the Master, at a cave called the Boar's Shelter (*Sūkharakhata-leṇa*), depending on Rājagaha for his alms food. Half a month after his ordination the Blessed One gave a discourse on the comprehension of feelings[5] to the Venerable Sāriputta's nephew, the wandering ascetic Dīghanakha. The Venerable Sāriputta was standing behind the Master, fanning him. While following with his thoughts the progress of the discourse, as though sharing the food prepared for another, the Venerable Sāriputta on that occasion reached the acme of "knowledge pertaining to a disciple's perfection and attained to arahatship together with the fourfold analytical knowledge (*paṭisambhidā-ñāṇa*)."[6] And his nephew, at the end of

3. *Carita-vasena.* This refers to the types of character (*carita*) as explained in *The Path of Purification* (*Visuddhimagga*, Ch. III).

4. This is a reference to the discourse in the AN 7:58/A IV 85.

5. *Dīghanakha Sutta*, MN 74.

6. The fact of his attainment to analytical knowledge, which has here been added to the commentarial text, was mentioned by the Venerable Sāriputta himself in AN 4:172.

the sermon, was established in the Fruition of stream-entry.[7]

Now it may be asked, "Did not the Venerable Sāriputta possess great wisdom; and if so, why did he attain to the disciple's perfections later than the Venerable Mahā Moggallāna?" The answer is because of the greatness of the preparations necessary for it. When poor people want to go anywhere they take to the road at once; but in the case of kings, larger preparations are required, as for instance to get ready the elephants and chariots, and so on. Thus it was in this case.

On that same day, when the evening shadows had lengthened, the Master caused his disciples to assemble and bestowed upon the two elders the rank of chief disciples. At this, some monks were displeased and said among themselves, "The Master should have given the rank of chief disciples to those who were ordained first, that is, the group of five disciples. If not to them, then either to the group of two hundred and fifty bhikkhus headed by Yasa, or to the thirty of the auspicious group (*bhaddavaggiya*), or else to the three Kassapa brothers. But passing over all these Great Elders, he has given it to those whose ordination was the very last of all."

The Master inquired about the subject of their talk. When he was told, he said, "I do not show preference, but give to each what he has aspired to. When, for instance, Kondañña in a previous life gave alms food nine times during a single harvest, he did not aspire to Chief Discipleship; his aspiration was to be the very first to penetrate to the highest state, arahatship. And so it came about. But when Sāriputta and Mahā Moggallāna many aeons ago, at the time of the Buddha Anomadassi, were born as the brahmin youth Sarada and landowner Sirivaḍḍhaka, they made the aspiration for Chief Discipleship. This, O bhikkhus, was the aspiration for these, my sons, at that time. Hence I have given them just what they aspired to, and did not do it out of preference."

This account of the beginning of the Venerable Sāriputta's career is taken from the commentary to the *Etad-agga* chapter of the Aṅguttara Nikāya, with some passages from the parallel version in the Dhammapada commentary. From it some of the

7. The Venerable Sāriputta refers to his way of attaining arahatship in Th 995–96.

principal traits of the Venerable Sāriputta's character are already discernible. His capacity for deep and constant friendship showed itself while he was still a worldling, a youth nurtured in luxury and pleasure, and it persisted after he had abandoned the household life. On receiving his first insight into the Dhamma, and before proceeding any further, his first thought was for his friend Kolita and the vow they had sworn together. His penetrating intellect is revealed in the promptness with which he grasped the essence of the Buddha's teaching from a few simple words. And, most rare of all, he combined that intellectual power with a modesty and sweetness of nature that expressed itself in gratitude and reverence for anyone, even the misguided Sañjaya, who had taught him things of value. It was no wonder, therefore, that throughout his life he continued to show respect for the Venerable Assaji, from whom he had gained his introduction to the Buddha's Teaching. We are told in the commentary to the *Nāvā Sutta* (Sutta-Nipāta), and also in the commentary to v. 392 of the Dhammapada, that, whenever the Venerable Sāriputta lived in the same monastery as the Elder Assaji, he always went to pay obeisance to him immediately after having done so to the Blessed One. This he did out of reverence, thinking, "This venerable one was my first teacher. It was through him that I came to know the Buddha's Dispensation." And when the Elder Assaji lived in another monastery, the Venerable Sāriputta used to face the direction in which the Elder Assaji was living, and to pay homage to him by touching the ground at five places (with the head, hands and feet), and saluting with joined palms.

But this led to misunderstanding, for when other monks saw it they said, "After becoming a Chief Disciple, Sāriputta still worships the heavenly quarters! Even today he cannot give up his brahmanical views!" Hearing these remarks, the Blessed One said, "It is not so, bhikkhus. Sāriputta does not worship the heavenly quarters. He salutes him through whom he came to know the Dhamma. It is him he salutes, worships and reveres as his teacher. Sāriputta is one who gives devout respect to his teacher." It was then that the Master preached to the monks assembled there the *Nāvā Sutta*,[8] which starts with the words:

8. Sutta Nipāta, vv. 316ff. (Also called "*Dhamma Sutta.*")

"As gods their homage pay to Indra,
So should a man give reverence to him
From whom he learned the Dhamma."

Another example of the Venerable Sāriputta's gratitude is given in the story of Rādha Thera. The commentary to v. 76 of the Dhammapada relates that there was, living at Sāvatthī, a poor brahmin who stayed in the monastery. There he performed little services such as weeding, sweeping and the like and the monks supported him with food. They did not, however, want to ordain him. One day the Blessed One, in his mental survey of the world, saw that this brahmin was mature for arahatship. He inquired about him from the assembled monks, and asked whether any one of them remembered to have received some help from the poor brahmin. The Venerable Sāriputta said that he remembered that once, when he was going for alms in Rājagaha, this poor brahmin had given him a ladle full of alms food that he had begged for himself. The Master asked Sāriputta to ordain the man, and he was given the name Rādha. The Venerable Sāriputta then advised him time and again as to what things should be done, and always Rādha received his admonitions gladly, without resentment. And so, living according to the elder's advice, he attained arahatship in a short time.

This time the bhikkhus remarked on Sāriputta's sense of gratitude and said that he who himself willingly accepts advice obtains pupils who do the same. Commenting on this, the Buddha said that not only then, but also formerly Sāriputta had showed gratitude and remembered any good deed done to him. And in that connection the Master told the *Alīnacitta Jātaka*, the story of a grateful elephant.[9]

9. Jātaka No. 156.

Part II

Maturity of Insight

Friendships

If Sāriputta was notable for his lasting sense of gratitude, he was no less so for his capacity for friendship. With Mahā Moggallāna, the friend and companion of his youth, he maintained a close intimacy, and many were the conversations they held on the Dhamma. One of these, which is of special interest as throwing light on the process of Venerable Sāriputta's attainment, is recorded in the Aṅguttara Nikāya, Catukka-Nipāta, No. 167. It relates that once the Venerable Mahā Moggallāna went to see the elder and said to him:

> "There are four ways of progress, brother Sāriputta: difficult progress, with sluggish direct-knowledge; difficult progress, with swift direct-knowledge; easy progress, with sluggish direct-knowledge; easy progress, with swift direct-knowledge.
>
> "By which of these four ways of progress, brother, was your mind freed from the cankers without remnants of clinging?" To which the Venerable Sāriputta replied, "By that of those four ways of progress, brother, which is easy and has swift direct-knowledge."

The explanation of this passage is that, if the suppression of the defilements preparatory to absorption or insight takes place without great difficulty, progress is called "easy" (*sukha-paṭipadā*); in the reverse case it is "difficult" or "painful" (*dukkha-paṭipadā*). If, after the suppression of the defilements, the manifestation of the Path, the goal of insight, is quickly effected, the direct-knowledge (connected with the Path) is called "swift" (*khippābhiññā*); in the reverse case it is "sluggish" (*daṇḍābhiññā*). In this discourse the Venerable Sāriputta's statement refers to his attainment of arahatship. His attainment of the first three Paths, however, was, according to the commentary to the above text, connected with "easy progress and sluggish direct-knowledge."

In such ways as this did the two friends exchange information about their experience and understanding of the Dhamma. They were also frequently associated in attending to affairs of the Saṅgha. One such occasion was when they combined in winning back certain monks who had been led astray by Devadatta. There is an interesting passage[10] in this connection which shows that the Venerable Sāriputta's generous praise of Devadatta's achievements before the latter brought about a schism in the Saṅgha was the cause of a slight embarrassment. It relates that when the Buddha asked Sāriputta to proclaim in Rājagaha that Devadatta's deeds and words should no longer be regarded as connected with the Buddha, Dhamma, and Saṅgha, the Venerable Sāriputta said, "Formerly I spoke at Rājagaha in praise of Devadatta's magical powers. How can I now make that declaration about Devadatta?" The Buddha asked, "Did you not speak truthfully, Sāriputta, when you praised Devadatta's magical powers?" "Yes, Lord," the Elder replied. "So you will now speak truthfully also, Sāriputta, when you make this proclamation about Devadatta." So, after receiving the formal approval of the Saṅgha, the Venerable Sāriputta, together with many monks, went to Rājagaha and made the declaration about Devadatta.

When Devadatta had formally split the Saṅgha by declaring that he would conduct Saṅgha-acts separately, he went to Vultures' Peak with five hundred young monks who through ignorance had become his followers. To win them back, the Buddha sent Sāriputta and Mahā Moggallāna to Vultures' Peak, and while Devadatta was resting, the two Chief Disciples preached to the monks, who attained to stream-entry and went back to the Master.[11]

Another time when the Venerable Sāriputta and the Venerable Mahā Moggallāna worked together to restore order in the Saṅgha was when a group of monks led by Assaji (not the Elder Assaji referred to earlier) and Punnabbassu, living at Kīṭāgiri, were misbehaving. In spite of repeated admonitions, these monks would not mend their ways, so the two chief disciples were sent to pronounce the penalty of *pabbājaniya-kamma* (excommunication) on those who would not submit to the discipline.[12]

10. Cv VII 3.2/Vin II 189.
11. Cv VII 4.3/Vin II 200.
12. Cv I 13–17/Vin II 200. *Saṅghādisesa* 13, Vin III 179ff.

Venerable Sāriputta's devotion to his friend was fully reciprocated; we are told of two occasions when Sāriputta was ill, and Mahā Moggallāna attended to him and brought him medicine.

Yet there was nothing exclusive about the Venerable Sāriputta's friendships, for according to the commentary to the *Mahāgosinga Sutta* there was also a bond of mutual affection between him and the Elder Ānanda. On the part of Sāriputta it was because he thought, "He is attending on the Master—a duty which should have been performed by me"; and Ānanda's affection was due to the fact that Sāriputta had been declared by the Buddha as his foremost disciple. When Ānanda gave Novice Ordination to young pupils he used to take them to Sāriputta to obtain higher ordination under him. The Venerable Sāriputta did the same in regard to Ānanda, and in that way they had five hundred pupils in common.

Whenever the Venerable Ānanda received choice robes or other requisites he would offer them to Sāriputta, and in the same way, Sāriputta passed on to Ānanda any special offerings that were made to him. Once Ānanda received from a certain brahmin a very valuable robe, and with the Master's permission he kept it for ten days awaiting Sāriputta's return. The sub-commentary says that later teachers commented on this, "There may be those who say, 'We can well understand that Ānanda, who had not yet attained to arahatship, felt such affection. But how is it in the case of Sāriputta, who was a canker-free arahant?' To this we answer, 'Sāriputta's affection was not one of worldly attachment, but a love for Ānanda's virtues (*guṇa-bhatti*).'"

The Buddha once asked the Venerable Ānanda, "Do you, too, approve of Sāriputta?" And Ānanda replied, "Who, O Lord, would not approve of Sāriputta, unless he were childish, corrupt, stupid or of perverted mind! Learned, O Lord, is the Venerable Sāriputta; of great wisdom, O Lord, is the Venerable Sāriputta; of broad, bright, quick, keen and penetrative wisdom is the Venerable Sāriputta; of few wants and contented, inclined to seclusion, not fond of company, energetic, eloquent, willing to listen, an exhorter who censures what is evil."[13]

13. SN 11:2/S I 112.

In the Theragāthā (v. 1034f) we find the Venerable Ānanda describing his emotion at the time of Sāriputta's death. "When the Noble Friend (Sāriputta) had gone," he declares, "the world was plunged in darkness for me." But he adds that after the companion had left him behind, and also the Master had passed away, there was no other friend like mindfulness directed on the body. Ānanda's sorrow on learning of the Venerable Sāriputta's death is also described very movingly in the *Cunda Sutta.*[14]

Sāriputta was a true friend in the fullest sense of the word. He well understood how to bring out the best in others, and in doing so did not hesitate sometimes to speak straightforwardly and critically, like the ideal friend described by the Buddha, who points out his friend's faults. It was in this way that he helped the Venerable Anuruddha in his final break-through to arahatship, as recorded in the Aṅguttara Nikāya (Tika-Nipāta No. 128):

> Once the Venerable Anuruddha went to see the Venerable Sāriputta; when they had exchanged courteous greetings, he sat down and said to the Venerable Sāriputta, "Friend Sāriputta, with the divine eye that is purified, transcending human ken, I can see the thousandfold world-system. Firm is my energy, unremitting; my mindfulness is alert and unconfused; the body is tranquil and unperturbed; my mind is concentrated and one-pointed. And yet my mind is not freed from cankers, not freed from clinging."
>
> "Friend Anuruddha," said the Venerable Sāriputta, "that you think thus of your divine eye, this is conceit in you. That you think thus of your firm energy, your alert mindfulness, your unperturbed body and your concentrated mind, this is restlessness in you. That you think of your mind not being freed from the cankers, this is worrying[15] in you. It will be good, indeed, if the Venerable Anuruddha, abandoning these three states of mind and paying no attention to them, will direct the mind to the Deathless Element."

14. See p. 60.

15. Conceit (*māna*) and restlessness (*uddhacca*) are two of the three fetters (*saṃyojana*) which are destroyed only at the stage of Arahatship. Worry (or scruples: *kukkucca*), however, is removed already at the stage of non-returner (*anāgāmi*).

> And the Venerable Anuruddha later on gave up these three states of mind, paid no attention to them and directed his mind to the Deathless Element. And the Venerable Anuruddha, living then alone, secluded, heedful, ardent, with determined mind, before long reached in this very life, understanding and experiencing it by himself, that highest goal of the Holy Life, for the sake of which noble sons go forth entirely from home into homelessness. And he knew, "Exhausted is rebirth, lived is the holy life, the work is done, nothing further remains after this." Thus the Venerable Anuruddha became one of the arahats.

Sāriputta must have been stimulating company, and sought after by many. What attracted men of quite different temperament to him and his conversation can be well understood from the incident described in the *Mahāgosinga Sutta* (Majjhima Nikāya No. 32). One evening the Elders Mahā Moggallāna, Mahā Kassapa, Anuruddha, Revata and Ānanda went to Sāriputta to listen to the Dhamma. The Venerable Sāriputta welcomed them, saying, "Delightful is this Gosinga Forest of Sāla trees; there is moonlight tonight, all the Sāla trees are in full bloom, and it seems that heavenly perfume drifts around. What kind of monk, do you think, Ānanda, will lend more lustre to this Gosinga Sāla Forest?"

The same question was put to the others as well, and each answered according to his individual nature. Finally, Sāriputta gave his own answer, which was as follows:

> "There is a monk who has control over his mind, who is not under the control of his mind.[16] In whatever (mental) abiding or attainment he wishes to dwell in the forenoon, he can dwell in it at that time. In whatever (mental) abiding or attainment he wishes to dwell at noon, he can dwell in it at that time. In whatever (mental) abiding or attainment he wishes to dwell in the evening, he can dwell in it at that time. It is as though a king's or royal minister's cloth chest were full of many-coloured garments; so that whatever pair of garments he wishes to wear in the morning, or at noon, or in the evening, he can wear it at will at those times. Similarly

16. Is not subject to the vagaries of the mind.

it is with a monk who has control over his mind, who is not under the control of his mind; in whatever (mental) abiding or attainment he wishes to dwell in the morning, or at noon, or in the evening, he can do so at will at those times. Such a monk, Friend Moggallāna, may lend lustre to this Gosinga Sāla Forest."

They then went to the Buddha, who approved of all their answers and added his own.

We see from this episode that Sāriputta, with all his powerful intellect and his status in the Saṅgha, was far from being a domineering type who tried to impose his views on others. He understood well how to stimulate self-expression in his companions in a natural and charming way, conveying to them the pensive mood evoked by the enchanting scenery. His own sensitive nature responded to it, and drew a similar response from his friends.

There are many such conversations recorded between Sāriputta and other monks, not only the Venerables Mahā Moggallāna, Ānanda and Anuruddha, but also Mahā Koṭṭhita, Upavāna, Samiddhi, Savittha, Bhūmija and many more. It seems that the Buddha himself liked to talk to Sāriputta, for he often did so, and many of his discourses were addressed to his "Marshal of the Law," to use the title he gave him.

Once, Sāriputta repeated some words the Master had spoken to Ānanda on another occasion. "This is the whole of the life of purity (*brahmacariya*); namely, noble friendship, noble companionship, noble association."[17]

There could be no better exemplification of that teaching than the life of the Chief Disciple himself.

The Helper

Among the bhikkhus, Sāriputta was outstanding as one who helped others. We find a reference to this in the *Devadaha Sutta.*[18] Some visiting monks, about to return to their own places, took formal leave of the Buddha. He then advised them to see the Venerable Sāriputta and take leave of him also, telling them,

17. SN 45:2/S V 2.
18. SN 22:2/S III 5.

"Sāriputta, O bhikkhus, is wise, and a helper of his fellow monks." The commentary, in explanation of these words, says, "Sāriputta was a helper in two ways: by giving material help (*āmisānuggaha*) and the help of the Dhamma (*dhammānuggaha*)."

The Elder, it is said, did not go on alms round in the early morning hours as the other bhikkhus did. Instead, when they had all gone he walked around the entire monastery grounds, and wherever he saw an unswept place, he swept it; wherever refuse had not been removed, he threw it away; where furniture such as beds, chairs, etc., or earthenware had not been properly arranged, he put them in order. He did that lest other, non-Buddhist ascetics, visiting the monastery, might see some disorderliness and speak in contempt of the bhikkhus.

Then he used to go to the hall for the sick, and having spoken consoling words to the patients he would ask them about their needs. To procure their requirements he took with him young novices, and went in search of medicine either by way of the customary alms round or to some appropriate place. When the medicine was obtained he would give it to the novices, saying, "Caring for the sick has been praised by the Master! Go now, good people, and be heedful!" After sending them back to the monastery sick room, he would go on the alms-round or take his meal at a supporter's house. This was his habit when staying for some time at a monastery.

But when going on a journey on foot with the Blessed One, he did not go with the very first of the monks, shod with sandals and umbrella in hand, as one who thinks, "I am the Chief Disciple." But letting the young novices take his bowl and robes, sending them ahead with the others, he himself would first attend to those who were old, very young, or unwell, making them apply oil to any sores they might have on their bodies. Then, either later on the same day or on the next day, he would leave together with them.

Once, when for that reason the Elder Sāriputta had arrived particularly late at the place where the others were resting, he did not get proper quarters for the night, and seated himself under a tent made from robes. The Master saw this, and next day he caused the monks to assemble and told them the story of the elephant, the monkey, and the partridge, who, after deciding which was the eldest of them, lived together showing respect for the seniormost.[19] He then laid down the rule that "lodgings should be allocated according to seniority."[20]

In this way the Venerable Sāriputta was a helper by giving material help.

Sometimes he would give material help and the help of the Dhamma together, as when he visited Samitigutta, who suffered from leprosy, in the infirmary. The Theragāthā commentary tells us that he said to Samitigutta, "Friend, so long as the aggregates (*khandhā*) continue, all feeling is just suffering. Only when the aggregates are no more is there no more suffering." Having thus given him the contemplation of feelings as subject of meditation, Sāriputta went away. Samitigutta, following the Elder's instruction, developed insight and realised the six supernormal powers (*chaḷabhiññā*) as an arahat.[21]

Again, when Anāthapiṇḍika was lying on his deathbed, Sāriputta visited him, accompanied by Ānanda. Sāriputta preached to the dying man on non-attachment, and Anāthapiṇḍika was greatly moved by the profound discourse.[22]

Another sickbed sermon given by the Elder to Anāthapiṇḍika is preserved in the Sotāpatti-Saṃyutta (SN 55:26). In this discourse, Anāthapiṇḍika is reminded that those things which lead to rebirth in states of woe are no longer in him, but that he possesses the four basic qualities of stream-entry (*sotāpattiyaṅga*) and the eight path factors: in considering this, his pains would subside. As the result, his pains did subside.

Once the Elder Channa was lying ill and in great pain. The Venerable Sāriputta paid him a visit, in company with the Elder Mahā Cunda. Seeing the sick monk's agonies, Sāriputta at once offered to go in search of medicines and suitable food for him. But Channa told them he had decided to take his life, and after they had left he did so. Afterwards the Buddha explained that the Elder Channa's act was without demerit and blameless, since he had attained arahatship while dying. This story is found in the *Channovāda Sutta* (MN 144).

---

19. Tittita Jātaka (No. 37).
20. Cv VI 6.4/Vin II 162.
21. Theragāthā v. 81 and commentary.
22. MN 143.

It is said that whenever Sāriputta gave advice, he showed infinite patience; he would admonish and instruct up to a hundred or a thousand times, until his pupil was established in the Fruition of stream-entry. Only then did he discharge him and give his advice to others. Very great was the number of those who, after receiving his instruction and following it faithfully, attained to arahatship. In the *Saccavibhaṅga Sutta* (MN 141) the Buddha says, "Sāriputta is like a mother who brings forth, while Moggallāna is like a nurse of that which has been brought forth. Sāriputta trains to the Fruit of stream-entry, and Moggallāna trains to the highest goal."

Explaining this passage, the commentary says, "When Sāriputta accepted pupils for training, whether they were ordained by him or by others, he favoured them with his material and spiritual help, looked after them in sickness, gave them a subject of meditation and at last, when he knew that they had become stream-winners and had risen above the dangers of the lower worlds, he dismissed them in the confident knowledge that 'Now they can, by their own manly strength, produce the higher stages of saintship.' Having thus become free from concern about their future, he instructed new groups of pupils. But Mahā Moggallāna, when training pupils in the same way, did not give up concern for them until they had attained arahatship. This was because he felt, as was said by the Master, 'As even a little excrement is of evil smell, I do not praise even the shortest spell of existence, be it no longer than a snap of the fingers.'"

But although the Majjhima commentary says that Sāriputta used to lead his regular pupils only up to stream-entry, in individual cases he helped monks to attain the higher stages. The Udāna commentary, for example, says that "at that time bhikkhus in higher training (*sekhā*) often used to approach the Venerable Sāriputta for a subject of meditation that could help them to attain the three higher Paths." It was after taking instruction from Sāriputta that the Elder Lakuṇṭika Bhaddiya ("The Dwarf") attained arahatship,[23] having been a stream-winner at the time. There is also the case of the Venerable Anuruddha, referred to above.

It was in this manner that the Venerable Sāriputta gave

23. Ud 7.1.

the help of the Dhamma. He was a great leader of men and an outstanding spiritual adviser. To the latter task he brought not only a keen and perceptive understanding of the human mind, but also a warm, human interest in others which must have been a great encouragement to those under his spiritual guidance. We have already seen how ready he was to give generous praise where it was due; he was also keen at all times to meet noble monks, particularly those whom the Master had commended. One such was the Elder Puṇṇa Mantāṇiputta; when Sāriputta learned that he had come on a visit he went to meet him. Without telling him who he was, he listened to Puṇṇa's great discourse, the Stage Coach simile (MN 24), and when it was ended gave it high praise.

Administering to the physical as well as to the spiritual needs of the monks under his charge, restraining them with kindly admonitions and encouraging them with the praise their efforts deserved, guiding them on the Path, showing in all he did that vital sympathetic interest which draws forth the best from a pupil, Sāriputta combined the qualities of a perfect teacher with those of a perfect friend. He was ready to help in every way, in small things as in great. Filled with the virtue of the Holy Life himself, he was quick to see virtue in others, expert in developing it in those in whom it was latent, and among the first to extol it where it was in full flower. His was no cold, aloof perfection, but the richest intermingling of spiritual exaltation with the qualities that are finest and most endearing in a human being.

Attainment

Two stanzas in the Theragāthā (verses 995–96) relate, in words ascribed to the Venerable Sāriputta himself, the way in which he attained arahatship. There he tells us:

> "It was to another that the Blessed One was teaching the Dhamma; to the Dhamma-preaching I listened intently for my own good. And not in vain, for freed from all defilements, I gained release."

In the next two verses (996–97) the Elder declares that he felt no inclination to develop the five supernormal powers (*abhiññā*). However, the *Iddhividha-Kathā* of the *Paṭisambhidāmagga* credits him with possessing the intensive degree of meditative concentration called "the power of intervention by concentration" (*samādhi-vipphāra-iddhi*), which is capable of intervening in certain normal physiological processes or other natural events. This is illustrated by the anecdote in the *Visuddhimagga,* Ch. XII, which records that once, when the Venerable Sāriputta was living with the Elder Mahā Moggallāna at Kapotakandarā, he was sitting meditating in the open with his hair freshly shaved when he was given a malicious blow on the head by a mischievous spirit. The blow was a very severe one, but at the time it was given "the Elder was absorbed in meditative attainment; consequently he suffered no harm." The source of this story is the Udāna (4.4), which continues the account as follows:

> The Venerable Mahā Moggallāna saw the incident and approached the Venerable Sāriputta to ask how he fared. He asked him, "Brother, are you comfortable? Are you doing well? Does nothing trouble you?"
>
> "I am comfortable, brother Moggallāna," said the Venerable Sāriputta. "I am doing well, brother Moggallāna. Only my head troubles me a little."
>
> Whereupon the Venerable Mahā Moggallāna said, "O wonderful is it, brother Sāriputta! O marvellous is it, brother Sāriputta! How great is the psychic power, and how great is the might of the Venerable Sāriputta! For just now, brother Sāriputta, a certain demon gave you a blow on the head. And a mighty blow it was! With such a blow one might fell an elephant seven or seven and a half cubits high, or one might split a mountain peak. But the Venerable Sāriputta says only this, 'I am comfortable, brother Moggallāna. I am doing well, brother Moggallāna. Only my head troubles me a little.'"
>
> Then the Venerable Sāriputta replied, "O wonderful is it, brother Moggallāna! O marvellous is it, brother Moggallāna! How great is the psychic power and how great is the might of the Venerable Moggallāna, that he should see any demon at all! As for me, I have not seen so much as a mud-sprite!"

The *Anupada Sutta* (MN 111) contains a description of Sāriputta's attainments given by the Buddha himself. In it the Blessed One declares that the Venerable Sāriputta had mastered the nine meditative attainments, that is, the four fine-material and four immaterial *jhānas* and the cessation of perception and feeling. And in the *Sāriputta Saṃyutta*[24] the Venerable Elder mentions the fact himself, in speaking to Ānanda, adding that in all the stages he was free of any self-reference: "I had no such thoughts as 'I am entering the jhāna; I have entered it; I am rising from it.'" And on another occasion he describes to Ānanda how he attained to such developed concentration of mind that with regard to the earth element he was without earth perception of it. And so also, with regard to the other three elements and the four immaterial absorptions; he was without perception of them. Yet it seems that he was not entirely without perception of another kind, his only perception being that "Nibbāna is ceasing of coming-to-be" (*bhava-nirodha*).[25]

This detached attitude to the jhānic attainments may have been due to the meditative "abiding in voidness" (*suññatā-vihāra*) which the Venerable Sāriputta cultivated. We read in the *Piṇḍapāta-pārisuddhi Sutta* (MN 151) that the Buddha once remarked on the Venerable Sāriputta's radiant features and asked him by which state of mind this radiance had been caused.[26] The Venerable Sāriputta replied that he frequently practiced the abiding in voidness, upon which the Buddha said that this was the abode of great men, and proceeded to describe it in detail. The Udāna records that on three occasions the Master saw the Venerable Sāriputta seated in meditation outside the monastery and uttered verses (*udāna*) in praise of a firm and calm mind.

We may perhaps imagine the Venerable Sāriputta seated in meditation in a bower such as that mentioned in the *Devadaha Sutta* (SN 22:2), where it is said, "Once the Blessed One lived in the Sākya country, at Devadaha, a market town of the Sākyas. At that time the Venerable Sāriputta was seated not far from the Blessed One, under an Eḷagalā bush." The commentary to the text tells us, "At Devadaha there was a bower under an Eḷagalā bush.

24. SN 28:1/S III 225f.

25. AN 10:7/A V 8ff.

26. The Buddhas, although they are able to divine such matters themselves, ask questions for the instruction and illumination of others.

This bush grows where there is a constant supply of flowing water. People had made a bower with four posts over which they let the bush grow, forming a roof. Under it they made a seat by placing bricks there and strewing it with sand. It was a cool place for the daytime, with a fresh breeze blowing from the water." It may well have been in some such rustic shelter as this that the Buddha saw Sāriputta deep in meditation, on those occasions when he extolled his disciple's tranquillity and detachment.

Concerning his attainment to analytical knowledge (*paṭisambhidā-ñāṇa*), the Venerable Sāriputta speaks of it in the Aṅguttara Nikāya (AN 4:172), where he says:

> "It was half a month after my ordination, friends, that I realised, in all their parts and details, the analytical knowledge of meaning, the analytical knowledge of the Dhamma, the analytical knowledge of language, the analytical knowledge of perspicuity. These I expound in many ways, teach them and make them known, establish and reveal them, explain and clarify them. If anyone has any doubt or uncertainty, he may ask me and I shall explain (the matter). Present is the Master who is well acquainted with our attainments."

From all of this it is evident that the Venerable Sāriputta was a master of all the stages of attainment up to and including the highest insight-knowledge. What could be more aptly said of him than this, in the Buddha's own words:

> "If one could ever say rightly of one that he has come to mastery and perfection in noble virtue, in noble concentration, in noble wisdom and noble liberation, it is of Sāriputta that one could thus rightly declare.
>
> "If one could ever say rightly of one that he is the Blessed One's true son, born of his speech, born of the Dhamma, formed of the Dhamma, heir to the Dhamma, not heir to worldly benefit, it is Sāriputta that one could thus rightly declare.
>
> "After me, O monks, Sāriputta rightly turns the supreme Wheel of Dhamma, even as I have turned it." (MN 111, *Anupada Sutta*)

The Turner of the Wheel

The discourses of Sāriputta and the books attributed to him form a comprehensive body of teaching that for scope and variety of exposition can stand beside that of the Master himself. Sāriputta understood in a unique way how to organize and present the rich material of the Dhamma lucidly, in a manner that was intellectually stimulating and also an inspiration to practical effort. We find this exemplified in two classic discourses of the Majjhima Nikāya, the *Sammā-diṭṭhi Sutta* (MN 9) and the *Greater Sutta on the Elephant Footprint Simile* (MN 28).

The *Greater Discourse on the Elephant Footprint Simile*[27] is a masterpiece of methodical treatment. It begins with the statement that the Four Noble Truths comprise everything that is salutary, and then singles out the Truth of Suffering as being identifiable with the five aggregates of personality. From these, the aggregate of corporeality is chosen for detailed investigation; it is shown to consist of the four great elements, each of which is said to be internal and external. The bodily parts and functions belonging to the internal element are stated in detail, and it is said of both the internal and external elements that they neither belong to a self, nor constitute a self. This insight leads to disgust and detachment regarding the elements.

The discourse then goes on to show the impermanence of the mighty external elements when they are involved in great upheavals of nature, and against that background it is stressed that this tiny body, the product of craving, can never be regarded as "I" or "mine" or considered in the sense of "I am." And when a monk who has this firm and deeply rooted insight meets with abuse, blame and hostility on the part of others, he is able to analyse the situation soberly and so remain master of it. He recognises that the painful feeling that has arisen in him is produced by ear-contact, which is in itself no more than a conditioned phenomenon; and of all the constituent parts of the situation he knows that they are impermanent. This he discerns with reference to contact, feeling, perception, formations and consciousness. At this point of the discourse we see that the other four aggregates, the mental

27. See *Wheel* No. 101.

components of personality, are introduced in an organic context, together with the already mentioned factor of contact. The discourse then continues, "Then his mind, just by taking only the elements as its object, becomes elated, gladdened, firm and intent; and even if he is beaten and injured he will think, 'This body is of such a nature that is liable to such injuries.'" Thereupon he recollects the Master's Simile of the Saw and will resolve to follow the Buddha's injunction to suffer all injuries in patience, whatever may happen to him.

But, the sermon continues, if when thus remembering the Buddha, Dhamma and Saṅgha, the monk's equanimity does not endure, he will be stirred by a sense of urgency and feel ashamed that, in spite of that recollection of the Triple Gem, he could not remain constant. On the other hand, if his endurance persists he will experience happiness. "Even to this extent, much has been achieved by that monk," he says.

Here all the four elements are treated identically. The concluding section starts by comparing the body and its constituent parts with a house, which is made up of its various components. After that follows an exposition of the conditioned arising of the sixfold perceptual consciousness. In mentioning the five sense-organs and sense-objects as the basic conditions for the arising of five-sense consciousness, derived corporeality is here introduced by means of a prominent part of it, thus completing the treatment of the corporeal aggregate. With the state of consciousness having thus arisen, all five aggregates are given, and in that way their conjunction can be understood, as well as their dependent origination. And in this connection Sāriputta quotes the Master, "He who understands dependent origination understands the Dhamma; and he who understands the Dhamma understands dependent origination." Desire, inclination and attachment in regard to the five aggregates is the *origin of suffering.* Removal of that desire, inclination and attachment is the *cessation of suffering.* And of the monk who has understood this it is said, "Even to this extent, much has been achieved by that monk." Thus the exposition is rounded off with the Four Noble Truths. This discourse is indeed like an intricate and beautifully constructed piece of music ending on a solemn and majestic chord.

Another model exposition of the Venerable Sāriputta's is the *Sammā-diṭṭhi Sutta*.[28] This is a masterpiece of teaching, which also provides a framework for further elaboration, such as given in the extensive commentary to it. The commentary says, "In the Buddha Word as collected in the five great Nikāyas there is no discourse other than the Discourse on Right Understanding, wherein the Four Noble Truths are stated thirty-two times, and thirty-two times the state of arahatship." The same discourse also gives us an original exposition of dependent origination, with slight, but very instructive, variations. Each factor of dependent origination is used, as are also the additional sections, to illustrate the right understanding of the Four Noble Truths, the comprehension of which is thus greatly enhanced, broadened, and deepened. This discourse has been widely used for instructional purposes throughout the centuries down to the present day.

Another of the Venerable Sāriputta's discourses is the *Samacitta Sutta*,[29] which was listened to by the "devas of tranquil mind." It is concerned with the first three stages of sanctitude: the stream-winner, the once-returner and the non-returner. Its purpose is to clarify the question of their residuum of rebirths, in the five-sense world or in the fine-material and non-material worlds, which depends upon their mode of practise and on the fetters of existence still remaining. It is a very short discourse, but had a singular impact on the huge assembly of devas, who, according to tradition, assembled to hear it. It is said that a very large number of them attained arahatship, and innumerable were those who reached stream-entry. This discourse of the Venerable Sāriputta is, in fact, counted among the few which had unusually far-reaching results among beings of the higher worlds; and although it is a very brief text rather cryptic without the commentarial explanation, it had a high reputation in succeeding centuries. It is the sermon that was preached by the arahat Mahinda on the evening of his arrival in Ceylon, and the *Mahāvaṃsa* (XIV, 34ff), Ceylon's famous chronicle, relates that on this occasion, also, numerous devas listened and achieved penetration of the Dhamma.

---

28. See Bhikkhu Bodhi, *Discourse on Right View,* Wheel Publication 377/379, BPS, Kandy.
29. AN 2:4.5/A I 63.

The high regard in which the discourse is held, and the strong impact ascribed to it, may be attributed to the fact that it helps those on the Path to define their position as to the kind of rebirths still to be expected by them. Devas on higher levels of development are sometimes inclined to regard their heavenly status as final, and do not expect to be reborn in the five-sense world, as may sometimes be the case. The Great Elder's discourse gave them a criterion by which to judge their position. For worldlings still outside the Path, as well, it must have offered valuable orientation for the direction of their efforts.

The *Saṅgīti Sutta* ("The Recital") and *Dasuttara Sutta* ("Up to Ten"), two more of the Venerable Sāriputta's sermons, are the last two texts of the Dīgha Nikāya, the Collection of Long Discourses. Both these texts are compilations of doctrinal terms, in which a large number of topics are classified as falling into groups of from one to ten members. The reason for bringing the compilation only up to ten may have been that there are only very few groups of doctrinal terms extending beyond ten members, and these could be supposed to be well known and easily remembered. The *Saṅgīti Sutta* was preached in the presence of the Buddha, and at its conclusion received his express approval.

While in the *Saṅgīti Sutta* the doctrinal terms are arranged solely in numerical groups of one to ten, in the *Dasuttara Sutta* each of these ten groups has tenfold subdivision which serves to bring out the practical significance of these groups, for example:

> "One thing (1) is of great importance, (2) should be developed, (3) should be fully known, (4) should be abandoned, (5) implies decline, (6) implies progress, (7) is hard to penetrate, (8) should be made to arise, (9) should be directly known, (10) should be realised. What is the one thing of great importance? Heedfulness in salutary things..."

These texts must have been compiled at a fairly late period of the Buddha's and the Venerable Sāriputta's life, when there was already in existence a large body of doctrine and carefully transmitted discourses which required organising for ready use, and also anthologies of salient features of the Dhamma became a useful aid in a comprehensive study of the Teaching. The *Saṅgīti Sutta* was delivered at the time of Nigaṇṭha Nāṭaputta's death, on the date of which, however, scholars differ. It was, in fact, this event that occasioned the preaching of the sutta, for it speaks of the dissensions, schisms and doctrinal disagreements that arose among the Jains immediately after the death of their Master, Nigaṇṭha Nātaputta, otherwise known as Mahāvīra. This was taken as a warning example by the Venerable Sāriputta, who in his discourse stresses that this text "should be recited by all in concord and without dissension, so that the Holy Life should last long for the welfare and happiness of gods and men." The commentators say that the *Saṅgīti Sutta* is meant to convey the "flavour of concord" (*sāmaggi-rasa*) in the Teaching, which is strengthened by doctrinal proficiency (*desanā-kusalatā*).

The purpose of the *Dasuttara Sutta* is indicated in the Venerable Sāriputta's introductory verses:

> The Dasuttara (Discourse) I shall proclaim—
> A teaching for the attainment of Nibbāna
> And the ending of suffering,
> The release from all bondage.[30]

It seems likely that these two suttas served as a kind of index to selected teachings. They may have been useful also to those monks who did not memorise a great many texts; to them they may have been helpful in presenting numerous aspects of the Teaching in a form that was easily memorised and assimilated. Both of these discourses admirably illustrate the Venerable Sāriputta's concern with the preservation of the Dhamma, and his systematic way of ensuring that it was transmitted intact in all its details. It was for that purpose that he provided "study aids" such as these and other discourses, together with works like the Niddesa.

* * *

A summary of other discourses given by the Venerable Sāriputta is included at the end of this book. We shall now turn to a consideration of larger canonical works attributed to him.

The first is the Niddesa, which belongs to the Khuddaka

30. *Dasuttaram pavakkhāmi, dhammaṃ nibbānapattiyā dukkhas' antakiriyāya, sabbaganthappamocanaṃ.*

Nikāya of the Sutta Piṭaka. It is the only work of an exclusively commentarial character included in the Pāli Tipiṭaka. Of its two parts, the Mahā Niddesa is a commentary to the Aṭṭhaka-vagga of the Sutta Nipāta, while the Cūla Niddesa comments on the Parāyaṇa-vagga and the *Khaggavisāṇa Sutta*, likewise of the Sutta Nipāta.

The Aṭṭhaka-vagga and the Parāyaṇa-vagga are the last two books of the Sutta Nipāta, and doubtlessly belong to the oldest parts not only of that work but of the entire Sutta Piṭaka. They were highly appreciated even in the earlier days of the Saṅgha, and of the Buddhist laity as well, as is testified by the fact that the Udāna records a recital of the Aṭṭhaka-vagga by Soṇa Thera and the Aṅguttara Nikāya a recital of the Parāyaṇa-vagga by the female lay disciple Nandamātā. On at least five occasions the Buddha himself has given explanations of verses contained in these two parts of the Sutta Nipāta. Apart from the high esteem in which they were evidently held, the fact that these two verse collections contain numerous archaic words and terse aphoristic sayings makes it understandable that in very early days a commentary on them was composed which was later included in the canonical scriptures. The traditional attribution of it to the Venerable Sāriputta must be regarded as highly plausible.[31] It is quite in character with the great Elder's concern with the methodical instruction of bhikkhus that the Niddesa contains not only word explanations, clarifications of the context and supporting quotations from the Buddha Word, but also material obviously meant for linguistic instruction, such as the addition of many synonyms of the word explained. On this subject, Prof. E. J. Thomas writes as follows: [32]

> The most characteristic feature of the Niddesa consists of a list of synonyms of the words commented on. Such lists are not used to explain the meaning of a word in a particular context. They are repeated in the same form wherever the word occurs and were evidently intended to be learned in the same way as the modern *kośa* (dictionary). Much of this

31. The Commentary to the Theragāthā, by Bhadantācariya Dhammapāla, quotes from the Niddesa and attributes it to Sāriputta (Dhammasenāpati).

32. See "Buddhist Education in Pāli and Sanskrit Schools," by E. J. Thomas, in *Buddhistic Studies*, ed. by B. C. Law (Calcutta, 1931), pp. 223ff.

is also found in the Abhidhamma books, but in the Niddesa it is used as general matter applied to passages for which it was not immediately intended. This shows a system for learning the vocabulary of the Canon, and for explaining archaic forms, but no further grammatical teaching occurs apart from the description of certain terms as particles in the Niddesa; we thus have direct evidence of a general system of instruction applied to a definite work, consisting of interpretation, doctrinal teaching and the verbal expositions of the beginnings of grammar. The Abhidhamma books and related works like the Paṭisambhidāmagga give other traces of its existence. It appears to be this system which is expressly referred to in the Niddesa (1, 234) and other places as the four kinds of analysis (*paṭisambhidā*); the analysis of meanings (*attha*), of conditions (*dhamma*), of grammatical analysis (*nirutti*), and clearness of insight (*paṭibhāna*). The Nirutti of the Niddesa is of the kind that we should expect to exist when Pāli was a living language. All the grammatical analysis that was required was a knowledge of those words in the Scriptures that had become obsolete, and the explanation of unusual grammatical forms by means of current expressions. We can see from its different forms and readings that it underwent changes and received additions, and in the case of a work used continually for instruction this would be inevitable.

The Venerable Sāriputta states that he attained to the four kinds of analytical knowledge (*paṭisambhidā*) two weeks after his ordination, that is, on attaining arahatship.[33] This fact, and the extensive application of *nirutti-paṭisambhidā*, "grammatical analysis," in the Niddesa, make it quite probable that he was actually the author of both the Niddesa and the Paṭisambhidāmagga.

The Mahā Niddesa contains also the commentary on the *Sāriputta Sutta* (also called the "*Therapañhā Sutta*"), which forms the last text of the Aṭṭhaka-vagga. The first part of this text, with verses in praise of the Master and questions put to him, is ascribed to Sāriputta. The Mahā Niddesa explains the opening stanza as

33. AN 4:173/A II 160;

referring to the Buddha's return from Tāvatiṃsa heaven after he had preached the Abhidhamma there. Apart from that it contains only his questions, the essential part of the text being the Buddha's replies.

The Paṭisambhidāmagga has the appearance of a manual of higher Buddhist studies, and its range is as broad as that of the mind of its reputed author. At the beginning it presents treatises on seventy-two types of knowledge (*ñāṇa*) and on the types of wrong speculative views (*diṭṭhi*), both of which show the methodical and penetrative mind of the Venerable Sāriputta. In the Treatise on Knowledge, as well as in other chapters of the work, a large number of doctrinal terms appear for the first time and only in the Paṭisambhidāmagga. It also contains elaborations of terms and teachings that are mentioned only briefly in other and older parts of the Sutta Piṭaka. In addition to this, it contains material on meditation of great practical value, as for example on mindfulness of breathing,[34] *mettā-bhāvanā*, and numerous insight-exercises. There is also, to give variety to the subject matter, a passage of hymnlike character and great beauty, on the Great Compassion of the Tathāgata. Mahānāma Thera of Ceylon, who wrote the *Saddhammappakāsinī*, the commentary to the work, confidently ascribes it to the Venerable Sāriputta, and in the introductory stanzas gives eloquent praise of the great Elder. In the Paṭisambhidāmagga itself, Sāriputta is mentioned twice, once as being one who possesses *samādhi-vipphāra-iddhi* (in the Iddhividha-kathā) and again in the Mahā-paññā-kathā, Soḷasa-paññā-niddesa, where it is said, "Those whose wisdom is equal to that of Sāriputta, they partake to some extent of the Buddha-knowledge."

We come now to one of the most important contributions made by the Venerable Sāriputta to Buddhist teaching. According to tradition (e.g., in the *Atthasālinī*), the Buddha preached the Abhidhamma in the Tāvatiṃsa heaven to his mother, Queen Māyā, who had been reborn as a deva in that world. He did this for three months, and when returning daily to earth for his meals, he gave to the Venerable Sāriputta the "method" (*naya*) of that portion of Abhidhamma he had preached. The *Atthasālinī* says:

34. Translated in *Mindfulness of Breathing* by Ñāṇamoli Thera, BPS, Kandy.

"Thus the giving of the method was to the Chief Disciple, who was endowed with analytical knowledge, as though the Buddha stood on the edge of the shore and pointed out the ocean with his open hand. To the Elder the doctrine taught by the Blessed One in hundreds and thousands of methods became very clear." Thereafter, the Elder passed on what he had learned to his five hundred disciples.

Further it is said, "The textual order of the Abhidhamma originated with Sāriputta; the numerical series in the Great Book (Paṭṭhāna) was also determined by him. In this way the Elder, without spoiling the unique doctrine, laid down the numerical series in order to make it easy to learn, remember, study and teach the Law."

The *Atthasālinī*, the commentary to the Dhammasaṅgaṇī, also ascribes to Sāriputta the following contributions to the canonical Abhidhamma:

(a) The 42 couplets (dyads; *duka*) of the Suttanta Mātikā, which follow the Abhidhamma Mātikā, both of which preface the seven Abhidhamma books. The 42 Suttanta couplets are explained in the Dhammasaṅgaṇī and this likewise has probably to be ascribed to the Elder.
(b) The fourth and last part of the Dhammasaṅgaṇī, the Atthuddhārakaṇḍa, the "Synopsis."
(c) The arrangement for the recitation of the Abhidhamma (*vācanamagga*).
(d) The Numerical Section (*gaṇanacāra*) of the Paṭṭhāna.

In the *Anupada Sutta* (MN 111) the Buddha himself speaks of the Venerable Sāriputta's analysis of meditative consciousness into its chief mental concomitants, which the Elder undertook from his own experience, after rising from each of the meditative attainments in succession. This analysis may well be either a precursor or an abridgment of the detailed analysis of jhāna-consciousness given in the Dhammasaṅgaṇī.

Concerning the Venerable Sāriputta's mastery of the Dhamma, and its exposition, the Buddha had this to say:

> The Essence of Dhamma (*dhammadhātu*) has been so well penetrated by Sāriputta, O monks, that if I were to question him therein for one day in different words and phrases,

> Sāriputta would reply likewise for one day in various words and phrases. And if I were to question him for one night, or a day and a night, or for two days and nights, even up to seven days and nights, Sāriputta would expound the matter for the same period of time, in various words and phrases. (Nidāna Saṃyutta, No. 32)

And on another occasion the Master employed this simile:

> If he is endowed with five qualities, O monks, the eldest son of a World-ruling Monarch righteously turns the Wheel of Sovereignty that had been turned by his father. And that Wheel of Sovereignty cannot be overturned by any hostile human being. What are the five qualities? The eldest son of a World-ruling Monarch knows what is beneficial, knows the Law, knows the right measure, knows the right time and knows the society (with which he has to deal, *parisā*).
>
> Similarly, O monks, is Sāriputta endowed with five qualities and rightly turns the supreme Wheel of Dhamma, even as I have turned it. And this Wheel cannot be overturned by ascetics or priests, by deities or Brahma, nor by anyone else in the world. What are those five qualities? Sāriputta, O monks, knows what is beneficial, knows the Teaching, knows the right measure, knows the right time and knows the assembly (he is to address). (Aṅguttara Nikāya, 5. 132)

Other Theras were not behind in their appreciation. The Elder Vaṅgisa, in his encomium in the Theragāthā (vv. 1231–3) praises Sāriputta, who "teaches in brief and also speaks in detail," while in the same compilation other great Elders, Mahā Kassapa (vv. 1082–5) and Mahā Moggallāna (vv. 1158; 1176–7; 1182), also give their reward of praise. And the Venerable Mahā Moggallāna, at the end of Sāriputta's Discourse on Guiltlessness, (MN 5) uttered these words of tribute to his friend's sermon, "To (virtuous and earnest) monks who have heard the exposition of the Venerable Sāriputta it will be like food and drink to their ears and mind. How well does he lift up his fellow-monks from what is unwholesome, and confirm them in what is good!"

The relationship in which the two Chief Disciples stood to one another in the matter of teaching was explained by the Buddha when he said:

> Associate, O monks, with Sāriputta and Moggallāna; keep company with them! They are wise bhikkhus and helpers of their fellow-monks. Sāriputta is like a mother who brings forth, and Moggallāna is like a nurse to what has been brought forth. Sāriputta trains (his pupils) in the Fruition of stream-entry, and Moggallāna trains them for the highest goal.
>
> Sāriputta is able to expound the Four Noble Truths in detail, to teach them and make them intelligible, to proclaim, reveal and explain them, and make them clear. (MN 141, *Saccavibhaṅga Sutta*)

And in the Aṅguttara Nikāya (AN 2:12):

> A monk of faith, O bhikkhus, should cherish this right aspiration, "Oh, may I become such as Sāriputta and Moggallāna!" For Sāriputta and Moggallāna are the model and standard for my bhikkhu-disciples.

That the Venerable Sāriputta's great reputation as a teacher of the Dhamma long survived him, to become a tradition among later Buddhists, is shown by the concluding passages of the *Milinda-pañha,* written some three hundred years later. There, King Milinda compares Nāgasena Thera to the Venerable Sāriputta, saying, "In this Buddha's Dispensation there is none other like yourself for answering questions, except the Elder Sāriputta, the Marshal of the Law."

That grand reputation still lives today, upheld by the cherished teachings of the Great Disciple, preserved, and enshrined in some of the oldest books of Buddhism alongside the words of his Master.

The Elder's Relatives

As we have already seen, the Venerable Sāriputta was born into a brahmin family of Upatissa village (or Nālaka), near Rājagaha, his father's name being Vaganta and his mother's Sāri. He had three brothers: Cunda, Upasena and Revata, and three sisters named Cālā, Upacālā and Sisūpacālā. All six took ordination and attained arahatship.

Cunda was known by the name Samaṇuddesa, meaning "the Novice" in the Saṅgha, even after becoming a bhikkhu; this was to distinguish him from the Elder Mahā Cunda. At the time of

Sāriputta's death, Cunda was his attendant and it was he who informed the Buddha of his passing away, bringing with him the Chief Disciple's relics. The story is told in the *Cunda Sutta,* an outline of which will be given elsewhere in this book.

Upasena, who came to be known as Vagantaputta, or "Son of Vaganta," as Sāriputta is "Son of Sāri," was said by the Buddha to be foremost among those of all-pleasing deportment (*samantapāsādika*). He died of a snakebite, as is related in the SN 35:69/S IV 41).

Revata was the youngest of the brothers, and their mother, wishing to prevent his seeking ordination, had him married when he was a very young boy. But on the wedding day he saw the grandmother of his future wife, an old woman of 120, stricken with all the signs of decrepitude. At once he became disgusted with worldly life. Escaping from the wedding procession by a ruse, he fled to a monastery and was ordained. In later years he was on his way to see the Buddha when he stopped at a forest of acacia trees (*khadira-vana*), and while spending the rainy season there he attained Arahatship. After that he became known as Revata Khadiravaniya—"Revata of the Acacia Forest." The Buddha distinguished him as being the foremost among forest dwellers.

The three sisters, Cālā, Upacālā and Sisūpacālā, wishing to follow their brothers' example, became nuns after their marriage. In marriage, each of them had a son who was named after his mother Cālā (or Cālī) and so on. These three sons were also ordained, being received as novices by Revata Khadiravaniya. Their good conduct was praised by the Venerable Sāriputta, who met them when he went to see his youngest brother who was ill. This is recorded in the commentary to the Theragāthā, v. 42.

Cālā, Upacālā and Sisūpacālā as nuns are said to have been approached by Mara with taunting and tempting questions, to which they gave excellent replies. These are recorded in the Therīgāthā and Bhikkhunī Saṃyutta.

In contrast to all these, Sāriputta's mother was a staunch brahmin and hostile to the Buddha's Teaching and his followers. In the commentary to the Dhammapada (v. 400) it is related that once, when the Venerable Sāriputta was in his own village of Nālaka with a large retinue of monks, he came to his mother's house in the course of his alms round. His mother gave him a seat and served him with food, but while she did so she uttered abusive words, "Oh, you eater of others' leavings!" she said. "When you fail to get leavings of sour rice-gruel, you go from house to house among strangers, licking the leavings off the backs of ladles! And so it was for this that you gave up eighty crores of wealth and became a monk! You have ruined me! Now go on and eat!"

Likewise, when she was serving food to the monks, she said, "So! You are the men who have made my son your page boy! Go on, eat now!"

Thus she continued reviling them, but the Venerable Sāriputta spoke not a word. He took his food, ate it and in silence returned to the monastery. The Buddha learned of the incident from the Venerable Rāhula, who had been among the monks at the time. All the bhikkhus who heard of it wondered at the Elder's great forbearance, and in the midst of the assembly the Buddha praised him, uttering the stanza:

> He that is free from anger, who performs his duties faithfully.
> He that guards the precepts, and is free from lust;
> He that has subdued himself, he that wears his last body—
> He it is I call a brahmin.

It was not until right at the close of Sāriputta's life that he was able to convert his mother; that story will be told later on. But the incident that has been related here leads us to a consideration of the great Elder's most pleasing characteristics, his humility, patience and forbearance.

The Unresentful

It is the neighbourhood of Jetavana, where the Buddha is residing. Some men are in a group, talking about the noble qualities of the Elder Sāriputta. "Such great patience has our noble Elder," they are saying, "that even when people abuse him and strike him, he feels no trace of anger."

"Who is this that never gets angry?" The question is from a brahmin, a holder of false views. And when they tell him, "It is our Elder, Sāriputta," he retorts. "It must be that nobody has ever provoked him."

"That is not so, brahmin," they reply. "Well, then, I will provoke him to anger." "Provoke him to anger if you can!" "Leave it to me," says the brahmin. "I know just what to do to him."

The Venerable Sāriputta enters the city on his round for alms. Approaching him from behind, the brahmin strikes him in a tremendous blow on the back. "What was that?" says the Venerable Sāriputta; and without so much as turning to look, he continues on his way.

The fire of remorse leaps up in every part of the brahmin's body. Prostrating himself at the Elder's feet he begs for pardon. "For what?" asks the Elder, mildly. "To test your patience I struck you," the penitent brahmin replies. "Very well, I pardon you."

"Reverend sir," the brahmin says, "if you are willing to pardon me, hereafter please take your food only at my house." With these words he takes the Elder's alms-bowl, which the Elder willingly yields, and leading him to his house serves him with food.

But those who saw the assault are enraged. They gather at the brahmin's house, armed with sticks and stones, to kill him. When the Venerable Sāriputta emerges, accompanied by the brahmin carrying his bowl, they cry, "Reverend sir, order this brahmin to turn back!"

"Why, lay disciples?" asks the Elder. They answer, "The man struck you. We are going to give him what he deserves!"

"But what do you mean? Was it you, or me, he struck?"

"It was you, reverend sir." "Well, if it was me he struck, he has begged my pardon. Go your ways." And so, dismissing the people and permitting the brahmin to return, the great Elder calmly makes his way to the monastery.

This incident, recorded in the Dhammapada Commentary, was the occasion of the Buddha's uttering the verses 389 and 390 of the Dhammapada, which are among those that give the Buddha's definition of what constitutes a brahmin, that is to say, rectitude of conduct rather than birth or rank.

Let none strike a brahmin;
Let no brahmin return a blow.
Shame on him that strikes a brahmin!
More shame on the brahmin who returns the blow!
Not small is the gain to a brahmin

Who restrains his mind from what is dear;
As fast as the will to injure wanes
So fast indeed does suffering decline.

(Dhammapada, vv. 389, 390)

The Venerable Sāriputta's humility was as great as his patience. He was willing to receive correction from anyone, not only with submission but with gratitude. It is told in the commentary to the Devaputta Saṃyutta, *Susīma Sutta,* that once, through a momentary negligence, a corner of the Elder's under-robe was hanging down, and a seven-year-old novice, seeing this, pointed it out to him. The Venerable Sāriputta stepped aside at once and arranged the garment in the proper equally-circular way. Then he stood before the novice with folded hands, saying, "Now it is correct, teacher!"[35]

There is a reference to this incident in the *Questions of Milinda,* where these verses are ascribed to the Venerable Sāriputta:

> One who this very day, at the age of seven, has gone forth—
> If he should teach me, I accept it with (bended) head.
> At sight of him, I give him ardent zeal and regard.
> With respect may I again and again set him in the teacher's place!

On one occasion the Buddha mildly reproved Sāriputta for not having carried his teaching far enough. When the brahmin Dhānañjāni was on his deathbed, he was visited by the Venerable Sāriputta. The Elder, reflecting that brahmins are bent on the Brahma-world (or "union with Brahmā") taught the dying man the way to it through the Brahma-vihāras. As a result, it is said, the brahmin was in fact reborn there.

When the Venerable Sāriputta returned from the visit, the Master asked him, "Why, Sāriputta, while there was more to do, did you set the brahmin Dhānañjāni's thoughts on the inferior Brahma-world, and then rising from your seat, leave him?" The Venerable Sāriputta replied, "I thought, 'These brahmins are bent

35. A slightly different version of this is found in the Commentary to the Theragāthā, where it deals with Sāriputta's verses.

on the Brahma-world. Should I not show the brahmin Dhānañjāni the way to the communion with Brahmā?'"

"The brahmin Dhānañjāni has died, Sāriputta," said the Buddha, "and he has been reborn in the Brahma-world."

This story, which is found in the *Dhānañjāni Sutta* of the Majjhima Nikāya (No. 97), is interesting as an illustration of the undesirability of rebirth in an inferior Brahma-world for one who is capable of bringing rebirth entirely to an end. For while the Buddha himself sometimes showed only the way to Brahma, as for example in the *Tevijjā Sutta,* it seems probable that in the case of Dhānañjāni the Master saw that he was fit to receive a higher teaching, while the Venerable Sāriputta, lacking the capacity of knowing others' hearts (*lokiya-abhiññā*), was not able to discern that fact. The result is that Dhānañjāni will spend an incalculable period in the Brahma-world and will have to take human birth again before he can achieve the goal.

The Venerable Sāriputta received another gentle reproof when, having asked the Buddha why it was that the Sāsana (Dispensation) of some of the Buddhas of the past did not last very long, and the Buddha had replied that it was because those Enlightened Ones did not preach very much Dhamma, did not lay down regulations for the disciples, nor institute the recital of the Pātimokkha, Sāriputta said that it was now time for the Blessed One to promulgate the regulations and to recite the Pātimokkha, so that the Holy Life might last for a long period. The Buddha said, "Let it be, Sāriputta! The Tathāgata himself will know the time for it. The Master will not lay down regulations for the disciples nor recite the Pātimokkha until signs of corruption have appeared in the Saṅgha."[36]

The disciple's concern that the Sāsana should endure as long as possible is characteristic of Sāriputta; equally characteristic was it of the Buddha that he did not wish to lay down regulations until such time as it was absolutely necessary to do so. He went on to explain that at that time the least-advanced member of the Saṅgha was a Sotāpanna (perhaps a fact of which the Venerable Sāriputta was not aware), and therefore it was not yet necessary to lay down the rules of the bhikkhu life.

---

36. Pārājika Pāḷi I 3.4/Vin III 9f.

The *Cātumā Sutta* (MN 67) records another occasion when the great Elder was admonished by the Master. A large number of monks, newly ordained, as the commentary tells us, by the Venerable Sāriputta and Mahā Moggallāna, had come with the latter to pay their respects to the Buddha for the first time. On arrival they were allotted quarters and started chatting with the resident monks of Cātumā. Hearing the noise, the Buddha summoned the resident monks to question them about it, and was told that the commotion was caused by the new arrivals. The text does not say whether the visiting monks were present at the time, but they must have been, for the Buddha addressed them with the words, "Go away, monks, I dismiss you. You should not stay with me."

The newly ordained monks left, but some persons intervened in their behalf and they were allowed to return.

The Buddha then said to the Venerable Sāriputta, "What did you think, Sāriputta, when I dismissed that group of monks?"

The Venerable Sāriputta replied, "I thought, 'The Blessed One wishes to remain unconcerned and to abide in the state of happiness here-and-now; so we too shall remain unconcerned and abide in the state of happiness here-and-now.'"

"Hold, Sāriputta! Do not allow such a thought ever to arise in you again!" the Buddha said. Then turning to Mahā Moggallāna, he put the same question.

"When the Blessed One dismissed those monks," replied Mahā Moggallāna, "I thought, 'The Blessed One wishes to remain unconcerned and to abide in the state of happiness here-and-now. Then I and the Venerable Sāriputta should now look after the community of monks.'"

"Well spoken, Moggallāna, well spoken!" said the Master. "It is either myself or Sāriputta or Moggallāna who should look after the community of monks."

The sutta account is lacking in certain details which would place the story in the proper light necessary for an understanding of all its implications, but it is possible that since the monks who had been dismissed were pupils of Sāriputta and Mahā Moggallāna, the Elder wished to show his displeasure with them and to indicate by his aloofness that they had behaved badly.

Once, when the Buddha was residing at Jetavana, the Venerable Sāriputta was the victim of a false accusation. It so happened that at the end of the rains the Elder took leave of the Master and departed with his own retinue of monks on a journey. A large number of monks also took leave of Sāriputta, and in dismissing them he addressed those who were known by their personal and family names, by those names. Among them there was a monk who was not known by his personal and family name, but a strong desire arose in him that the Chief Disciple should address him by those names in taking his departure.

In the great throng of monks, however, the Venerable Sāriputta did not give him this distinction, and the monk was aggrieved. "He does not greet me as he does the other monks," he thought, and conceived a grudge against Sāriputta. At the same time it chanced that the hem of the Elder's robe brushed against him, and this added to his grievance. He approached the Buddha and complained: "Lord, the Venerable Sāriputta, doubtless thinking to himself, 'I am the Chief Disciple,' struck me a blow that almost damaged my ear. And having done that without so much as begging my pardon, he set out on his journey."

The Buddha summoned Sāriputta into his presence. Meanwhile, the Venerable Mahā Moggallāna and the Venerable Ānanda, knowing that a calumny was about to be exposed, summoned all the monks, convoking an assembly. "Approach, venerable sirs!" they called. "When the Venerable Sāriputta is face to face with the Master, he will roar the roar of a lion!"[37]

And so it came about. When the Master questioned the great Elder, instead of denying the charge, he said, "O Lord, one who is not firmly established in the contemplation of the body with regard to his body, such a one may be able to hurt a fellow monk and leave without apologising." Then followed the Venerable Sāriputta's lion's roar. He compared his freedom from anger and hatred with the patience of the earth, which receives all things, clean and unclean; his tranquillity of mind to a bull with severed horns, to a lowly outcast youth, to water, fire and wind, and to the removal of impurity; he compared the oppression he felt from his own body to the oppression of snakes and corpses, and the maintenance of his body to that of fatty excrescences. In nine

37. A "lion's roar" (*sīha-nāda*) is a weighty and emphatic utterance, made with assurance.

similes he described his own virtues, and nine times the great earth responded to the words of truth. The entire assembly was moved by the majestic force of his utterance.

As the Elder proclaimed his virtues, remorse filled the monk who had unjustly traduced him. Immediately, he fell at the feet of the Blessed One, admitting his slander and confessing his fault. Thereupon the Buddha said, "Sāriputta, pardon this deluded man, lest his head should split into seven pieces." Sāriputta's reply was, "Venerable sir, I freely pardon this venerable monk." And, with joined palms, he added, "May this venerable monk also pardon me if I have in any way offended him."

In this way they were reconciled. The other monks were filled with admiration, saying, "See, monks, the surpassing goodness of the Elder! He cherishes neither anger nor hatred against this lying, slanderous monk! Instead, he crouches before him, stretches his hands in reverence and asks his pardon."

The Buddha's comment was, "Bhikkhus, it is impossible for Sāriputta and his like to cherish anger or hatred. Sāriputta's mind is like the great earth, firm like a gate post, like a pool of still water."

> Unresentful like the earth, firm like a gate post,
> With mind like a clear pool, such is the virtuous man
> For whom the round of births exists no more.[38]

Another incident of this nature, in the early Saṅgha, did not end so happily, for the calumniator refused to admit his fault. He was a monk named Kokālika, who approached the Buddha with a slander against the two Chief Disciples: "Sāriputta and Moggallāna have bad intentions, O Lord!" he said. "They are in the grip of evil ambition."

The Master replied, "Do not say so, Kokālika! Do not say so! Have friendly and trustful thoughts towards Sāriputta and Moggallāna! They are of good behaviour, and lovable!"

But the misguided Kokālika paid no heed to the Buddha's words. He persisted with his false accusation, and soon after that his whole body became covered with boils, which continued to grow until eventually he died of his illness.

38. Dhammapada, v. 95.

This incident was well-known. It is recorded in the following places in the Sutta-Piṭaka: Brahma Saṃyutta No. 10; Sutta Nipāta, Mahāvagga No. 10; Aṅguttara Nikāya 5. 170, and Takkariya Jātaka (No. 481). A comparison of these two incidents reveals the importance of penitence. Neither the Venerable Sāriputta nor Mahā Moggallāna bore the monk Kokālika any ill-will for his malice, and his apologies, had he offered them, would have made no difference to the attitude of the two Chief Disciples. But they would have benefitted the erring monk himself, averting the consequences of his bad kamma. Evil rebounds upon those who direct it towards the innocent, and so Kokālika was judged and punished by himself, through his own deeds.

Part III

The Further Shore

The Last Debt Paid

We now come to the year of the Master's Parinibbāna. The Blessed One had spent the rainy season at Beluva village,[39] near Vesāli, and when the Retreat was over he left that place and, going by the way he had come, returned by stages to Sāvatthī and arrived at the Jeta Grove Monastery.

There the Elder Sāriputta, the Marshal of the Law, paid homage to the Blessed One and went to his day quarters. When his own disciples had saluted him and left, he swept the place and spread his leather mat. Then, having rinsed his feet, he sat down cross-legged and entered into the state of the Fruition Attainment of Arahatship.

At the time predetermined by him, he arose from the meditation, and this thought occurred to him, "Do the Enlightened Ones have their final passing away first, or the Chief Disciples?" And he saw that it is the Chief Disciples who pass away first. Thereupon he considered his own life-force, and saw that its residue would sustain him only for another week.

He then considered, "Where shall I have my final passing away?" And he thought, "Rāhula finally passed away among the deities of the Thirty-three, and the Elder Kondañña the Knower at the Chaddanta Lake.[40] Where, then, will be my place?"

While thinking this over repeatedly he remembered his mother, and the thought came to him, "Although she is the mother of seven arahats[41] she has no faith in the Buddha, the Dhamma and the Saṅgha. Has she the supportive conditions in her to acquire that faith or has she not?"

---

39. See *Mahā-Parinibbāna Sutta*, Ch. II (*Last Days of the Buddha*, BP 213). It was during his stay at Beluva that the Master fell gravely ill.

40. In the Himālayas.

41. Sāriputta himself and his younger brothers and sisters.

Investigating the matter he discerned that she had the supportive conditions for the Path-intuition (*abhisamaya*) of stream-entry. Then he asked himself, "Through whose instruction can she win to the penetration of truth?"

And he saw that not through anyone else's but only through his own instruction in the Dhamma could it come about. And following upon that came the thought, "If I now remain indifferent, people will say, 'Sāriputta has been a helper to so many others; on the day, for instance, when he preached the *Discourse to the Deities of Tranquil Mind*, a large number of devas attained arahatship, and still more of them penetrated to the first three Paths; and on other occasions there were many who attained to stream-entry, and there were thousands of families who were reborn in heavenly worlds after the Elder had inspired them with joyous confidence in the Triple Gem. Yet despite this, he cannot remove the wrong views of his own mother? Thus people may speak of me. Therefore I shall free my mother from her wrong views, and shall have my final passing away in the very chamber where I was born."

Having made that decision, he thought, "This very day I shall ask the Master's permission and then leave for Nālaka." And, calling the Elder Cunda, who was his attendant, he said, "Friend Cunda, please ask our group of five hundred bhikkhus to take their bowls and robes, for I wish to go to Nālaka." And the Elder Cunda did as he was bidden.

The bhikkhus put their lodgings in order, took their bowls and robes, and presented themselves before the Elder Sāriputta. He, for his own part, had tidied up his living quarters and swept the place where he used to spend the day. Then, standing at the gate, he looked back at the place, thinking, "This is my last sight of it. There will be no more coming back."

Then, together with the five hundred bhikkhus, he went to the Blessed One, saluted him and spoke, "May, O Lord, the Blessed One permit, may the Exalted One consent, the time of my final passing away has come, I have relinquished the life-force."

Lord of the World, O greatest Sage!
From life I soon shall be released.
Going and coming no more shall be;

This is the last time that I worship thee.
Short is the life that now remains to me;
But seven days from now, and I shall lay
This body down, throwing the burden off.
Grant it, O Master! Give permission, Lord!
At last for me Nibbāna's time has come,
Relinquished have I now the will to live.

Now, says the text, if the Enlightened One were to have replied, "You may have your final passing away," hostile sectarians would say that he was speaking in praise of death; and if he had replied, "Do not have your final passing away," they would say that he extolled the continuation of the round of existence. Therefore the Blessed One did not speak in either way, but asked, "Where will your final passing away take place?"

The Venerable Sāriputta replied, "In the Magadha country, in the village called Nālaka, there in the chamber of my birth shall I finally pass away."

Then the Blessed One said, "Do, Sāriputta, what you think timely. But now your elder and younger monks in the Saṅgha will no longer have the chance to see a bhikkhu like you. Give them once more a discourse on Dhamma."

The great Elder then gave a discourse, displaying all his wondrous powers; rising to the loftiest heights of truth, descending to mundane truth, rising again, and again descending, he expounded the Dhamma directly and in symbols. And when he had ended his discourse he paid homage at the feet of the Master; embracing his legs, he said, "So that I might worship these feet I have fulfilled the Perfections throughout an aeon and a hundred thousand kalpas. My heart's wish has found fulfilment. From now on there will be no more contact or meeting; severed now is that intimate connection. The City of Nibbāna, the unaging, undying, peaceful, blissful, heat-assuaging and secure, which has been entered by many hundreds of thousands of Buddhas—I too shall enter it now.

"If any deed or word of mine did not please you, O Lord, may the Blessed One forgive me! It is now time for me to go."

Now, once before the Buddha had answered this, when he said, "There is nothing, be it in deeds or words, wherein I should have to reproach you, Sāriputta. For you are learned, Sāriputta, of great wisdom, of broad and bright, quick, keen and penetrative wisdom." (SN 8:7/S I 190f)

So now he made answer in the same way, "I forgive you, Sāriputta," he said. "But there was not a single word or deed of yours that was displeasing to me. Do now, Sāriputta, what you think timely."

From this we see that on those few occasions when the Master seemed to reproach his Chief Disciple, it was not that he was displeased with him in any way, but rather that he was pointing out another approach to a situation, another way of viewing a problem.

Immediately after the Master had given his permission and the Venerable Sāriputta had risen from paying homage at his feet, the Great Earth cried out, and with a single huge tremor shook to its watery boundaries. It was as though the Great Earth wished to say, "Though I bear these girdling mountain ranges with Mount Meru, the encircling mountain walls (*cakkavāḷa*) and the Himavant, I cannot sustain on this day so vast an accumulation of virtue!" And mighty thunder split the heavens, a vast cloud appeared and heavy rain poured down.

Then the Blessed One thought, "I shall now permit the Marshal of the Law to depart," and he rose from the seat of the Law, went to his Perfumed Cell and there stood on the Jewel Slab. Three times the Venerable Sāriputta circumambulated the cell, keeping it to his right, and paid reverence at four places. And this thought was in his mind, "An aeon and a hundred thousand kalpas ago it was, when I fell down at the feet of the Buddha Anomadassi and made the aspiration to see you. This aspiration has been realiased, and I have seen you. At the first meeting it was my first sight of you; now it is my last, and there will be none in the future." And with raised hands joined in salutation he departed, going backwards until the Blessed One was out of sight. And yet again the Great Earth, unable to bear it, trembled to its watery boundaries.

The Blessed One then addressed the bhikkhus who surrounded him. "Go, bhikkhus," he said. "Accompany your elder brother." At these words, all the four assemblies of devotees at once went out of the Jeta Grove, leaving the Blessed One there alone. The citizens of Sāvatthī also, having heard the news, went out of the city in an unending stream carrying incense and flowers in their hands; and with their hair wet (the sign of mourning), they followed the Elder lamenting and weeping.

The Venerable Sāriputta then admonished the crowd, saying, "This is a road that none can avoid," and asked them to return. And to the monks who had accompanied him, he said, "You may turn back now! Do not neglect the Master!"

Thus he made them go back, and with only his own group of disciples, he continued on his way. Yet still some of the people followed him, lamenting. "Formerly our venerable went on journeys and returned. But this is a journey without return!" To them the Elder said, "Be heedful, friends! Of such nature, indeed, are all things that are formed and conditioned!" And he made them turn back.

During his journey the Venerable Sāriputta spent one night wherever he stopped, and thus for one week he favoured many people with a last sight of him. Reaching Nālaka village in the evening, he stopped near a banyan tree at the village gate. It happened that at the time a nephew of the Elder, Uparevata by name, had gone outside the village and there he saw the Venerable Sāriputta. He approached the Elder, saluted him, and remained standing.

The Elder asked him, "Is your grand-aunt at home?" "Yes, venerable sir," he replied. "Then go and announce our coming," said the Elder. "And if she asks why I have come, tell her that I shall stay in the village for one day, and ask her to prepare my birth chamber and provide lodgings for five hundred bhikkhus."

Uparevata went to his grand-aunt and said, "Grandaunt, my uncle has come."

"Where is he now?" she asked.

"At the village gate."

"Is he alone, or has someone else come with him?"

"He has come with five hundred bhikkhus."

And when she asked him, "Why has he come?" he gave her the message the elder had entrusted to him. Then she thought, "Why does he ask me to provide lodgings for so many? After becoming a monk in his youth, does he want to be a layman again in his old age?" But she arranged the birth chamber for the Elder and lodgings for the bhikkhus, had torches lit and then sent for the Elder.

The Venerable Sāriputta then, accompanied by the bhikkhus, went up to the terrace of the house and entered his birth chamber. After seating himself, he asked the bhikkhus to go to their quarters. They had hardly left, when a grave illness, dysentery, fell upon the Elder, and he felt severe pains. When one pail was brought in, another was carried out. The brahmin lady thought, "The news of my son is not good," and she stood leaning by the door of her own room.

And then it happened, the text tells us, that the Four Great Divine Kings asked themselves, "Where may he now be dwelling, the Marshal of the Law?" And they perceived that he was at Nālaka, in his birth chamber, lying on the bed of his Final Passing Away. "Let us go for a last sight of him," they said.

When they reached the birth chamber, they saluted the Elder and remained standing.

"Who are you?" asked the Elder.

"We are the Great Divine Kings, venerable sir."

"Why have you come?"

"We want to attend on you during your illness."

"Let it be!" said the Venerable Sāriputta. "There is an attendant here. You may go."

When they had left, there came in the same manner Sakka the king of the gods, and after him, Mahā Brahma, and all of them the Elder dismissed in the same way.

The brahmin lady, seeing the coming and going of these deities, asked herself, "Who could they have been, who came and paid homage to my son, and then left?" And she went to the door of the elder's room and asked the Venerable Cunda for news about the Elder's condition. Cunda conveyed the inquiry to the Elder, telling him, "The Great Upāsikā (lay devotee) has come."

The Venerable Sāriputta asked her, "Why have you come at this unusual hour?"

"To see you, dear," she replied. "Tell me, who were those who came first?"

"The Four Great Divine Kings, Upāsikā."

"Are you, then, greater than they?" she asked.

"They are like temple attendants," said the Elder. "Ever since our Master took rebirth they have stood guard over him with swords in hand."

"After they had left, who was it that came then, dear?"

"It was Sakka the king of the gods."

"Are you, then, greater than the king of gods, dear?"

"He is like a novice who carries a bhikkhu's belongings," answered Sāriputta. "When our Master returned from the heaven of the Thirty-three (Tāvatiṃsa), Sakka took his bowl and robe and descended to earth together with him."

"And when Sakka had gone, who was it that came after him, filling the room with his radiance?"

"Upāsikā, that was your own Lord and Master, the Great Brahma."

"Then are you greater, my son, even than my Lord, the Great Brahma?"

"Yes, Upāsikā. On the day when our Master was born, it is said that four Great Brahmas received the Great Being in a golden net."

Upon hearing this, the brahmin lady thought, "If my son's power is such as this, what must be the majestic power of my son's Master and Lord?" And while she was thinking this, suddenly the fivefold rapture arose in her, suffusing her entire body.

The Elder thought, "Rapture and joy have arisen in my mother. Now is the time to preach the Dhamma to her." And he said, "What was it you were thinking about, Upāsikā?"

"I was thinking," she replied, "if my son has such virtue, what must be the virtue of his Master?"

The Venerable Sāriputta answered, "At the moment of my Master's birth, at his Great Renunciation (of worldly life), on his attaining Enlightenment and at his first turning of the Dhamma Wheel—on all these occasions the ten-thousandfold world-system quaked and shook. None is there who equals him in virtue, in concentration, in wisdom, in deliverance, and in the knowledge and vision of deliverance." And he then explained to her in detail the words of homage, "Such indeed is that Blessed One..." (*Iti pi so Bhagavā...*). And thus he gave her an exposition of the Dhamma, basing it on the virtues of the Buddha.

When the Dhamma talk given by her beloved son had come to an end, the brahmin lady was firmly established in the Fruition of stream-entry, and she said, "Oh, my dear Upatissa, why did you act like that? Why, during all these years, did you not bestow on me this ambrosia (the knowledge of the Deathless)?"

The Elder thought, "Now I have given my mother, the brahmin lady Rūpa-Sārī, the nursing-fee for bringing me up. This should suffice," and he dismissed her with the words, "You may go now, Upāsikā."

When she was gone, he asked, "What is the time now, Cunda?"

"Venerable sir, it is early dawn."

And the Elder said, "Let the community of bhikkhus assemble."

When the bhikkhus had assembled, he said to Cunda, "Lift me up to a sitting position, Cunda." And Cunda did so.

Then the Elder spoke to the bhikkhus, saying, "For forty-four years I have lived and travelled with you, my monks. If any deed or word of mine was unpleasant to you, forgive me, monks."

And they replied, "Venerable sir, not the least displeasure has ever come from you to us, who followed you inseparably like your shadow. But may you, venerable sir, grant forgiveness to us!"

After that the Elder gathered his large robe around him, covered his face and lay down on his right side. Then, just as the Master was to do at his Mahā Parinibbāna, he entered into the nine successive attainments of meditation, in forward and reverse order, and beginning again with the first absorption he led his meditation up to the fourth absorption. And at the moment after he had entered it, just as the crest of the rising sun appeared over the horizon, he utterly passed away into the Nibbāna-element which is without any remnant of clinging.

And it was the full-moon day of the month Kattikā, which by the solar calendar is between October and November.

The brahmin lady in her room thought, "How is my son? He does not say anything." She rose, and going into the Elder's room she massaged his legs. Then, seeing that he had passed away, she fell at his feet, loudly lamenting: "O my dear son! Before this, we did not know of your virtue. Because of that, we did not gain the good fortune to have seated in this house, and to feed, many a hundred bhikkhus! We did not gain the good fortune to have built many monasteries!" And she lamented thus up to sunrise.

As soon as the sun was up, she sent for goldsmiths and had the treasure room opened and had the pots full of gold weighed on a large scale. Then she gave the gold to the goldsmiths with the order to prepare funeral ornaments. Columns and arches were erected, and in the centre of the village the Upāsikā had a pavilion of heart-wood built. In the middle of the pavilion a large, gabled structure was raised, surrounded by a parapet wall of golden arches and columns. Then they began the sacred ceremony, in which men and deities mingled.

After the great assembly of people had celebrated the sacred rites for a full week, they made a pyre with many kinds of fragrant woods. They placed the body of the Venerable Sāriputta on the pyre and kindled the wood with bundles of Usīra roots. Throughout the night of the cremation the concourse listened to sermons on the Dhamma. After that the flames of the pyre were extinguished by the Elder Anuruddha with scented water. The Elder Cunda gathered together the relics and placed them in a filter cloth.

Then the Elder Cunda thought, "I cannot tarry here any longer. I must tell the Fully Enlightened One of the final passing away of my elder brother, the Venerable Sāriputta, the Marshal of the Law." So he took the filter cloth with the relics, and the Venerable Sāriputta's alms-bowl and robes, and went to Sāvatthī, spending only one night at each stage of the journey.

These are the events related in the commentary to the *Cunda Sutta* of the Satipaṭṭhāna Saṃyutta, with additions from the parallel version in the commentary to the *Mahā-Parinibbāna Sutta.* The narrative is taken up in the *Cunda Sutta,* which follows.

Cunda Sutta[42]

Once the Blessed One was dwelling at Sāvatthī, in Anāthapiṇḍika's park. At that time the Venerable Sāriputta was at Nālaka village in the Magadha country, and was sick, suffering, gravely ill. The Novice Cunda[43] was his attendant.

And the Venerable Sāriputta passed away finally through that very illness. Then the Novice Cunda took the alms-bowl and robes of the Venerable Sāriputta and went to Sāvatthī, to the

42. SN 47:13/S V 161ff.

43. Cunda Samaṇuddesa. Comy: "He was the Venerable Sāriputta's younger brother. Before he received Higher Ordination the bhikkhus used to call him so, and even when he was an Elder he was still so addressed."

Jeta Grove, Anāthapiṇḍika's park. There he betook himself to the Venerable Ānanda and, having saluted him, seated himself at one side. Thus seated, he spoke to the Venerable Ānanda saying, "Venerable sir, the Venerable Sāriputta has had his final passing away. These are his bowl and robes."

"On this matter, Cunda, we ought to see the Blessed One. Let us go, friend Cunda, and meet the Master. Having met him, we shall acquaint the Blessed One with that fact."

"Yes, venerable sir," said the Novice Cunda.

They went to see the Blessed One, and having arrived there and saluted the Master, they seated themselves at one side. Then the Venerable Ānanda addressed the Blessed One:

"O Lord, the Novice Cunda has told me this, 'The Venerable Sāriputta has had his final passing away. These are his bowl and robes.' Then, O Lord, my own body became weak as a creeper; everything around became dim and things were no longer clear to me, when I heard about the final passing away of the Venerable Sāriputta."

"How is this, Ānanda? When Sāriputta had his final passing away, did he take from you your portion of virtue, or your portion of concentration, or your portion of the knowledge and vision of deliverance?"

"Not so, Lord. When the Venerable Sāriputta had his final passing away he did not take my portion of virtue... concentration... wisdom... deliverance, or my portion of the knowledge and vision of deliverance. But O Lord, the Venerable Sāriputta has been to me a mentor, teacher and instructor, one who rouses, inspires and gladdens, untiring in preaching Dhamma, a helper of his fellow monks. And we remember how vitalising, enjoyable and helpful his Dhamma instruction was."

"Have I not taught you before, Ānanda, that it is the nature of all things near and dear to us that we must suffer separation from them, and be severed from them? Of that which is born, come to being, put together, and so is subject to dissolution, how should it be said that it should not depart? That, indeed, is not possible. It is, Ānanda, as though from a mighty hardwood tree a large branch should break off, so has Sāriputta now had his final passing away from this great and sound community of bhikkhus. Indeed, Ānanda, of that which is born, come to being, put together, and so is subject to dissolution, how should it be said that it should not depart? This, indeed, is not possible.

"Therefore, Ānanda, be ye an island unto yourself, a refuge unto yourself, seeking no external refuge; with the Teaching as your island, the Teaching your refuge, seeking no other refuge."

The commentary takes up the narrative thus:

> The Master stretched forth his hand, and taking the filter with the relics, placed it on his palm, and said to the monks:
>
> "These, O monks, are the shell-coloured relics of the bhikkhu who, not long ago, asked for permission to have his final passing away. He who fulfiled the perfections for an incalculable period and a hundred thousand aeons—this was that bhikkhu. He who helped me in turning the Wheel of the Law that was first turned by me—this was that bhikkhu. He who obtained the seat next to me—this was that bhikkhu. He who, apart from me, had none to equal him in wisdom throughout the whole ten-thousandfold universe—this was that bhikkhu. Of great wisdom was this bhikkhu, of broad wisdom, bright wisdom, quick wisdom, of penetrative wisdom was this bhikkhu. Few wants had this bhikkhu; he was contented, bent on seclusion, not fond of company, full of energy, an exhorter of his fellow monks, censuring what is evil. He who went forth into homelessness, abandoning the great fortune obtained through his merits in five hundred existences—this was that bhikkhu. He who, in my Dispensation, was patient like the earth—this was that bhikkhu. Harmless like a bull whose horns had been cut—this was that bhikkhu. Of humble mind like an outcast boy—this was that bhikkhu.
>
> "See here, O monks, the relics of him who was of great wisdom, of broad, bright, quick, keen and penetrative wisdom; who had few wants and was contented, bent on seclusion, not fond of company, energetic—see here the relics of him who was an exhorter of his fellow monks, who censured evil!"

Then the Buddha spoke the following verses in praise of his Great Disciple:

"To him who in five times a hundred lives
Went forth to homelessness, casting away
Pleasures the heart holds dear, from passion free,
With faculties controlled—now homage pay
To Sāriputta who has passed away!
To him who, strong in patience like the earth,
Over his own mind had absolute sway,
Who was compassionate, kind, serenely cool,
And firm as earth withal—now homage pay
To Sāriputta who has passed away!
Who, like an outcast boy of humble mind,
Enters the town and slowly wends his way
From door to door with begging bowl in hand,
Such was this Sāriputta—now homage pay
To Sāriputta who has passed away!
One who in town or jungle, hurting none,
Lived like a bull whose horns are cut away,
Such was this Sāriputta, who had won
Mastery of himself—now homage pay
To Sāriputta who has passed away!"

* * *

When the Blessed One had thus lauded the virtues of the Venerable Sāriputta, he asked for a stupa to be built for the relics.

After that, he indicated to the Elder Ānanda his wish to go to Rājagaha. Ānanda informed the monks, and the Blessed One, together with a large body of bhikkhus, journeyed to Rājagaha. At the time he arrived there, the Venerable Mahā Moggallāna had also had his final passing away. The Blessed One took his relics likewise, and had a stupa raised for them.

Then he departed from Rājagaha, and going by stages towards the Ganges, he reached Ukkacelā. There he went to the bank of the Ganges, and seated with his following of monks he preached the *Ukkacelā Sutta*, on the Parinibbāna of Sāriputta and Mahā Moggallāna.

Ukkacelā Sutta

[44]"Once the Blessed One was dwelling in the Vajji country, at Ukkacelā on the bank of the river Ganges, not long after Sāriputta and Mahā Moggallāna had passed away. And at that time the Blessed One was seated in the open, surrounded by the company of monks.

The Blessed One surveyed the silent gathering of monks, and then spoke to them, saying:

"This assembly, O bhikkhus, appears indeed empty to me, now that Sāriputta and Mahā Moggallāna have passed away. This assembly was not empty for me [before], and I had no concern for whatever quarter Sāriputta and Mahā Moggallāna were dwelling in.

"Those who in the past have been Holy Ones, Fully Enlightened Ones, those Blessed Ones, too, had such excellent pairs of disciples as I had in Sāriputta and Mahā Moggallāna. Those who in the future will be Holy Ones, Fully Enlightened Ones, those Blessed Ones too will have such excellent pairs of disciples as I had in Sāriputta and Mahā Moggallāna.

"Marvellous it is, most wonderful it is, bhikkhus, concerning those disciples, that they will act in accordance with the Master's Dispensation, will act in accordance with his advice; that they will be dear to the four Assemblies, will be loved, respected and honoured by them. Marvellous it is, most wonderful it is, bhikkhus, concerning the Perfect Ones, that when such a pair of disciples has passed away there is no grief, no lamentation on the part of the Perfect One.

"For of that which is born, come to being, put together and so is subject to dissolution, how should it be said that it should not depart? That indeed, is not possible.

"Therefore, bhikkhus, be ye an island unto yourselves, a refuge unto yourselves, seeking no external refuge; with the Teaching as your island, the Teaching your refuge, seeking no other refuge."

* * *

---

44. SN 47:14/S V 163f.

And with that profound and deeply moving exhortation, which echoes again and again through the Buddha's Teaching up to the time of his own final passing away, ends the story of the youth Upatissa who became the Master's Chief Disciple, the beloved "Marshal of the Law." The Venerable Sāriputta died on the full moon of the month Kattikā, which begins in October and ends in November of the solar calendar. The death of Mahā Moggallāna followed a half-month later, on the Uposatha of the New Moon. Half a year later, according to tradition, came the Parinibbāna of the Buddha himself.

Could such an auspicious combination of three great personages, so fruitful in blessings to gods and men, have been brought about purely by chance? We find the answer to that question in the Milinda-pañhā,[45] where Nāgasena says:

> "In many hundred thousands of births, too, sire, the Elder Sāriputta was the Bodhisatta's father, grandfather, uncle, brother, son, nephew or friend."[46] So the weary round of becoming, which linked them together in time, came at last to its end; time which is but the succession of fleeting events became for them the Timeless, and round of birth and death gave place to the Deathless. And in their final lives they kindled a glory that has illumined the world. Long may it continue to do so!"

45. This is according to the Commentary to the *Ukkacelā Sutta*.
46. *Milinda's Questions* by I. B. Horner, Vol. I, p. 295. See also the chapter "Sāriputta in the Jātakas" (Part V below).

Part IV

Discourses of Sāriputta

The suttas attributed to the Venerable Sāriputta cover a wide range of subjects connected with the Holy Life, from simple morality up to abstruse points of doctrine and meditation practice. A list of them, together with a brief description of the subject matter of each, is given below. Their arrangement in the Sutta Piṭaka does not give any indication of the chronological order in which they were delivered. Some few, however, contain references to particular events which make it possible to assign to them a period in the Buddha's ministry. One such is the *Anāthapiṇḍika Sutta,* preached just before the great lay disciple's death.

Majjhima Nikāya

No. 3: Heirs of Dhamma (*Dhammadāyāda Sutta*)

> After the Buddha had discoursed on "heirs of Dhamma" and "heirs of worldliness" and had retired into his cell, the Venerable Sāriputta addresses the monks on how they should conduct themselves, and how not, when the Master goes into seclusion. They likewise should cultivate seclusion, should reject what they are told to give up and should be modest and lovers of solitude. He concludes by speaking on the evil of the sixteen defilements of mind[47] and says that the Middle Way by which they can be eradicated is the Noble Eightfold Path.

No. 5: Without Blemishes (*Anaṅgaṇa Sutta*)

> On four types of persons: those who are guilty of an offence and know it, and those who are guilty and unaware of it; those who are guiltless and know it, and those who are guiltless and unaware of it. The first of each pair is said to be the better one of the two, and the reason is explained. This discourse shows

47. See "The Simile of the Cloth" (MN 7) in *Wheel* No. 61/62.

the importance of self-examination for moral and spiritual progress.

No. 9: Right Understanding (*Sammā-diṭṭhi Sutta*)
No. 28: The Greater Discourse on the Elephant Footprint Simile (*Mahā-hatthipadopama Sutta*)
No. 43: The Greater Discourse on Explanations (*Mahā-vedalla Sutta*)

The Elder answers a number of questions put by the Venerable Mahā Koṭṭhita, who was foremost in analytical knowledge. Sāriputta matches the excellence of the questions with the clarity and profundity of his answers. The questions and answers extend from analytical examination of terms, through the position of wisdom and right understanding to subtle aspects of meditation.

No. 69: Discourse to Gulissāni (*Gulissāni Sutta*)

On the conduct and Dhamma-practice to be followed by a forest-dwelling monk. Questioned by the Venerable Mahā Moggallāna, the Elder confirms that the same duties apply also to monks living in the vicinity of towns and villages.

No. 97: Discourse to Dhānañjāni (*Dhānañjāni Sutta*)

The Venerable Sāriputta explains to the brahmin Dhānañjāni that the multifarious duties of a layman are no excuse for wrong moral conduct, nor do they exempt one from painful consequences of such conduct in a future existence.

Later, when Dhānañjāni was on his deathbed he requested the Elder to visit him, and the Venerable Sāriputta spoke to him, on the way to Brahma through the Brahma-vihāras. The Buddha mildly reproached the Elder for not having led Dhānañjāni to a higher understanding.

No. 114: To Be Practised and Not To Be Practised (*Sevitabbāsevitabba Sutta*)

The Venerable Sāriputta elaborates upon brief indications given by the Buddha on what should be practised, cultivated or used, and what should not. This is shown with regard to threefold action in deed, word and thought; in relation to mental attitudes and views, the six sense objects and the monk's requisites.

No. 143: Discourse to Anāthapiṇḍika (*Anāthapiṇḍikovāda Sutta*)

The Venerable Sāriputta is called to Anāthapiṇḍika's deathbed and admonishes him to free his mind from any attachment whatsoever, beginning with the six sense organs, "Thus should you train yourself, householder, 'I shall not cling to the eye, and my consciousness will not attach itself to the eye.' Thus, householder, should you train yourself." This is repeated in full for each of the other five sense organs, the six sense objects, the sixfold consciousness, sixfold contact, sixfold feeling born of contact, the six elements, the five aggregates, the four incorporeal jhānas, and concludes with detachment from this world and all other worlds; detachment from all things seen, heard, sensed and thought; from all that is encountered, sought and pursued in mind.

In short, detachment should be practised as to the entire range of experience, beginning with what for a dying person will be his immediate concern, his sense faculties and their function.

This call for detachment, drawing ever wider circles and repeating the same mighty chord of thought, must have had a deeply penetrating impact and a calming, liberating, even cheering influence on the dying devotee's mind. This was what Sāriputta, the skilled teacher, obviously intended. And in fact his words had that impact because our text says that Anāthapiṇḍika was moved to tears by the loftiness of the discourse, one in profundity unlike any he had ever heard before. Anāthapiṇḍika passed away soon after, and was reborn as a deity in Tusita Heaven.

Dīgha Nikāya

No. 28: Faith-Inspiring Discourse (*Sampasādanīya Sutta*)

An eloquent tribute to the Buddha by Sāriputta, spoken in the Buddha's presence and proclaiming the peerless qualities (*anuttariya*) of his Teaching. It is an expression and at the same time a justification of Sāriputta's deep confidence in the

Buddha. It may be regarded as complementary to Sāriputta's "Lion's Roar," which forms the first section of the discourse and is repeated in the *Mahā-Parinibbāna Sutta*.[48]

No. 33: Doctrinal Recitation (*Saṅgīti Sutta*) and No. 34: Tenfold Series Discourse (*Dasuttara Sutta*)

Aṅguttara Nikāya

The first number denotes the number of the book (*Nipāta*) and the second the number of the sutta. The division of the suttas in the Aṅguttara Nikāya is only numerical.

2:37 (*Samacitta-Sutta*): On the stream-winner, the once-returner, and the non-returner, and on what determines the places of the rebirths they have still before them.

3:21: On another classification of noble persons (*ariya puggala*): the body-witness (*kāyasakkhi*), the one attained to right understanding (*diṭṭhippatto*) and the one liberated through faith (*saddha-vimutto*).

4:79: Sāriputta asks the Buddha why the enterprises of some people fail, those of others succeed, and those of others even surpass their expectations. The Buddha replies that one of the reasons is generosity, or lack of it, shown to ascetics, priests, and monks.

4:156: On four qualities indicative of loss or maintenance of wholesome states of mind.

> Here it is said that if one finds in oneself four qualities one can know for certain that one has lost wholesome qualities, and that this is what has been called deterioration by the Blessed One. These four are: excessive greed, excessive hate, excessive delusion, and lack of knowledge and wisdom concerning the diverse profound subjects (relating to wisdom).
>
> If on the other hand, one finds in oneself four other qualities, one can know for certain that one has not lost one's wholesome qualities, and that this is what has been called progress by the Blessed One. These four other qualities are: attenuated greed, attenuated hate, attenuated delusion, and

48. See *Wheel* No. 67/69.

the possession of knowledge and wisdom concerning the diverse profound subjects (relating to wisdom).

4:167f: The four types of progress on the Path.

4:171: Sāriputta elaborates a brief statement made by the Buddha on the four forms of personalised existence (*attabhāva*) and puts an additional question. The Buddha's reply to it was later elaborated by Sāriputta in the *Samacitta Sutta* (see above).

4:172: Sāriputta states that he attained to the fourfold analytical knowledge (*paṭisambhidā-ñana*) two weeks after his ordination (i.e., at his attainment of arahatship). He appeals to the Buddha for confirmation.

4:173: Discussion with Mahā Koṭṭhita on the limits of the explainable. The Venerable Sāriputta says: "As far, brother, as the six bases of sense-impression (*phassāyatana*) reach, so far reaches the (explainable) world of diffuseness (*papañca*); and as far as the world of diffuseness reaches, so far reach the six bases of sense-impression. Through the entire fading away and cessation of the six bases of sense impression, the world of diffuseness ceases and is stilled."

4:175: On the need of both knowledge and right conduct (*vijjācaraṇa*) for the ending of suffering.

4:179: On the reasons for obtaining, and not obtaining, Nibbāna in the present life.

5:165: Five reasons why people ask questions: through stupidity and foolishness; with evil intentions and through covetousness; with a desire to know; out of contempt; with the thought: "If he answers my question correctly, it is good; if not, then I shall give the correct answer."

5:167: On how to censure fellow-monks.

6:14–15: Causes of a monk's good or bad dying.

6:41: Sāriputta explains that a monk with supernormal powers may, if he so wishes, regard a tree trunk merely as being solid, or as liquid, fiery (calorific) or airy (vibratory), or as being either pure or impure (beautiful or ugly), because all these elements are to be found in the tree.

7:66: On respect and reverence, Sāriputta says that these are helpful in overcoming what is unwholesome and developing what is wholesome: that is, respect and reverence towards the Master, the Teaching, the Community of Monks, the training, meditation, heedfulness (*appamāda*) and towards the spirit of kindliness and courtesy (*paṭisanthāra*). Each of these factors is said to be a condition of the one following it.

9:6: On the two things needful to know about people, robes, alms-food, lodging, villages, towns and countries: that is, whether one should associate with them, use them, or live in them, or whether one should not.

9:11: A second "Lion's Roar" of Sāriputta, uttered in the Master's presence on the occasion of a monk's false accusation; with nine similes proclaiming his freedom from anger, detachment from the body and his inability to hurt others.

9:13: A discussion with the Venerable Mahā Koṭṭhita about the purpose of living the Holy Life.

9:14: The Venerable Sāriputta questions the Venerable Samiddhi about the essentials of the Dhamma and approves of his answers.

9:26: This text illustrates the Venerable Sāriputta's scrupulous fairness even towards antagonists. He corrects a statement attributed to Devadatta which was probably wrongly formulated by one of Devadatta's followers who reported it to Sāriputta. Later, Sāriputta speaks to that monk on the fully developed and steadfast mind, which is not shaken by even the most attractive sense impressions.

9:34: On Nibbāna, which is described as happiness beyond feelings.

10:7: Sāriputta describes his meditation, during which he had only the single perception that "Nibbāna is the ceasing of existence." See p. 12.

10:65: To be reborn is misery; not to be reborn is happiness.

10:66: To have delight in the Buddha's Teaching and Discipline is happiness; not to have delight in them is misery.

10:67–68: Causes of progress and decline in the cultivation of what is salutary.

10:90: On the ten powers of a canker-free arahat that entitle him to proclaim his attainment.

Saṃyutta Nikāya

Nidāna Saṃyutta

24: Sāriputta rejects the alternatives that suffering is produced either by oneself or by another, and explains the conditioned arising of suffering through the (sixfold sense-) contact (*phassa*).

25: The same is stated with regard to both happiness and suffering (*sukha-dukkha*).

31: On the conditioned arising of existence from nutriment.

32: *Kalāra Sutta.* Questioned by the Buddha, Sāriputta says that the knowledge inducing him to declare his attainment of arahatship was that he knew: the cause of birth being extinct, the result (i.e., future birth) becomes extinct. Hence he was able to say, in the words of the stock formula declaring Arahatship: "Extinct is birth..." (*khiṇā jāti*). He then replies to further questions of the Buddha about the cause and origin of birth, becoming and the other terms of dependent origination, leading up to feeling, the contemplation of which had served the Venerable Sāriputta as the starting-point for his attainment of Arahatship. He says that, as he sees impermanence and suffering in all three kinds of feeling, there is in him no arising of any hedonic gratification (*nandi*).

Khandha Saṃyutta

1: Sāriputta explains in detail the Buddha's saying: "Even if the body is ill, the mind should not be ill."

2: Monks going to distant border districts are instructed by Sāriputta on how to answer questions posed to them by non-Buddhists. He tells them that the removal of desire for the five aggregates is the core of the Teaching.

122–123: On the importance of reflecting on the five aggregates. If one who possesses virtue (or, in text 123, learning) contemplates the five aggregates as impermanent, bound up with suffering and void of self, he may be able to attain to stream-entry. If a stream-winner, once-returner or non-returner thus contemplates, he may be able to win to the next higher stage. An arahat should also contemplate the five aggregates thus, as it will conduce to his happiness here and now, as well as to mindfulness and clear comprehension.

126: On ignorance and knowledge.

Sāriputta Saṃyutta

1–9: In these nine texts Sāriputta speaks of his having developed all nine meditative attainments, i.e., from the first jhāna up to the cessation of perception and feeling; and states that in doing so he was always free of any self-affirmation.

10: Once, at Rājagaha, after the alms round the Venerable Sāriputta was taking his food near a wall. A female ascetic called Sucimukhī (Bright-face) approached him and asked whether when eating he turned to one or other of the directions, as done by some non-Buddhist ascetics. Sāriputta denied it for every one of the directions, explaining them in his own way as being several means of livelihood that are wrong for ascetics, such as geomancy, astrology, going on errands, etc. He said that he did not turn to any of those wrong directions, but sought his alms-food in the right manner; and what he had thus obtained righteously, that he would eat. Sucimukhī was deeply impressed, and thereafter went from street to street and place to place loudly proclaiming: "The Sakya ascetics take their food righteously! They take their food blamelessly! Please give alms-food to the Sakya ascetics!"[49]

Salāyatana Saṃyutta

232: Not the senses and their objects, but the desire for them is the fetter that binds to existence.

49. Sāriputta's method of teaching in this discourse invites comparison with the Buddha's in the *Sigalovāda Sutta* (DN 31).

Jambukhādaka Saṃyutta

Sāriputta replies to questions put by his nephew, Jambukhādaka, who was a Paribbājaka, i.e., a non-Buddhist ascetic.

1–2: He defines Nibbāna and Arahatship as the elimination of greed, hatred and delusion.

3–16: He replies to questions about those who proclaim truth: about the purpose of the Holy Life; about those who have found true solace. He explains feeling, ignorance, the taints, personality, etc., and speaks on what is difficult in the Buddha's Doctrine and Discipline.

Indriya Saṃyutta

44: Questioned by the Buddha, Sāriputta says that not out of faith in him, but from his own experience, he knows that the five spiritual faculties (confidence, etc.) lead to the Deathless.

48–50: On the five spiritual faculties. (These texts are translated in Wheel No. 65/66, *The Way of Wisdom.*)

Sotāpatti Saṃyutta

55: On the four conditioning factors of stream-entry (*sotāpattiyaṅga*).

Part V

Sāriputta in the Jātakas

As might be expected, the Venerable Sāriputta makes frequent appearances in the Jātakas, the stories of the Buddha's previous lives. In these, the Bodhisatta and Sāriputta assume various roles; in some existences we find Sāriputta as the teacher and the Bodhisatta as pupil, as for example in the Susīma (163), Cūla Nandiya (223), Sīlavimaṃsa (305), Kārandiya (356) and Mahā Dhammapāla (447) Jātakas. In the last-mentioned Jātaka, however, the Bodhisatta, as pupil, gives his teacher, Sāriputta, a valuable lesson: not to give the five precepts indiscriminately to those who have no desire to accept them nor the intention to observe them.

In several births Sāriputta appears as a human being and the Bodhisatta an animal. Some examples are the Cūla Nandiya Jātaka (223), the Romaka Jātaka (277)—where Sāriputta, as a wise ascetic, instructs a partridge, the Bodhisatta—the Bhojajāniya Jātaka (23) and the Dummedha Jātaka (122).

In other stories the roles are reversed, as in the Jarudapāna (256) and Kuṇḍakakucchi Sindhava (254) Jātakas (for the latter, see below), where Sāriputta is an animal and the Bodhisatta human. Sometimes, as in the Kurungamiga Jātaka (206), both are animals.

The following are summaries of Jātakas in which the Venerable Sāriputta's previous personalities appear.

Lakkhaṇa Jātaka (11): As the wise one of two brother stags, each leader of a herd, Sāriputta brings his herd safely back to the hills from a dangerous track, while his foolish brother (Devadatta) loses his whole herd.

Bhojajāniya Jātaka (23): The Bodhisatta is a superb war-steed, while Sāriputta is a knight entrusted with the task of capturing seven hostile kings. He succeeds, thanks to the endurance and sacrificing spirit of the steed.

Visavanta Jātaka (69): Sāriputta is a snake which refuses to suck back its poison from a man bitten by it, preferring death. This Jātaka was told when Sāriputta, the Great Disciple, gave up the eating of meal cakes, which he enjoyed, and never went back on his resolution.

Parosahassa Jātaka (99): Sāriputta, as pupil of a hermit teacher, is able to understand short, enigmatic sayings. A comment on his penetrative mind.

Dummedha Jātaka (122): Sāriputta, as a king of Benares, is able to appreciate excellence when he sees it. The Bodhisatta is a superb white elephant. Devadatta, as king of Magadha, had owned that elephant but lost it through jealousy.

Rajovāda Jātaka (151): Sāriputta and Mahā Moggallāna are both charioteers of powerful kings. Meeting one another on a narrow road, each expects the other to give way, and they decide the issue by proclaiming the virtues of their respective monarchs. Sāriputta, whose king is the Bodhisatta, wins the contest by showing that his master's virtue is superior: he is not only good to those who are good, he is good to the bad as well.

Alīnacitta Jātaka (156): Sāriputta, as an elephant, shows the virtue of gratitude.

Kurungamiga Jātaka (206): Sāriputta as a woodpecker and Mahā Moggallāna as a tortoise save the life of the Bodhisatta, who is an antelope, from a hunter (Devadatta). Later, the woodpecker saves the imprisoned tortoise.

Cūla Nandiya Jātaka (223): As a wise brahmin teacher, Sāriputta advises his pupil, Devadatta, not to be harsh, cruel and violent, but his exhortation is in vain.

Kuṇḍakakucchi Sindhava Jātaka (254): Sāriputta, as a wondrous horse owned by the Bodhisatta, a horse-dealer, benefits an impoverished old woman who had owned the horse previously.

Jarudapāna Jātaka (256): Sāriputta, as a Naga king, helps the Bodhisatta, a merchant, to transport some treasure which the latter had found.

Vyaggha Jātaka (272): In a former life as a Yakkha, the monk Kokālika could not live together with Sāriputta and Mahā Moggallāna, nor could he live without them.

Romaka Jātaka (277): Sāriputta, as a wise ascetic, instructs a partridge, the Bodhisatta.

Abbhantara (281) and Supatta (292) Jātakas: Incidents of Sāriputta's last life. Rāhula, whose mother is a bhikkhunī, requests the Venerable Sāriputta to get sugared mango juice as a medicine for her flatulence, which he does. In (292), for another illness of hers, the Venerable Sāriputta procures rice cooked with ghee and flavoured with red fish (*rohita-maccha*).

Sayha Jātaka (310): Ānanda, as a king, sends his courtier, Sayha (Sāriputta) to a friend of his youth (the Bodhisatta) who had become an ascetic, asking him in vain to return and be the court brahmin.

Khantivādi Jātaka (313): When the Bodhisatta was a wise ascetic, the preacher of patience (*khantivādi*), and was tortured by King Kālabu (Devadatta), Sāriputta was that king's commander-in-chief of the army. Sāriputta bandaged the Bodhisatta's wounds.

Maṃsa Jātaka (315): Sāriputta was a hunter and the Bodhisatta a merchant's son. Addressing the hunter as "friend," and winning him over with kind words, the Bodhisatta persuaded him to give up his cruel profession.

Vaṇṇoroha Jātaka (361): In their last lives, when the Great Disciples Sāriputta and Mahā Moggallāna were living in solitude, a beggar who attended on them and ate the remnants of their food, tried to set them at variance but failed. Each of them just smiled at the calumnies and told him to go away. The Jātaka relates that the same had happened in an earlier life when the beggar was a jackal and Sāriputta and Mahā Moggallāna were a lion and a tiger.

Koṭisimbali Jātaka (412): Sāriputta, as a king of the Garudas (*sūpaṇṇa-rāja*), saves a tree which was the home of a tree spirit, the Bodhisatta.

Kaṇhadipāyana Jātaka (444): Sāriputta is the ascetic Aṇimaṇḍaviya. Impaled by the king on a false accusation, he bears the torture patiently and without resentment, knowing it to be the result of past evil kamma. The Bodhisatta is his brother-ascetic, Kaṇhadipāyana, who in an Act of Truth confesses that all throughout he has lived the ascetic life unwillingly, except for the first week.

Mahā Paduma Jātaka (472): Sāriputta, as a hill spirit, saves the life of the Bodhisatta, who is Prince Mahā Paduma.

Appendix

A Note on the Relics of Sāriputta and Mahā Moggallāna

On Sāñchī Hill forty-five kilometers northeast of the city of Bhopal in the centre of India are the remains of ten stupas which are among the oldest buildings still standing in India. By their architectural features and sculpture they have always been recognised as belonging to the high noon of Buddhist art, the characters in which their numerous inscriptions are written placing them at about the period of Asoka; that is, some time around the middle of the third century B.C. Some are in good preservation, while others have been reduced in the course of centuries to mere mounds of earth and stone.

It was in one of these, the now famous Third Stupa, that Sir Alexander Cunningham discovered the sacred Body Relics of the Buddha's Chief Disciples, Sāriputta and Mahā Moggallāna, in 1851. At about the same time, more relics of the two great Arahats were found in a stupa at Satadhāra, about six miles distant from Sāñchī.

On sinking a shaft in the centre of the stupa on Sāñchī Hill, Cunningham came upon a large stone slab, upwards of five feet in length, lying in a direction from north to south. Beneath the slab were found two boxes of gray sandstone, each with a brief inscription in Brahmi characters on the lid. The box to the south was inscribed "*Sāriputasa*" "(Relics) of Sāriputta," while that to the north bore the legend "*Mahā-Mogalānasa*" "(Relics) of Mahā Moggallāna."

The southernmost box contained a large flat casket of white steatite, rather more than six inches broad and three inches in height. The surface was hard and polished and the box, which had been turned on a lathe, was a beautiful piece of workmanship. Around this casket were some fragments of sandalwood believed to have been from the funeral pyre, while inside it, besides the relic, various precious stones were found. This casket contained a single bone relic of the Venerable Sāriputta, not quite one inch in length.

The stone box to the north enclosed another steatite casket, similar to that of Sāriputta but slightly smaller and with a softer surface. Inside it were two bone relics of the Venerable Mahā Moggallāna, the larger of them being somewhat less than half an inch in length.

Each of the two steatite caskets had a single ink letter inscribed on the inner surface of the lid: "*Sā*" for Sāriputta on the southern and "*Mā*" for Mahā Moggallāna on that to the north. In Cunningham's words: "Sāriputta and Mahā Moggallāna were the principal followers of the Buddha, and were usually styled his right and left hand disciples. Their ashes thus preserved after death the same positions to the right and left of Buddha which they had themselves occupied in life."[50] This is explained by the fact that the Buddha customarily sat facing east.

In the stupa at Satadhāra, one of a group which Cunningham noted was called locally "Buddha Bhīṭā" or "Buddha Monuments," he discovered two caskets of pale mottled steatite. These were inscribed, like those at Sāñchī, "*Sāriputasa*" and "*Mahā Mogalānasa*" respectively. This stupa showed signs of having been violated by robbers, but the bone relics had been left undisturbed. Cunningham, who was a very capable archaeologist, has left a detailed account of everything his excavations brought to light in these and other stupas, and it is thanks to him that the authenticity of the relics is established beyond all doubt.

The relics from both stupas were removed to England and placed in the Victoria and Albert Museum, but some discrepancies between Cunningham's description of the caskets and the actual boxes in which the relics were deposited gives reason to believe that he, or someone else, transferred the relics from Sāñchī to the caskets discovered at Satadhāra, and what became of the Sāñchī steatite caskets is not known for certain.

The sacred relics were preserved in the Victoria and Albert Museum until 1939, when the Mahā Bodhi Society approached the British government with a request that they be returned to India. The request was at once granted, but owing to the outbreak of the Second World War in that year, the actual transfer was delayed for reasons of safety until February 24, 1947. On that date

---

50. *Bhilsa Topes*, Alexander Cunningham, 1854, p. 300.

they were handed over to the representatives of the Mahā Bodhi Society at the Victoria and Albert Museum, and so began their journey back to the land of their origin.

Before being restored to India, however, the relics were taken to Sri Lanka, where they were received with great honour and amid general rejoicing. For two and a half months in 1947, they were displayed for public worship at the Colombo Museum, where it has been estimated that well over two million people paid homage to them. It is said that not only Buddhists but Hindus, Christians and Muslims joined in paying reverence to them.[51]

The next stage of their journey to the new Vihāra that was being erected for their re-enshrinement at Sāñchī was Calcutta. There the relics were displayed for public homage at the Dharmarājika Vihāra, headquarters of the Mahā Bodhi Society of India. The same scenes of religious devotion were enacted there. Every day for two weeks an unbroken stream of people filed past the shrine where the relics were exposed, from morning until late evening. Most of the devotees were Hindus, but there was also a large number of Muslims among them, and the reverence shown by all was a deeply impressive sight. Many had come from distant parts to pay their respects to the remains of these great sons of India.

Next came a request from Burma that the relics should be taken for exposition here. This was readily granted. The reception given to them in that country revived all the pomp and religious fervour of ancient times. In order that everyone in Burma should be given an opportunity of worshipping them, the relics were conducted on a riverine tour along the Irrawaddy from Mandalay to Rangoon. Boats decorated in traditional Burmese style escorted the steamer that conveyed them, and at every town along the river the relics were taken ashore in procession for worship at the chief pagoda. At the same time religious meetings were held, drawing vast crowds of people from the adjacent villages to hear sermons and the recitation of suttas, which usually continued all through the night.

Subsequently, at the request of the respective governments, the relics were taken for exposition to Nepal and Ladakh.

---

51. *The Cynosure of Sāñchi*, p. 28.

After they were returned to India, the Burmese government asked that a portion of the Sacred Relics should be given to Burma. The Mahā Bodhi Society of India agreed to this, and the then Prime Minister of Burma went in person to Calcutta to receive them. They were ceremonially transferred to him on the 20th October 1950. The portion allotted to Burma was afterwards enshrined in the Kaba Aye Zedi (World Peace Pagoda), built on the site of the Sixth Great Buddhist Council, close to Rangoon. The elaborate ceremonies connected with the crowning of the pagoda and the installation of the relics lasted from the 5th to 11th of March 1952.

Another portion was given to Sri Lanka to be enshrined in a new stupa built by the Mahā Bodhi Society of Sri Lanka to receive them. At the time of writing they are housed in the temple of the Mahā Bodhi Society, Colombo, awaiting the completion of the building.

On the 30th November 1952, the remaining relics were duly enshrined at Sāñchī on completion of the new Cetiyagiri Vihāra built to receive them. There they remain, objects of the deepest veneration to pilgrims from every Buddhist country, and a lasting reminder of the lives of those in whom the Buddha's Teaching bore its finest fruit.

The Eight Marvellous and Wonderful Truths

from the Mahāvastu
A Visākha Offering

by

Bhikkhu Khantipālo

WHEEL PUBLICATION NO. 93

Namo tassa bhagavato arahato sammāsambuddhassa

Sukho Buddhānaṃ uppādo,
Sukhā Saddhammadesanā,
Sukhā Saṅghassa sāmaggī,
Samaggānaṃ tapo sukho.

Happy is the birth of Buddhas,
Happy is the Dhamma's teaching,
Happy is the Sangha's harmony,
Of those in harmony, happy is their striving.

Dhammapada 194

Sources

The text used here is that in the *Mahāvastu* (III 200ff), which is close to the Dīgha Nikāya version (at D II 220ff). Due to the imperfect state of the *Mahāvastu* text, only six or seven truths appear in the text as we have it (according to whether one counts the statement about the celestials as a truth or not (and here it has been transferred to the opening section), instead of the required number of eight. There are two truths which are found in Pali but absent from the *Mahāvastu* and these have therefore been inserted (numbers two and five) and cast in the form of the *Mahāvastu*. Brackets in the text of these two truths indicate that the material so enclosed has been drawn from the Sanskrit and added to give a uniform appearance. Quotations of the remaining truths and other passages are from *The Mahāvastu*, Volume III, translated by J. J. Jones, in the *Sacred Books of the Buddhists*, Volume XIX. A few minor changes have been made. For the sake of uniformity, Sanskrit forms of Buddhist terms are used throughout.

The Eight Marvellous and Wonderful Truths

Everyone devoted to the Buddhadhamma or sympathetic to that Teaching, and all those who take interest in the welfare of mankind, can only be glad if indeed not joyful upon the Visākha day (Vesak), which celebrates three great events in the life of the Sage of the Sakyas: his Birth, his Enlightenment and his Parinibbāna. When we reflect upon the life and practice of the Enlightened One and how he undertook the difficult life of a wandering bhikkhu, not only for the sake of those whom he taught personally but also for future generations, then dwells the mind in tranquil joy. The same infusion of peace that quiets turmoil and allays fears will be the fruit of reflection upon any, either one or all, of the Three Gems. Only peace and joy, tranquillity and sublime happiness result from such recollection whether the mind is turned upon the Buddha, the Dhamma (Teaching) or the Sangha (Community). A reflection of this type which actually covers all Three Jewels is found in the ancient *Mahāgovinda Sutta* of the Long Discourses (Dīgha Nikāya) and in the Sanskrit of the *Mahāvastu* (*Mahāgovindiya Sūtra*). In both cases this discourse is related to Lord Buddha by Pañcasikha the celestial minstrel.

The events it describes are set in the celestial realm of the Thirty-three Gods and most of the extract with which we are concerned quotes the speech of Sakra (Pali: *Sakka*), sovereign of celestials. He is addressing them in the presence of the great Brahma, who has come there on "some business of the celestials." It so happened that many new celestial beings had been reborn there later than the rest, but who excelled them in the five celestial (deva) attributes of length of life, power, glory, honour and retinue. Whereupon some other celestials said:

> "Verily, friends, these are disciples of the Exalted One. They lived the life of purity, and at death upon the dissolution of the body they were reborn in heaven among the celestials of the Thirty-three. ..."

Then, Lord,[1] some others of the celestials said, "Friends, would it be possible that four ... three ... two ... Tathāgatas, Arhans and Perfect Buddhas arose in the world (together) and taught Dharma. It would be for the welfare of celestials and men. The hosts of titans (asura) would wane; the hosts of celestials (deva) would wax."

When this had been said, Lord, Sakra, sovereign of celestials, spoke to the celestials of the Thirty-three, saying, "But this too, friends, is impossible and inopportune, that at one and the same time, four ... three ... two ... Tathāgatas, Arhans and Perfect Buddhas should appear in the world and teach Dharma."

... "When, friends," said he, "(just one) Exalted One, Arhan and Perfect Buddha has arisen in the world, the hosts of celestials wax."

If we think about it, this appears to be a rather clever statement on the part of Sakra. He does not launch straight into a description of the Eight Marvellous and Wonderful Truths about to be expounded. Rather than to begin by telling the celestials of deep truths of the Dharma, he first prepares their minds using a well-known device in teaching: he catches their interest by referring to a situation in which they themselves are involved.

This statement by Sakra implies of course that, due to the teaching of Dhamma, men take up the good life of giving, pure moral conduct and the cultivation of the sublime states and mind-development and so after death arise in the celestial worlds. Their foes, the titans, do not receive "reinforcements" in this way since there are fewer men who misuse power or wrongly crave for it.

If the waxing of the celestial hosts and the waning of the titans give but little comfort to us on earth, even though the lutes of heaven resound with accompanying joyful deva-anthems, there is yet another interpretation of this statement possible. It is sure that upon the appearance of a Buddha in the world all the noble qualities in mankind receive encouragement to develop. Either men hear the Dharma directly from Lord Buddha or they receive

1. As mentioned above, Pañcasikha, the celestial minstrel, is speaking to Lord Buddha.

it from one of his enlightened disciples. At the same time, the hosts of low and unprofitable states are seen as such in the clear light of the Dharma. These are the titan hosts in every man—the greed, envy, sensuality, stubbornness, pride, conceit, malice, grudge-bearing, hatred, dislike, stupidity and ignorance; it is natural that they should wane where a Buddha teaches Dharma. The celestial hosts which wax upon this joyful occasion are of course generosity, gentleness, compassion, altruistic joy, patience, energetic striving, gratitude, humility, wisdom and so forth.

> ... And when Sakra, lord of the celestials of the Thirty-three, saw that the celestials were glad, thrilled, elated, joyful and pleased, he said, "If, friends, you were to hear the Eight Marvellous and Wonderful Truths about the Exalted One, Arhan and Perfect Buddha, you would be still more glad, thrilled, elated, joyful and pleased."
>
> When this had been spoken, Lord, the celestials of the Thirty-three said to Sakra, their sovereign, "Lord Kausika, we should like you then to proclaim the Eight Marvellous and Wonderful Truths about the Exalted One, Arhan and Perfect Buddha."

First Marvellous and Wonderful Truth

> "Friends, I do not see, whether I survey the past or present, any master arisen in the world who has so wrought for the welfare of the multitude like this Exalted One, Arhan and Perfect Buddha. For the beautifully proclaimed Dharma and Discipline of the Tathāgata, Arhan and Samyak Sambuddha bears on this present life and is independent of time. It welcomes and it guides and is for the inward comprehension of those who are wise. For this well-proclaimed Dharma and Discipline means the crushing of pride, the suppression of longing, the destruction of clinging, the breaking-up of sensorial states, the end of craving, passionlessness, cessation and Nirvana. Again, friends, I say that I do not see, whether I survey the past or present, any teacher of such a Dharma and Discipline arisen in the world other than this Exalted One, Arhan and Perfect Buddha."

How is it that Lord Buddha *has so wrought for the welfare of the multitude*? Seeing beings adrift upon the ocean of saṃsāra, has he not out of compassion shown the advantages of moral conduct, the fruits of generosity, the results of actions good or ill, the way to develop the mind and to remove the hindrances, the further reaches of the way wherein the nature of the world is seen in clarity and the highest benefit—the ending of dukkha with ultimate perfection experienced? After the Enlightenment, he determined to teach because great compassion was born after seeing the wretched conditions of beings subject all to birth-and-death. For forty-five years out of compassion for beings he travelled about teaching anyone who wished to learn. The Teacher, having compassion for us, left us his greatest gift, the Jewel of the Dharma.

Every day thousands, millions recite the ancient description of this fine Dharma Jewel. In Pali, this runs: *Svākkhāto Bhagavatā Dhammo, sandiṭṭhiko akāliko, ehipassiko, opanayiko, paccattaṃ veditabbo viññūhīti*—"The Dhamma of the Exalted One is beautifully proclaimed, bears on this present life and is independent of time. It welcomes and it guides and is for the inward comprehension of those who are wise."

Well or *beautifully proclaimed* means that the Dharma is not a patchwork system but has an underlying unity. It is Dharma (from *dhṝ* = to uphold), being that law which supports or upholds and governs both physical and psychological phenomena. It has a *bearing on this present life* and one should not think of waiting to see its results after death or in another life. "Whether Tathāgatas arise or whether they do not arise—this being, that becomes; by the arising of this, that arises; this not being, that becomes not; from the cessation of this, that ceases"—so is the Dharma *independent of time*. It did not begin at any particular time and while the forces of conditionality act and react it will continue to be true. Was there ever another religious teaching in which one was invited by the founder to "come-and-see"? Not to come-and-believe, which is the usual cry, but to come and judge from what one learns. This is what BuddhaDharma offers. Only a teacher who is quite fearless, having nothing to hide, can offer a Dharma which is *ehipassiko*. It *guides* one forward step by step. These steps along the Path are also described in great detail and clarity by the

Perfect Buddha who has himself already travelled along that way. We are not expected to vault or leap along the Path for its steps are well-graded. We are told elsewhere that just as the great ocean shelves out gently, gradually deepening, so does Dharma-practice gradually deepen to Dharma-realisation. Naturally enough this is for *the inward comprehension of those who are wise.*

In many places we are told that the Dharma taught by Lord Buddha is not just a system of philosophy beaten out and devised by him and thus must not be treated as being merely such. No one does justice to Lord Buddha who merely studies Buddhism (or only interests himself in the Pali language) in the same way as one may study algebra or zoology. No Buddhist "philosophy" exists only to be studied; for whatever is found in all the voluminous pages of the various Collections and in the even greater piles of Commentaries, all this is meant to illumine the way that is to be trodden. Just as Lord Buddha practised what he taught (*yathā vādī tathā kārī*), so should we as students of the Way do likewise. To make this possible, the Teaching is divided into two aspects. Firstly, indispensable for realisation of Dharma is Discipline (Vinaya), which includes all the various groups of moral precepts and steps of training. These, when practised in our everyday lives, give rise to excellent conduct (*caraṇa*). Secondly is learning and practise of Dharma, which in due time ripens to the fruit of wisdom (*vidyā*).

Not only the Perfect Buddha should be described as *vidyācaraṇa* (possessed of wisdom and conduct), so too we, his followers, should endeavour that this description becomes true of us.

Those who are wise practise this Dharma so that it comes to be clearly seen and attained to by them. Apart from blind faith, apart from books, apart from lectures and discussions, apart from intellectual considerations, this Dharma comes to shine in the hearts of those who have made it their own. It shines there always, quite independently of all accidents of place and circumstance. And in the face of this light, Māra and his daughters and armies have been put to precipitate flight. Precisely what this Dharma-realisation means, for one who has experienced it, is given in the third part of this truth, where is listed the end *of pride, longing, clinging, craving* and *the breaking up of the dominance of sensorial states*, while *passionlessness, cessation and Nirvana* are the positive side to this supreme experience.

Surely this is enough to make one feel *glad, thrilled, elated, joyful and pleased*; but a further truth is to come ...

Second Marvellous and Wonderful Truth

> "Again (friends), the Exalted One (Arhan and Perfect Buddha) has in truth well pointed out: 'this is skilful'; and well pointed out: 'that is unskilful'; that 'this is with obstruction and that without obstruction'; that 'this should be followed and that should not be followed'; that 'this is base and that exalted'; that 'this pertains to brightness and that to darkness'—this pair of opposites has also been pointed out. And a master of such a character, (friends), who discloses knowledge thus of these pairs of opposites, namely: the skilful-unskilful, obstructing-unobstructing, the followable and not-followable, the base and exalted, the bright and the dark (I[2] do not see arisen in the world whether I survey the past or present, other than this Exalted One, Arhan and Perfect Buddha)."

Very exactly has the Great Teacher outlined the profitable way to go. Very carefully has he guarded his followers against all the dangers that could easily arise for them should they stray off the Path. Here, however, he differs from other religious teachers for they have delimited their religious doctrines by saying, "You must believe this thing or that and believe in this way—to believe otherwise is to be heretical and damnable." Not so Lord Buddha, who was not concerned with enforcing mere beliefs, tangles of views or the endless wilderness of religious dogmas upon others, but who was very much concerned with which spiritual path of practice people set their feet to. He therefore instructs, not in terms of beliefs but having regard for what is profitable, what is skilful, for that which leads to growth among the "celestial hosts" of noble qualities in man—that is Dharma.

To do this, he frequently contrasted the effects of practising in one way with that of practising the opposite. That is, by

2. The Pali here is in the first person plural.

presenting the contrast in pairs of opposite factors, he outlined clearly what is the true Path. One factor of a pair would lead, if practised, to the increase of the interior "titan hosts" and thus should be carefully avoided. It is for this reason that Buddhist terminology speaks of 'unskilful' (*akusala*) rather than the vague and unmeaning "bad." The reverse applies to the opposite factor which since it increases what is Dharma, is spoken of as "skilful" (*kusala*) and not as merely "good."

Very definitely, certain actions if practised are said to act as *obstructions* to one's progress on the Path. They are, literally, "that-which-is-to-be-avoided." In spite of the very clear directions of Lord Buddha on this point, at least one disciple is known to us by name (Ariṭṭha, formerly of the vulture-killers; see MN No. 22) who somehow persuaded himself that, "There are things called 'obstructions' by the Exalted One. As I understand His teaching, these things are not necessarily obstructive to one who pursues them."[3] As this disciple was a bhikkhu and therefore, while he retained his robes, bound to uphold the celibate life, the Commentary tells us that in this instance the danger which he considered not dangerous, or the obstruction not obstructive, was the indulgence by a bhikkhu in sexual intercourse. This is but one example and many more might be found that are more or less serious. One that comes to mind is the person who eagerly takes up the practice of meditation while continuing to indulge in unrestrained and even unskilful conduct. One who regards obstructions declared to be such by Lord Buddha as not really obstructive is placing himself in a very dangerous position where whatever he attempts of the training will be sure to go wrong, sometimes disastrously wrong.

That which is *without obstruction* implies at least that it does not lead to the diminution of Dharma in one's heart and may increase it. This very much depends on the state of mind which underlies certain actions. Thus, a Buddhist on a Holy Day goes and respects a stupa (relic-mound), builds miniature stupas of sand within the temple grounds, circumambulates a holy place, perhaps turning the prayer-wheels there, burns incense and makes prostrations, lights candles or lays flowers on a shrine. Does he do these things because

3. See *The Discourse on the Snake Simile* (The Wheel No. 48/49).

they are a tradition or just out of habit? If so, then his actions will certainly be *without obstruction* though not adding much to his practice of Dharma. Or does he perform such acts full of veneration and with a mind one-pointedly fixed upon those who have seen Enlightenment? If so, then he does indeed honour their memory because he sincerely and devotedly increases the power of Dharma in his own heart.

Much the same might be said of the next pair of opposites. There are whole discourses where Lord Buddha pointed out *what should be followed and what should not be followed* (see for instance, MN No. 8). Similarly, the Vinaya (Rules of Conduct for bhikkhus and bhikkhunīs) basically consists of stating what should not be done and indicating what is the proper course of conduct in any given situation. For lay-people there is a striking case of this in the Five Precepts, which should not be broken, while their positive counterparts, the Five Ennobling Virtues (loving-kindness, right livelihood, contentment, truthfulness and heedfulness), most certainly should be followed.

Again, that which is accounted "*base*" is whatever drags one's character down in the swamps of greed, into the fires of hatred, or within the mists of delusion. Conversely, the "*exalted*" raises one beyond the sway of these unskilful passions and gives rise to an increased ability to practise and a greater understanding of Dharma.

What is it that permits one to understand more? This is an action which is *bright* and which, far from obscuring intelligent practice, actually promotes it. The reverse of this is *darkness*, which hems one in and leads one nowhere except to greater confusion and misery.

And we, if we are followers of Lord Buddha, have such a Teacher who tirelessly pointed out these *pairs of opposites* and ever exhorted us to choose the skilful, the unobstructing, and so on. Should we not rejoice in this truth as did those celestials in ancient times and feel in our hearts *glad, thrilled, exalted, joyful and pleased*? But listen to the words of Sakra as he continues....

Third Marvellous and Wonderful Truth

"And friends, the Exalted One, Arhan and Perfect Buddha has won students who are entered into the Way, and Arhans who abide in immovable states. The Exalted One, Arhan and Perfect Buddha sends them away, and makes his home in the forests, which are remote, isolated, away from the habitations of men, abodes unknown to men, and most fitting for seclusion. There he dwells by himself aloof from the crowd, all alone, giving himself to concentration. A master so intent on concentration, friends, I do not see arisen in the world, whether I survey the past, or present, other than this Exalted One, Arhan and Perfect Buddha."

One of the blemishes of a religion mentioned in the Suttas is that when it is proclaimed by a teacher, none (or few) listen to the doctrine. Or if they do listen, they do not practise; or practising that teaching, due to its inherent defects few or none come to realise it. Hence it is significant that it is proclaimed here—*the Perfect Buddha has won disciples*, moreover that they are not only *students who are entered into the Way* (*sotāpanna, sakridāgāmin, anāgāmin*) but also the Consummate Ones, *Arhans who abide in immovable states*. To have the assurance that there are those "who abide in immovable states," so different from our frail, transitory and flickering minds, is a good reason indeed for the arising of profound joy.

At this point, our text relates something which at first looks rather strange. It says that Lord Buddha, *sends them* (the Arhans) *away*. It is possible that this is an allusion to the time when Lord Buddha sent forth the sixty Arhans to spread the Dharma saying: "Go, O bhikkhus, and wander forth for the gain of the many, for the welfare of the many, in compassion for the world, for the good, for the gain, for the welfare of celestials and men. Proclaim, O bhikkhus, the glorious Dharma, preach a life of holiness, perfect and pure."[4]

4. Possibly this also refers to the Buddha's frequent periods of seclusion when, as the texts say, he was to be approached only by the person bringing his meals. The Pali commentators remark that also in the midst of company the

However, it is not so much his life of teaching which is emphasised when we are told that the *Perfect Buddha...makes his home in the forests, which are remote...and most fitting for seclusion*, but rather the early period after the Enlightenment when quite often Lord Buddha dwelt alone. There is a good picture of this earliest life in the Sangha to be found in the *Rhinoceros Sutta* (Suttanipāta). The picture painted is of the outdoor life with bhikkhus living individually or in small groups in bamboo groves, sacred woods outside villages and towns or in the depths of the great forest which then covered so much of the Ganges valley.

Sometimes Lord Buddha lived in this way even after he had been presented with "parks" for the residence of the Sangha; but at other times both he and they wandered, unattached and with few needs from place to place discussing the Dharma with all those who were interested.

Aloof from the crowd he certainly was, even when dwelling near cities or visiting the courts of kings. He was aloof from the passions which throng the worldly man's mind and yet he was the Greatly Compassionate One. In purity and wisdom aloof, in compassion ever willing to help with Dharma those who wished for help.

Whether in populous or isolated places, the Buddha's mind remained quite naturally intent on concentration. Who could be other than *glad, thrilled, elated, joyful and pleased* at the marvel of the great Teacher *aloof from the crowd* and the wonder of the perfected disciples, *who abide in immovable states.* Another cause for marvel and wonder follows....

Buddha, entering the state of Fruition Attainment (*phalasamāpatti*), was able to be mentally aloof and detached; to "dismiss" mentally the thought of the company's presence—Ed.

Fourth Marvellous and Wonderful Truth

"Again, friends, the Exalted One, Arhan and Perfect Buddha gets choice solid and soft food of proper and exquisite flavour, and he makes his meals thereof. But he eats without indulgence and wantonness, being aware of the peril in pleasures of sense, knowing the way of escape and being free of intoxication. A master, friends, who eats his food so free from self-indulgence, I do not see arisen in the world, whether I survey the past or present, other than this Exalted One, Arhan and Perfect Buddha."

Just in case any of the celestials were beginning to let their attention stray, Sakra, who is obviously well-versed in the arts of teaching, introduces here a subject which may well be as much discussed in the realms of the Thirty-three as it is on earth. At the word "food" any minds which may have wandered from Sakra's truths will surely have returned, for it is said to have been of "exquisite flavour" a subject on which those celestials would doubtless have been experts. If it were not possible to account for the introduction of this truth in this way then it might seem that after the lofty heights of the fourth truth, Sakra strangely descends to a very mundane matter. But this is not so. He is intent on showing the celestials that Lord Buddha's transcendent attainments have very plain and practical consequences which all could see for themselves.

Religious history could furnish us with some interesting examples of "teachers" whose mighty attainments have been shown to be rather forced, if not altogether a pretence, in some trying or quite ordinary situation in which they exhibited signs of greed or hatred or fell into confusion. Further, we might learn how such inflated "teachers" had excused their still uncontrolled passions—perhaps they were just "testing the faith of their disciples," or posing that sages, such as they, dwelt on such mysterious, nay, incomprehensible planes, that their actions could not be equated with those of ordinary men. Their anger was, of course, always "righteous."

In contrast to this sort of hypocrisy, the example of the Perfect Buddha generated the utmost devotion in those who knew him intimately as well as in those who chanced to meet him. Even with *choice solid and soft food of proper and exquisite flavour* there could be no relapse into a state where greed would arise and likewise no possibility of dislike aroused when food was insufficient, coarse or unpleasing to the tongue. One who is a Samyak Sambuddha has no roots of unskill (*akusala-mūla*) remaining—and one who has them is no Buddha.

Sakra wishes to drive home his point and he repeats that the Exalted One *eats without indulgence and wantonness.* Now this is extraordinary for there is not an ordinary man or woman in the world who does not have his or her favourite foods and who is not willing to spend time and money upon obtaining them. Whether they are often able to indulge their appetites depends on whether their merit is such that it permits them to do so. Even though the Exalted One's food was sometimes (but not always) of exquisite flavour and he therefore had the chance to please the tongue, still no pleasure cravings were born of tongue-contact. He was aware, unlike the majority of men, of *the peril in pleasures of sense* and again unlike them took food as a sick man takes medicine—that his body might be preserved for use as an instrument of Dharma.

The subject of "food" has a very profound and extensive significance in BuddhaDharma. In this context, however, the other types of "food" (*āhāra*)—contact-food, the food of volitional thought and consciousness-food—are not mentioned. All foods whether nourishing the body or the mental functions are really ingestions of certain aspects of the world. They are appropriations, the making "mine" of what in no wise belongs to me. Appetites, physical and mental, sustain the illusion of the self; they stimulate an intoxication, making an "I" where no 'I' exists and creating the delusion of "mine" where nothing can possibly "belong to me."

From these perils and intoxications, however, the Perfect Buddha knows *the way of escape*—which is mindfulness (*smrti, sati*) and the recollections connected with it; besides he is one who eats his food *free from self-indulgence.* When the perfect knowledge (*ajñā, aññā*) dawns that in fact there is no self in what is normally taken to be one, how then can there be indulgence of a self? With this great truth Sakra and the celestials rejoiced, and surely we would be abject beings not to feel with them *glad, thrilled, elated, joyful and pleased.*

Fifth Marvellous and Wonderful Truth

"Again (friends), the Exalted One (Arhan and Perfect Buddha) in truth speaks according to his actions and acts according to his speech. And (friends), a master of such a character who has so practised as-speaking, so-doing; as-doing, so-speaking according to the truth of Dharma (I[5] do not see arisen in the world, whether I survey the past or present, other than this Exalted One, Arhan and Perfect Buddha)."

This is a marvellous quality of Lord Buddha and one can see in it a connection with the previous truth. Both there and here, Sakra is teaching us that Lord Buddha has no hypocrisy in his nature. He does not instruct in one way and then, when no one is looking, do something quite the reverse. Not one example of such a thing can be found in the forty-five years of his teaching. Is this not remarkable?

Let us make a comparison whereby we may understand just how remarkable this is. It seems that Napoleon, to take one example, was worshipped at a distance by many who had no idea of all sides of his character and who therefore made much of his glory and announced intentions. His aide-de-camp could take a different view since he knew well a side of the emperor not seen by outsiders. How was this in the case of Lord Buddha? The Venerable Ānanda was the disciple closest to him and for a great many years was the personal attendant of the Lord. Had there been any discrepancy between Lord Buddha's teaching and his personal actions, would these not have been known to him? Such defects cannot be hidden forever. In an uneventful life a person may seem calm and get along well in friendship with most people, but even then there always comes the testing-time, the time of some quite unexpected event for which he has not provided and cannot guard against. It is then that the roots of unskill (greed, hate and delusion) show themselves. Has not Lord Buddha said this himself on many occasions? (See MN No. 21, for a good example.)

But Lord Buddha led quite an eventful life of travel, forever meeting with new personalities and new situations. And yet these

5. Again the Pali here is in the first person plural.

unskilful qualities were never seen by the Venerable Ānanda, never seen by him during his twenty-five years devoted service to the Lord! He indeed deeply revered Lord Buddha and knew better than other disciples more distant from the Lord, that he was one who constantly and quite naturally practised *as-speaking, so-doing; as-doing, so-speaking*. And this was his constant way of life, the Enlightened way of life, the perfection of the Path, the natural way *according to the truth of Dharma*.

Not only was this apparent to those who were his devoted followers. It is related in the *Brahmāyu Sutta* (MN No. 91) how Brahmāyu, an aged brahmin, instructed his disciple Uttara to go and meet the revered Gotama. After he had met him, "for seven months the brahmin youth, Uttara, like a constant shadow, followed the Lord closely" from the time when he appeared in the morning until he saw him retire. Uttara, after having minutely observed and considered Lord Buddha's conduct, could report to his teacher at the end of seven months, that indeed the revered Gotama was exactly what was reported about him—an Exalted One, Arhan and Perfect Buddha.

If there had been the slightest difference between "speaking" and "doing" in the case of Lord Buddha, then his own words would have been sufficient to reveal the discrepancy. For he also advised bhikkhus to examine his words and conduct so as to satisfy themselves that no longer are any "mixed" states (of skill and unskill) or "dark" states remaining in the Tathāgata (See MN No. 47). Only one who has the fearlessness of complete and perfect Enlightenment is able to invite such critical inspection. The malodorous flowers of hypocrisy have no chance for growth in the pure garden of Enlightenment. One Enlightened has nothing to hide.

This is the end of all hypocrisy whatever, the end of all two-faced action. It is the abolition of all those mental tendencies which lead men to have "double standards of conduct"—to seem upright and honest but, when the veils are removed, to be revealed as corrupt, perverted and full of emotional conflicts. It is the end of being a log rotten within, a simile several times used by Lord Buddha to counter hypocrisy. One who has won to this state is no longer a "whited sepulchre," outwardly pleasing but inwardly foul.

It is a test of our practise of Dharma as to how far this conflict between appearances and reality is lessened. The more one finds oneself, *as-speaking, so-doing; as-doing, so-speaking*, the more has one made the true Dharma enter into one's heart. It has then certainly become a personal reason to join the celestials and feel with them *glad, thrilled, elated, joyful, and pleased.*

But Sakra goes on to tell of another truth to give us joy ...

Sixth Marvellous and Wonderful Truth

> "Again, friends, it is out of his knowledge that the Exalted One, Arhan and Perfect Buddha teaches the Dharma and Discipline, not out of unknowing.[6] And friends, a master so possessed of the method of teaching Dharma I do not see arisen in the world, whether I survey the past or present, other than this Exalted One, Arhan and Perfect Buddha."

Sakra now makes this very plain statement that the Teaching, some of which he has outlined in previous truths, is born of knowledge. The word for this is *abhijñā* (Pali: *abhiññā*) and by this term his listeners were meant to understand "the direct intuitional knowledge gained through discipline and meditation (*sīla-samādhi*)" and not the traditional priestly knowledge from texts handed down from teacher to pupil.

Although the conditions affecting the birth and growth of a new religion are many, of prime importance is the character of the founder. Naturally, characters may be widely different but two primary roots in such persons will affect their teachings one way or the other. The first is unknowing (*avidyā*) and the second knowledge (*jñāṇa*).[7] *Avidyā* has the sense of "not knowing completely, knowing only segmentally or partly" and therefore is better translated by "unknowing" since "ignorance" means "total lack of knowledge." There will be many species more or less highly evolved in the genus of teachers whose doctrines are taught *out of unknowing* but we are not concerned with them here, nor with their partial views of reality. But there can be only one

6. The translation has "ignorance" (see below).
7. The terms used in the Mahāvastu are *anabhijñā* and *abhijñā* respectively

species in the genus of those who teach Dharma out of knowledge since "Truth is one without a second" (Sn 884). They are called Perfectly Enlightened Ones.

Having declared to the celestials that the basis of Lord Buddha's Dharma is knowledge, Sakra goes on to praise the ways in which it was taught. Elsewhere the Buddha is frequently called *Sāstā devamanusyānāṃ* (Teacher of Celestials and Men), and this not for nothing, for he taught all who were able to understand him. We know of his discourses and answers to celestials and of his admonitions to demons (*yakṣa*); but outnumbering these by far are the teachings addressed to men. They were given to all men who questioned or who stood in need of Dharma. His explanations differed in range and content of subject just as the understanding and the requirements of men vary. He suited his replies to match exactly the character and knowledge of the inquirer. A farmer was answered in similes drawn from agriculture while learned brahmins were shown the greater knowledge of the Buddha drawn from a source beyond all their books. With this great ability to give everyone the right Dharma "food," it is not surprising that he came to be known as Teacher of Celestials and Men.

This unexcelled adaptation of his teaching to fit the needs of people and circumstances is known as skill-in-means (*upāya*). It was labelled by the envious disciples of other teachers "Gotama's enticing-device." The basis of his "enticing" was very simple: truth and penetrating wisdom, non-harming and compassion. These elements were often woven into a gentle dialectic which resolved the doubts and delusions of many, and brought to them devotion and appreciation (*pasāda*) of the Teaching. We know how often this happened since at the end of many discourses one passage in particular is repeated: "It is wonderful, Lord, marvellous indeed, Lord. As if, Lord, one were to turn up what was face down, to uncover what was concealed, to point the way to one who is lost, or to carry a lamp into the darkness with the thought." Also, "As those who have eyes will be able to see objects so has the Dharma been expounded in many ways by the Lord."

For being among those able to benefit from the Dharma so well-expounded out of knowledge, we cannot fail to be *glad, thrilled, elated, joyful and pleased*. But for the further benefit of celestials and men, Sakra now proceeds to the seventh truth....

Seventh Marvellous and Wonderful Truth

> "This Exalted One, Arhan and Perfect Buddha, friends, has crossed the sea of doubt, is rid of perplexity and has won assurance in good states. A master, friends, who has so passed beyond doubt I do not see arisen in the world, whether I survey the past or present, other than this Exalted One, Arhan and Perfect Buddha."

Sakra first tells the celestial hosts that the Buddha *has crossed the sea of doubt*. One who has doubts is not yet enlightened, for the possession of doubts implies incomplete understanding whereas a Perfect Buddha has penetrated to the whole truth. But, it might be objected, it is possible to be deceived about lack of doubts. Many teachers and philosophers have been quite sure that they were right. To provide for this objection, Sakra tells us that the Buddha is *rid of perplexity*.

Only one who is puzzled or has a desire to know will ask questions. The Buddhas need never question others (nor themselves) in order to understand the nature of Dharma. Certainty based on pride in one's own philosophic constructions is one thing while that arising through insight into the Three Marks (*lakṣana*) is quite another.

As if to give the greatest confidence to the celestials, Sakra finally says of the Buddha that he *has won assurance in good states*. This is the seal to his former statements for "assurance in good states" cannot ripen to perfection where the frost of doubt and the blight of perplexity are found.

The Buddha, having passed beyond doubt, established a Dharma where nothing need remain in doubt. Doubt (*vicikitsā*) is never in the Dharma but only in perplexed minds and as it is among the unskilful concomitants, Lord Buddha encourages everyone by wise examination of the Dharma to overcome their doubts.

Without doubt was the Exalted One! For *A master, friends, who has so passed beyond doubt* and who teaches the Dharma devoid of doubt—should not we all be *glad, thrilled, elated, joyful and pleased*?

The last and greatest truth Sakra has reserved until the minds of the celestials are steeped in tranquil joy....

Eighth Marvellous and Wonderful Truth

"Again, friends, Nirvana and the Way leading to Nirvana as taught by this Exalted One, Arhan and Perfect Buddha run together one into the other. Just as, friends, the waters of the Ganges and the Jumna flow one into the other and run together into the great ocean, so do Nirvana and the Way leading to Nirvana as taught by this Exalted One, Arhan and Perfect Buddha flow together. A master, friends, with such a well-revealed Nirvana and Way leading to Nirvana I do not see arisen in the world, whether I survey the past or present, other than this Exalted One, Arhan and Perfect Buddha."

Here is the cause for highest joy! Quite naturally the Way when practised leads to Nirvana and Nirvana is the natural outcome of that way.

In the simile, the lesser stream of the Jumna can be taken as the Way (*marga*) taught by Lord Buddha. It is the way of training for the man who sees his own mental afflictions (*klesa*) and is willing to make effort. He has wise faith that this way once led to the Enlightenment of Lord Buddha; he is one who not only places his trust in, but practises the way itself; and lastly he may have the benefit of a noble friend (a meditation master) who having travelled along that way can point it out to others. In brief, he has gone for Refuge to the Triple Gem. His faith in these refuges gives him the strength to go onward—even though obstacles appear to be very great. But it will be a great consolation to him if he realises that the Dharma is so to speak "on his side," for if his life truly accords with it he will progress quite naturally "towards" Nirvāna, just as the waters of the Jumna flow by nature onwards to their union with those of the Ganges.

The mighty spate of the Ganges into which the Jumna flows represents the experience during life of Nirvana, meaning here the most profound understanding of its nature. It is the fruit of perfection and the destruction of all the host of mental ills: greed, hatred, delusion and the rest. It is the summit of Buddhist endeavour so ardently longed for by those who practise the Holy Dharma.

Although people in Lord Buddha's days, as now, frequented the union of such rivers and regarded them as "holy" places, this simile shows that the real rivers, those of practice and attainment, are not to be found by going anywhere, nor ultimately is it places which are to be esteemed as "holy." Sakra, in using this simile and knowing well the sacred associations of the Ganges in India, has given a characteristically Buddhist meaning to these rivers and their union by pointing out that they flow within anyone who practises the Dharma. It is also fitting that the broad Ganges together with its famous and illimitable sands often used as a symbol for the inexpressible in Buddhist works, should here represent Nirvana, which is also the Inexpressible. For although one may consider Nirvana, under many aspects such as Enlightenment, gnosis, freedom or purity, a complete description forever evades one.

These two rivers, the Ganges and the Jumna, *flow one into the other and run together into the great ocean* and while the very perfection of the way is shown quite naturally to be the perfection of the fruit, how should the latter part of this phrase be interpreted? One who has experienced Enlightenment is said to have traversed the whole way with no need to strive further, nor any idea that he has yet anything left to do—he has "done what had to be done." The finest of fruits is his, no longer is Nirvana read about, talked about, thought about but is actually an experience he has and from which he cannot be separated. Such a sage, we are told, is aware of how the distortions (*vipallāsa*) used to play havoc with his perceptions, colouring his emotional reactions and affecting the concepts formed by him. Formerly he will have had such attitudes to saṃsāra, the wandering-on, as assuming its permanence, enjoyability, substantiality and beauty. After having the knowledge of Enlightenment it is said to look rather different, for the wandering-on is then, without any emotional attachment, seen to be a flux of changing events; that which is bound up with unsatisfactory experience being scarcely a place in which to "have fun"; further, that all its manifestations are without substance and in their nature void, while that which one formerly seized on as beautiful, being impelled to do so by the passions, is now seen as lacking inherently beautiful qualities.

On the other hand, one Enlightened sees permanence in quite another quarter, for Nirvana is called the Permanent. It is also known to him as the highest happiness and is seen by those who are truly noble (*arya*) as devoid of substance and lacking that which could be interpreted as a metaphysical self. As to beauty, both the Blessed One and his disciples who saw events-as-they-really-are, were appreciative of the fair aspects of the forest in which they lived without having greed or grasping for them. Most highly valued by them were surely the beautiful deeds (*kalyāṇa-karma*) with which then as now the wise man adorns his mind, speech and body.

Further, when we are unenlightened we have not only distorted impressions of saṃsāra, but also mistaken notions about Nirvana, the more so since words are no substitute for direct knowledge. Whether it is words in books, by way of conversation or lecture, or whether it is the interior stream of words, however precise we try to be concerning "what Nirvana must be like," Nirvana can never be adequately contained. Our distorted picture of both saṃsāra and Nirvana might in fact be compared to the belief that the waters in the Ganges and Jumna run upwards and backwards from the ocean to the mountains!

But we find that the text of this truth stresses that Nirvana is *well-taught and well-revealed*, so how can this be done apart from words? In formulating a reply, we should remember that Sakra has here some authority to speak from his personal experience, since his attainment of Stream-entry is recorded in the Suttas.[8] For him, as it must be for us, that well-taught and well-revealed Nirvana can only be found within the limits of "this six-foot carcass" and its consciousness. It is there that the arising and declining of the fivefold heaps (*skandha*) according to conditionality must be apprehended. If saṃsāra, the wandering-on, is "here" all around and in us and we are caught up in it as flies upon flypaper, then equally, Nirvana is "here." It is 'here' since the understanding of conditionality and in particular of the conditioned arising of dukkha, which is the gateway to Nirvana, cannot take place except within "our own" mentality and materiality (*nāma-rūpa*). Where else indeed could it take place? While this is easily and quickly said in words it is quite another matter directly to perceive Nirvana.

Just as a scientist who wishes to record infrared or ultraviolet light must use special equipment to allow him to investigate what his eyes are unable to see, so the followers of the Exalted One have to use the special equipment provided by him—the way consisting

8. See *Sakka's Quest* (The Wheel No. 10).

of the aspects of moral conduct, collectedness and wisdom. Only then shall we come to know the unknown, to "see" Nirvana with "the eyes of wisdom" (*prajñācaksuḥ*).

One who has done this—often called "One-who-knows, one-who-sees"—is a living example of the way come to its perfect fruit and while his life lasts he is like those two great rivers as they *run together into the great ocean.* In his life will be found all that has ever been most precious for those who follow the Buddhist way. From the seeds of his striving for purity in moral conduct grows in Enlightenment the white lotus of perfect purity in all the spheres of thought, speech and action. Since he has sincerely tried to make his life the active expression of loving-kindness, compassion and joy with others, Enlightened he is one who pours as from a vessel the ambrosia of perfect compassion upon those still trapped and wandering in saṃsāra. And, as during his training he developed a vigilant mindfulness becoming aware of unskilful thoughts as they arose so that they went to destruction, upon becoming one-who-knows-and-sees, he wields the sword of penetrative wisdom, instantly able to detect views which lead others astray (*mithyā drishti*).

Sages such as this, and such were the great disciples of the Buddha-time together with some teachers of today, as they pass in this way through their lives, in time come to the great ocean. No longer will the patchwork of the five heaps hold together. Ungrieving and unconcerned with what after all does not belong to him, such a sage lets what is material return to the four great elements and since, what is mental arises only in connection with a body, that he knows must cease when the body is no more. This state which he approaches is called Nirvana-without-substrata (of existence) and it is this which is compared to the great ocean of which the depths and the extent are not easy to gauge. Nirvana is known, just as the ocean is known by those in its midst as the Unlimited.

> When this had been said, Lord, the celestials of the Thirty-three were still more glad and thrilled, elated and joyful, pleased and happy.
>
> And they said to Sakra, sovereign of celestials, "Therefore, friend Kausika, we should like you to proclaim again the eight marvellous and wonderful truths about the Exalted One,

Arhan and Perfect Buddha."—"Well then, again friends..." and Sakra repeated those eight truths as before.

When he had so spoken the celestials of the Thirty-three were still more glad, thrilled, elated, joyful, and pleased.

Then, Lord, when the Great Brahma saw that the celestials of the Thirty-three were so increased in happiness, he said to Sakra, Lord of celestials: "Therefore, friend Kausika, we would like you to proclaim again the eight marvellous and wonderful truths about the Exalted One, Arhan and Perfect Buddha."

And at the end of this third recital, *the celestials of the Thirty-three were still more thrilled, elated, joyful and pleased,* Truly, they took delight in what was worth delighting in.

Who can fail to rejoice when following such a Master, the like of whom Sakra says, "I do not see arisen in the world, whether I survey the past or the present"! But why is this? We are told that many Buddhas have proclaimed the Dharma in the past and that many more will do so in the future. The answer to this lies in the timelessness of the Dharma. It is not limited to any particular time, place or person. As the Buddha is reported to have told Vakkali Thera: "Whoso sees the Dharma, he sees me."

How shall we see this Dharma? How shall we also be able to experience the joy aroused by Dharma among the celestials? This is not possible if we only beckon to the further shore to come here, or just contemplate from a distance what we imagine are its beauties. When, like a strong man, we bind our loincloth and plunge into the stream, then the Dharma is near at hand. On that further shore lie the real joys and peace of Dharma; but to enjoy them we must first get there. And to do this we need the practice of Dharma (*praṭipatti-dharma*).

Meanwhile it only remains to set out on the journey—which over 2500 years ago resulted in such a wonderful discovery. Whatever method we use to cross over, whether raft, boat or bridge, one aspiration we should bear in mind, however long the journey and however rough the waters: "May we, having crossed, lead others across; ourselves free, set others free; ourselves comforted, give comfort to others; ourselves released, give release to others. May this come to pass for the welfare and happiness of the multitude, out of compassion for the world, for the sake of the great multitude, and for the welfare and happiness of celestials and men."

The Truth of Anattā

By

Dr. G. P. Malalasekera

WHEEL PUBLICATION NO. 94

Prefatory Note

Anattā is the last of the "three characteristics" (*ti-lakkhaṇa*) or the general characteristics (*sāmañña-lakkhaṇa*) of the universe and everything in it. Like the teaching of the four Noble Truths, it is the teaching peculiar to Buddhas (*buddhānaṃ sāmukkaṃsikā desanā:* M I 380).

Etymologically, *anattā* consists of the negative prefix plus *attā* (cf. Vedic Sanskrit *ātman*). There are two Pali forms of the word, namely, *attā* (instr. *attanā*) and *atta* (instr. *attena*). Neither form seems to be used in the plural in the Tipiṭaka.

In the texts and the commentaries the words *attā* and *atta* are used in several senses: (1) chiefly meaning "one's self" or "one's own" e.g. *attahitāya paṭipanno no parahitāya* (acting in one's own interest, not in the interests of others); or *attanā vā kataṃ sādhu* (what is done by one's own self is good); (2) meaning "one's own person," the personality, including both body and mind, e.g., in *attabhāva* (life), *attapaṭilābha* (birth in some form of life); (3) meaning self, as a subtle metaphysical entity, *"soul,"* e.g., *atthi me attā* (Do I have a "soul"?), *suññaṃ idaṃ attena vā attaniyena vā* (this is void of a "self" or anything to do with a "self"), etc. It is with the third meaning that we are here concerned, the entity that is conceived and sought and made the subject of a certain class of views called in early Buddhist texts *attadiṭṭhi attānudiṭṭhi* (self-views or heresy of self) and *attagāha* (misconception regarding self).

The Truth of Anattā

In most systems of religion or philosophy the question of the nature of man and his destiny centres largely in the doctrine of the soul, which has been variously defined. Some call it the principle of thought and action in man or that which thinks, wills and feels, knows and sees and, also, that which appropriates and owns. It is that which both acts and initiates action. Generally speaking, it is conceived as a perdurable entity, the permanent unchanging factor within the concrete personality which somehow unites and maintains its successive activities. It is also the subject of conscious spiritual experience. It has, in addition, strong religious associations and various further implications, such as being independent of the body, immaterial and eternal.

What has been said above regarding systems of philosophy holds true about the history of thought in India also. The Sanskrit word *ātman,* of which *attā is* the Pali counterpart, is found in the earliest Vedic hymns, though its derivation and meaning are uncertain. It is sometimes held to have meant "breath," but breath in the sense of "life," or what might be called "self" or "soul" in modern usage. Thus, the sun is called the *ātman* of all that moves or stands still and the *soma* drink is said to be the *ātman* of the sacrifice. This *ātman* was something that could leave the body and return and, in that connection, *manas* was used as a synonym (e.g., Ṛg Veda V 58). Such conceptions, coming down from the earliest times, were continued in later systems such as those found in the *Upaniṣads.*

Very briefly stated, the old Indian religion was a kind of pantheism with Brahman (eternal, absolute, etc.) as the first cause of the universe. The manifestation of Brahman was sometimes personified and called Brahmā (God or the Great Self). Every human being had in him a part of Brahman, called *ātman* or the little self. Brahman and *ātman* were one, and of the same "substance." Salvation consisted in the little *ātman* entering into unity with Brahman. The *ātman* was eternal substance, exempt from the vicissitudes of change and incapable of entering into combination with anything else except itself.

In process of time, however, various theories grew up regarding the *ātman.* Many of these are to be found in the *Brahmajāla Sutta* of the Dīgha Nikāya (D I 44ff), which is assumed to contain the whole of what is possible to assert concerning the self (*attā*) and the universe, treated from every point of view—positively, negatively and both. Thus, some doctrines set forth that the self and the universe are eternal (*sassata-vāda*). Some hold that the self and the universe are in some respects eternal and in some not. Some teachers wriggled like eels and refused to give a clear answer. Some assert that the self and the universe have arisen without a cause (*adhicca-samuppanna*). These are theories concerned mainly with the origin of the self.

There are others dealing with its future destiny. Some hold that the soul exists as a conscious entity after death, others that it exists but is unconscious. Then, there are those who say that the individual ceases to exist after death and is annihilated (*ucchedavāda*). This annihilation is further elaborated by stating that it may take place (1) with the death of the body, (2) with the death of the divine *ātman* in the world of sense (*kama-loka*), (3) in the world of form (*rūpa-loka*) or (4) in one of the stages of the formless world (*arūpa-loka*). Whether all these doctrines were in actual existence or whether any of them were only possibilities, added to make the "net" complete is not certain. Some of them can be identified[1] with the actual teachings of certain schools of philosophy but not all.

In the history of Indian philosophic development it is in the *Upaniṣads* that we find formulated a doctrine of the self which has remained fundamental in Indian thought and, it is this, more than anything else, which needs investigation when dealing with the Buddhist teachings on the self. The *Upaniṣads* contain many descriptions of the *ātman* apart from those already quoted above from the Pali *Brahmajāla Sutta.* It is always assumed that there does exist a self (*ātman*) in one's personality and the problem—

1. In other texts, various other views are mentioned, e.g., that the soul has form and is minute; has form and is boundless; is formless and minute; is formless and boundless; is feeling; has feeling; is non-sentient; is not non-sentient. Also the body is the *attā* (like a flame and its colour); the body exists together with or because of *attā* (like the shadow and the tree); in the body there is the *attā* (like a jewel in a box); because of *attā* a body materialises (like scent emanating because of a flower).

where there is a problem—is to locate it. It is also assumed (e.g., in Chand. Up. 8 7. 1) that this *ātman* is free from death (*vimṝtyuḥ*), free from sorrow (*visokaḥ*) and has real thoughts (*satyasaṃkalpaḥ*). Sometimes the *ātman* is identified with the physical personality as seen reflected in a vessel of water. Elsewhere, the *ātman* is identified with the self in the dreamstate, or in the state of deep sleep (e.g., Bṝhad. Up. IV 3, 9; ibid., II 1. 16f). After death, the soul has form, because it appears in its own form and is without defect or disease. The soul, being conscious, can if it so desires be conscious of enjoyment with women, chariots or relations (Chand. Up. 8 12. 3). Then, there is, for instance, the conception of the self as something almost physical, the size of a thumb, which abides in the heart. There are a hundred and one channels radiating from the heart through any of which the *ātman* may leave the body in sleep. From the aperture at the top of the head it may pass on to immortality (Bṝhad. Up. IV 3. 13).

Some of the Upaniṣads hold (e.g., Kaṭha Up. II 3. 17) that the soul can be separated from the body like the sword from its scabbard, or the fibre from the stalk of grass. Thus, the soul can travel at will away from the body, especially in sleep. Some theories state that the *ātman* cannot be identified with any aspects of the personality, physical or psychological, and then proceed to the metaphysical assumption that the *ātman* is an unobservable entity, a "pure ego," within the personality with all its aspects and, like the air, rises up from the body and reaches the highest light and appears in its own form (ibid., 8 11. 3).

In the *Bṝhadāraṇyaka Upaniṣad* is the famous *neti neti* (not this, not this) doctrine attributed to *Yājñavalkya,* who speaks of the unknowableness of the *ātman* by any process of reasoning. The *ātman* cannot, according to him, be apprehended by any of the standard ways of knowing (Bṝhad. Up. It 4. 14). The thought implied here is that the supreme *ātman* (*Brahman*) is unknowable because he is the all-comprehending unity, whereas all knowledge presupposes a duality of subject and object. The individual *ātman* is also unknowable because in all knowledge he is the knowing subject and consequently can never be the object. But there were other thinkers in the time of the *Upaniṣads* who believed that the *ātman* could be known by all the usual ways of knowing, that it could be empirically perceived, be heard or heard of, and likewise metaphysically conceived of and rationally understood by thinking (e.g., Chand. Up. 8 8. I; III 13. 8; 7 I 3; 6 16. 3).

Many centuries later, even Saṃkara accepts that the *ātman* can be known through argument and reasoning (*tarkinopapattya*), this is in his comment on (Bṛhad. Up. IV 5.6). The middle and late Upaniṣads, however, seem to agree with Yājñavalkya, the *ātman* has to be seen, directly seen, but not by means of perception, with the eye, for instance (Kaṭha Up. II 3. 12). It cannot be attained by means of scriptural instructions (ibid., I 2. 23). It is not to be reasoned about (Maitri Up. 6 17) because it is inconceivable, being subtler than the subtle, and it cannot be apprehended by the intellect (Kaṭha Up. I. 2. 23; Maṇḍaka Up. II 2. s). The *ātman*, which is hidden within all things and does not shine forth, is seen by the subtle, awakened intuition, by the purification of knowledge and not by any of the senseorgans (Kaṭhā Up. I 3. 12; Mund. III 2. 8).

Sometimes the *ātman* is spoken of in spatial terms, but not metaphorically, since to speak of the size of the soul would be meaningless. It can be expressed only in contradictory terms: "more minute than the minute, greater than the great" (e.g., Chand. Up. 6 3, 14.) "That which is the most minute, this universe has it as its *ātman*. That is the real. That is the *ātman*. "That-thou-art" (*tat tvaṃ asi*) (ibid., 6 8. 6).

Apart from the teachers of the *Vedas*, the *Brāhmaṇas* and the *Upaniṣads*, there were in India also other thinkers who had their own views on the *ātman* or self, some of them contemporaries of the Buddha himself. Most important among them were the Jains and the Ājīvakas. For the Jains, the soul (*jīva*), which is identified with life, is finite and has variable though definite size and weight. It is not only human beings that have soul but also everything else in the universe. When Mahāvīra, one of the founders of Jainism, was asked whether the body was identical with the soul or different from it, he is said (Bhagavati Sūtra 13 7, 495) to have replied that the body is identical with the soul as well as different from it, probably meaning thereby that the soul is identical with the body from one point of view and different from it from another point of view. The soul was also considered by the Jains to be intrinsically omniscient but cluttered up by the material particles of karma. When the influx of karmic particles is at an end by the complete exhaustion of past karma, the soul shines forth with its natural vision and intrinsic lustre. Some of the Ājīvakas seem to have held the view that the soul was octagonal or globular and five hundred *yojanas* in extent. It was also blue in colour (A. L. Basham: *History and Doctrine of the Ājīvakas*, London, 1951, p. 270).

The *Sāṅkhyas* taught the existence of a plurality of souls on the one hand, and of unique, eternal pervasive substantial matter on the other. How many of these doctrines were extant in the time of the Buddha and were in fact known to him cannot be said with any definiteness. The Buddha makes no claim to omniscience in these respects but he does, by implication at least, claim to have had a total vision of reality (*yathābhūta*). There is no statement attributed to the Buddha in which he makes mention of Brahman (neuter) as the one reality or of any identity of this with the *ātman*. The Brahmā that is found so often mentioned in the sutta, is a personal god ruling over a particular region of the universe and born and reborn as inevitably as any other being. And this Brahmā is never brought into relation with the Buddhist theory of the "self." But, whatever be the theories enunciated by various thinkers regarding the self before the Buddha's day, during his lifetime and thereafter, it would seem correct to say that the Buddhist teaching of *anattā* or non-self contradicts them all in an all-embracing sweep.

The Buddha made no concessions at all to the doctrine of self. He denied the view that there is in man an *ātman* or a self that is permanent and unchanging, possessed of bliss and autonomous. He denied equally emphatically that at death man is utterly destroyed. He denied that man is divine, but he said that man should and could become divine by good thoughts, good words and good deeds. Man, in Buddhism, is a concrete, living, striving creature and his personality is something that changes, evolves and grows, as composite existent and changing. It is the concrete man, not the transcendental self, that ultimately achieves perfection by constant effort and creative will.

The Buddhist argument against the doctrine of *ātman* is twofold. In the first place the Buddha takes various aspects of the personality and contends that none of them can be identified with the *ātman* since they do not have characteristics of the *ātman*. Thus, the question is asked (e.g., in M I 232 ff): Is the body (the physical personality) permanent or impermanent? The answer is: It is impermanent. Is what is impermanent sorrowful or happy? Sorrowful. Of what is impermanent, sorrowful and liable to change, is it proper to regard it as "This is mine, this I am, this is my soul?" It is not. The canonical commentary, the *Paṭisambhidāmagga* (I 37), adds that *rūpa*, etc., is not self in the sense that it has no core (*sāra*).

The same argument is repeated for the other aspects of the personality such as feeling (*vedanā*), perception or ideation (*saññā*), dispositions or tendencies (*saṅkhāra*) and consciousness (*viññāṇa*).

A similar procedure is attributed to *Prajāpati* in the *Chāndogya Upaniṣad* (8 7-12) but there is a very great difference in the attitudes of the two questioners. *Prajāpati* assumes the existence of an *ātman* and, when he fails to identify it with any of the aspects of the person-personality, continues to assume that it must exist within it, somewhere, somehow, in spite of its failure to show up in a purely empirical investigation. The Buddha, on the other hand, accepts the definition of the *ātman* without assuming its existence or non-existence; and when the empirical investigation fails to reveal any such *ātman,* he concludes that no such ātman exists because there is no evidence for its existence.

The second argument of the Buddha is that belief in a permanent self would negate the usefulness of the moral life. More of this later. In the first discourse, the *Dhammacakkappavattana Sutta,* given after his Enlightenment, the Buddha set out the Four Noble Truths. In the second, the *Anattalakkhaṇa Sutta,*[2] he stated the characteristics of his doctrine of the not-self (*anattā*). Here he begins by emphasising that if there were a self it should be autonomous, but no such thing is to be found. Matter (*rūpa*) is not the self. Were matter self, then the body would not be subject to affliction; one should be able to say to it "Let my body be thus. Let my body be not thus." But this is not possible; the body is shifting and ever in change and, therefore, ever accompanied by misery and affliction. Accordingly, it cannot be the self. The same is repeated for the other aspects of the personality. The conclusion

2. Both this one and the *Dhammacakkappavattana Sutta* have been translated in *Three Cardinal Discourses of the Buddha,* by Ñāṇamoli Thera in *The Wheel* No. 17. See also *The Buddha's First Discourse* (Bodhi Leaves, B. L.).

is, therefore, reached that all these things, whether past, future or presently arisen, in one self or external, gross or subtle, inferior or superior, far or near, all are to be viewed thus: "This is not mine, this is not what I am, this is not my self." Then it is added, when a man realises that all these things are not the self he turns away from them and by the extinction of desire he attains release. Here we find for the first time indication of the Buddha's purpose in enunciating his doctrine. All misery, in his view, arises from the delusion of self, which causes man to strive to profit himself, not to injure others. The most effective therapeutic against the folly of seeking to gratify longings is the realisation that there is no truth in the doctrine of a permanent self.

The *Mahānidāna Sutta* of the Dīgha Nikāya (D II 66ff) puts the argument in a different way. Here, three hypotheses are selected for investigation. The first is that the self is feeling (*vedanā*). It is argued that feelings are threefold: pleasant, painful and neutral. They are impermanent they are products and certain to pass away. If then, when a pleasant feeling exists, the conclusion is drawn, "This is my self" then, when a painful feeling supersedes it, one must conclude "My self has passed away." To call, therefore, feeling the self is to regard self as impermanent, blended of happiness and pain and liable to begin and end. The next hypothesis is that the self is neither feeling nor is insentient, i.e., the soul and the body are identical. This would mean that where there is no feeling it is impossible to say "I am," for a self without self-reference has no meaning. Thirdly, the self is regarded as not identical with feeling but as possessing feeling. If so, were feeling of every kind to cease absolutely, then, there being no feeling whatever, no one could say "I myself am."

There are many such variations in the presentation of the doctrine. Thus, what is conditioned by not-self cannot be self. Matter (*rūpa*, etc.) is not self. The cause and condition for the arising of matter, etc., are not-self, so, it is asked, how could matter, etc., which is brought into being by what is not-self, be self (S III 24)? Or, again, here someone's view is this: "This is self, this is the world. After death I shall be permanent, everlasting ..." Then he hears the true doctrine for the exhaustion of craving, for cessation, for extinction (nibbāna). Then he thinks: "So, I shall be annihilated! So, I shall be lost! So, I shall be no more!" Then he sorrows and laments. That is how there is anguish about what is non-existent in oneself (M I 133 ff). Some shrink back in that way from the truth, but some go too far the other way. Being ashamed and disgusted with being (*bhava*), they relish the idea of non-being (*vibhava*), saying: "When this self is annihilated on the dissolution of the body after death, that is peace. This is the supreme goal, that is reality (It 43–44). But one who has eyes sees how what is (*bhūta*) has come to be, and by so doing practises the way to dispassion for it" (ibid). In certain discourses the doctrine is very succinctly stated, thus: "The eye (ear, nose, tongue, body and mind and their six external objects) is impermanent; what is impermanent is fraught with sorrow; what is fraught with sorrow is not self" ; or, "All is not self. And what is the all that is not self? The eye is not self ..." (S IV 28); or, again, "All things (*dhamma*) are *not* self" (Dhammapada, verse 279). It is worth noting that whereas in the case of the two characteristics *anicca* (impermanence) and *dukkha* (affliction) it is the *saṅkhāra* (all component things) that are so described, in the case of the third characteristic *anattā* (not-self) all *dhamma,* i.e., everything without exception, is so described. This is because even Nibbāna, which being *asaṅkhata* (uncompounded) is not a *saṅkhāra,* is also without self.

In all the statements attributed to the Buddha regarding the doctrine of not-self there is complete consistency. When, for instance, he is asked who, in the absence of a self, is it that has feeling or other sensations, his answer is that there is no one who feels, but there is feeling, which is a totally different proposition. Similarly, it is not correct to ask who becomes old, who dies and who is reborn. There is old age, there is death and rebirth (S II 62). Indeed, if any assertion can be made about a self, it will be more correct to call the body the self because, whereas the body may endure as long as a hundred years, the mind in all its forms is in constant flux like an monkey in a forest which seizes one branch only to let it go and grasp another (S II 94f). The doctrine of not-self is a necessary corollary to the teaching of *anicca* (impermanence). Since all things are impermanent, they are fraught with sorrow and since bliss is the characteristic of the self, they are without self. Thus, there is no self in things. This is one interpretation of the three characteristics (*ti-lakkhaṇa*). Another is that all things, being impermanent, are fraught with suffering because they are without self, in as much as they are not autonomous. Existence is nothing but existence depending on a series of conditions; hence their existence is a conditional one and there is nothing in the universe that is permanent, i.e., independent of conditions. All things, matter and mind (*nāma-rūpa*), have no abiding self-reality. What appears to be real is temporary existence, an instant in a conditional sequence, the effect of two or more conditions combined.

This is rather dramatically expressed in a conversation between Māra, the Evil One, and the nun Vajirā. By whom is the person (*satta*) produced? asks Māra. Who is the creator of the person? Where is the person who comes into being? Where is the person who disappears?

Vajirā points out to him that there is no such thing as person but merely a collection of changing aggregates (*khandha*) and she illustrates her meaning by the simile of the chariot which is merely the name for a collection of various parts (S I 134f). In a late work, the *Milindapañhā*, the illustration is elaborated in great detail and it is pointed out that when a person is indicated by giving him a name it does not denote a soul but is merely an appellation for the five aggregates which constitute the empirical individual (*Milindapañhā*, pp. 25ff).

The Buddhist conception of the individual, the person, is a quite definite theory, expressed in different ways but all of them essentially the same. The individual consists of *nāma* and *rūpa*, "name" and "form," mind and matter, or mind and body. More usually, he is said to consist of five *khandhas* (groups, masses, aggregates), given as *rūpa* (the physical body), *vedanā* (feelings, sensations), *saññā* (perceptions, ideations), *saṅkhāra* (variously translated as tendencies, dispositions, character-complexes) and *viññāṇa* (cognition, consciousness, intellect). Body corresponds to *rūpa* and the four other *khandhas* to *nāma*, mind. Elsewhere (e.g., in the *Sammādiṭṭhi Sutta*, M I 53f) *nāma* is said to consist of feeling (*vedanā*), perception (*saññā*), volition (*cetanā*), contact (*phassa*) and attention (*manasikāra*), while *rūpa* is defined as being made up of the four great elements (*mahābhūtā*): earth (*pathavī-dhātu*), water (*āpo-dhātu*), wind (*vāyo-dhātu*) and fire (*tejo-dhātu*), which are common both to the world and to the individual. But the distinction between the elements in the world and those that are part of the complex which constitutes the individual is clearly defined in the texts (e.g., M III 239f). The latter are described as being *upādinna,* appropriated, taken-up, assimilated by the consciousness (*viññāṇa*) in order to continue the existence to which it is bound by its earlier activities (see also A I 175; D II 63).

These conceptions are elsewhere found further expanded. Just as the human being was analysed into its component parts, so was the external world with which he entered into relationship. This relationship is one of cognition (*viññāṇa*) and, in discussing how this cognition is established, mention is made of faculties (*indriya*) and their objects are called *āyatana*. The term simply means "place" or "sphere" or "entrance" and is used to include both sense and sense-object, the meeting of which two is necessary for cognition. These three factors that together comprise a condition, i.e., the sense faculty, the sense object and the resultant consciousness, are classified under the name *dhātu.* The human personality and the external world with which it enters into relationship are thus divided into *khandha, āyatana* and *dhātu.* The generic name for all three of them is *dhamma,* which in this context is translated as element of existence. Hence, the significance of the formula already referred to: *sabbe dhamma anattā*: All existence is not-self (without self).

The universe is made up of *saṅkhāras* or component things and since these are *anicca* or impermanent, they are regarded as being in a state of ceaseless movement. And since they have nothing perdurable or stable in them, they are in a condition not of static being but of perpetual becoming (*bhava*). The phenomenal world is therefore a world of continuous flux or flow (*santāna*), a congeries of ever-changing elements in a process of ceaseless movement. All things without exception, are nothing but strings or chains of events, instantaneous "bits" of existence. In the Buddhist view not only are eternal entities such as God, Soul, Matter denied reality but even the simplest stability of empirical objects is regarded as something constituted by our imagination. The empirical thing is a thing constructed by the synthesis of our productive imagination on the basis of sensation. It is nothing but an imagined mental computation.

How then is the illusion produced of a stable, material world and of the perdurable personalities living in it? It is in order to explain this that the Buddha taught the doctrine of *paṭicca-samuppāda* (dependent origination or conditional causation).[3] According to this doctrine, all things that exist in time as well as all space are subject to definite laws, the laws of causation. There is nothing haphazard or pre-determined. Every element (*dhamma*), though appearing only for a single instant (*khaṇa*), is a "tiny element," i.e., it depends for its origin on what had gone before it. Thus existence becomes "dependent existence" and is expressed by the formula: If there is this, there comes to be that; in the absence of this, that too is absent (*asmiṃ sati idaṃ hoti asmiṃ na sati idaṃ na hoti*). The relationship is one of "consecution" rather than of causation. There is no destruction of one thing and no creation of another, no influx of one substance into the other. There is only a constant, uninterrupted, infinitely graduated change.

Accordingly, the personality in which other systems of thought imagine the presence of a permanent spiritual principle, a self or soul (*attā*) is, from the point of view of the Buddha, only a bundle of elements or forces (*saṅkhāra*) and a stream or a series of successive states (*santāna*) originating and existing in dependence on other, previous states. Everything is a succession; there is nothing substantial or permanent. The human individual does not remain the same for two consecutive moments. The "spiritual" part (*nāma*) of the human being and its physical frame (*rūpa*) are linked together by causal laws. The individual is entirely phenomenal, governed by the laws of life, without any extra-phenomenal self or soul within him. Thus, in place of the *Upaniṣad* teaching, "Let no man try to find what speech is, let him know the speaker, let him not try to find what the seen-thing is, let him know not what the doing is, but the doer, etc." The Buddha says, "There is no doer, only doing; no seer, only a seeing, etc." The *attavādin* (believer in the soul-doctrine) would say that when a patch of colour is cognised by someone his soul is the agent, the sense of vision is the instrument. Finding its procedure would consist in light travelling from the eye to the object, seizing its form and coming back in order to deliver its impression to the soul. The Buddha would repudiate the whole of this construction as mere imagery. There are the senses, he would say, and there are the *sensibilia* or

3. See *Dependent Origination* by Piyadassi Thera, *The Wheel* No. 15.

objects of sense. Then there is a functional interdependence or relationship between them. There are sensations and conceptions, and there is a coordination between them.

The absence in the human being of a soul, an unchanging, undying essence, does not mean that the Buddha taught the annihilation of body and mind at death. For, besides all the doctrines mentioned earlier, he also taught the doctrine of *kamma*, the doctrine of the transmitted force of the act, both physical and mental. The living being is a *khandha*-complex, ever changing, but ever determined by its antecedent actions. The long-drawn-out line of life is but a fluctuating curve of inner experience. A man is a compound of body and its organs of sense, of feelings and perceptions, by which he is in constant contact with the external world, of disposition, aptitudes and abilities, and summing them all up, of thought, covering the whole group of mental activities. When he began this present life, he brought as his inheritance the kamma of his many previous lives. During the course of his existence in this world he is always accumulating fresh kamma, through his actions, his thoughts and desires, his affections and passions, and these affect every moment of his life, constantly changing its character. At death when the corporeal bond which held him together falls away, he undergoes only a relatively deeper change. The unseen potencies of his kamma beget a new person. His new body, determined by his kamma, becomes one fitted to that sphere in which he is born.

When a new life is thus produced its components are present from its very inception, although in an undeveloped condition. The first moment of new life is called *viññāṇa*; in the formula of the *paṭicca-samuppāda* its antecedents are the *saṅkhāra*, the prenatal forces which contain latent in them the *anusaya*, the resultant of all the impressions made in that particular flux of elements (*santāna*), conventionally called an individual, in the whole course of its repeated births and deaths, its faring through life (*saṃsāra*). The new person, psychologically if not physically, is continuous with the deceased and suffers or enjoys what his "predecessor" had prepared for him by his behaviour. The elements that contribute to the empirical individual are constantly changing but they will never totally disappear till the conditions and causes that hold them together and impel them to rebirth, the craving (*taṇhā*) and the grasping (*upādāna*) and the desire for separate existence are finally extinguished.

The teaching that *viññāṇa* (consciousness) forms the connecting link between one life and the next has had various interpretations, though it is clear there is no indication at all of an autonomous consciousness persisting unchanged, but only of a continuity of consciousness. The Buddha was once asked (S III 103): "If there is no permanent self, then who is affected by the acts which the not-self has performed?' The Buddha reproves this saying: "Shall one who is under the dominion of desire, think to go beyond the mind of the Master?", meaning thereby, perhaps, that the question is wrongly put because there is an assumption in it of a permanent self.

The *Mahātaṇhakkhaya Sutta* (M I 256ff) relates the story of a monk, Sāti, who went about saying that, according to the Buddha's doctrine, one's consciousness runs on and on and continues without break of identity (*anañña*). It is said (M-a I 477) Sāti's view was due to his having heard various characters in the Jātakas identified with the Buddha. Sāti's colleagues tried to point out his error and when they failed they brought him before the Buddha, who explained to him that, according to his teaching, consciousness arises only by causation and that without assignable conditions, consciousness does not come about.

The *Mahānidāna Sutta* (D II 63f) contains the assertion that there is a "descent" of the consciousness into the womb of the mother preparatory to rebirth. Commentators have differed in regard to the question whether, in addition to the continuity of consciousness between the old and the new lives, there is also some sort of corporeal accompaniment, some kind of subtle matter. For instance, Buddhaghosa denies that the consciousness is accompanied by any physical form and holds it is in process of constant change. The "descent" is only an expression to denote the simultaneity of death and rebirth.

The continuity of consciousness is also the theme of the amusing tale of Godhika (S I 120f). He made various attempts to win arahantship but disease prevented him from maintaining his state of trance long enough. In the end he decided to commit suicide and cut his throat. But before he died, he put forth a final effort and won Nibbāna. Māra, the Evil One, not being fully aware of what had happened, and seeing only the suicide, assumed the form of a cloud of smoke and went about searching for the "rebirth-consciousness" of the sage. When he failed to find it he reported this to the Buddha, who explained that his search was in vain because Godhika had gone beyond Māra's sphere. The question is: Does the story mean that the rebirth consciousness is something visible or is the conception of "visibility" purely metaphorical? It also asserts the doctrine of the moral responsibility of the individual for his actions, for it is not only his continuity that is stressed but also his identity.

This idea is emphasised with a wealth of illustration. To give only two—the milk turns into curds, the curds into butter and butter into ghee—The thief of a mango cannot escape punishment because the mango he stole was not the mango the owner planted. The *Milindapañhā* (pp. 40f) explicitly raises the question: Is the infant the same as the man? Is the mother of the child the same as the mother of the man? and so on. Each succeeding state is neither the same as the one that precedes, nor yet another. The being that is born into a new life is likewise neither the same nor different from his "predecessor." One comes into being and another passes away and the rebirth is, as it were, simultaneous.

The statement has been sometimes made that, although the Buddha has denied self as belonging to visible form (*rūpa*) or to mind (*nāma*), he has not said that there is no self at all, anywhere, of any kind at all. It is objected that to infer the absence of self altogether from the denial of self in either body or mind, is unjustified, because to do so would be to assume that the self if it is to be found at all, must be entirely comprised under and within body and mind. "If I pull my typewriter to pieces," so runs the argument, 'I shall find in it no typist; would it be correct, therefore, to say that there is no typist at all?"

The argument is evidently due to a confusion of thought. In Buddhism it is not only the typewriter that has been analysed; the typist has been analysed as well, and both man and machine have been discovered to be "bundles" of *khandhas*, the typewriter having only *rūpa* (matter) in it while the typist has *nāma* (mind) as well. From the point of view of Buddhism, typist and machine agree in this, that they are both *anattā*, without self of any kind. If it is suggested, however, that there is an *attā* outside and apart from body and mind, which uses body and mind for its expression and manifestation, in the same way as a typist uses a typewriter, it must be asserted that such a supposition finds no support in any of the records of the Buddha, as has already been stated, that the Buddha never recognised the presence of an *attā* of any nature or description either in the universe or out of it. If it be true to say that the Buddha has nowhere explicitly stated in so many words, that the "being" (*satta*) is composed only of the *khandhas,* it would be a hundred times truer to say that nowhere has he said of "being" that it comprises anything else at all, of any description whatsoever, apart from the five *khandhas.*

Numerous passages can be quoted from the Piṭakas which show beyond all possible doubt that, in Buddhist ontology, when "being" (*satta*) is resolved into the five *khandhas,* there is no residuum whatever left. It is clearly stated in one passage (e.g., S III 46f) that "all *samaṇas* and *brāhmaṇas,* who talk about the soul which is variously described by them, talk about it in reference to the five *khandhas* or one or other of them." Buddhaghosa says (*Visuddhimagga* 14 218) that the five *khandhas* were selected for this very purpose for examination to show that there was no residual self. So does Vasubandhu in the *Abhidharmakoṣa* (Chap. 9), where it is stated that *anātman is* synonymous with *skandha, āyatana* and *dhātu.*

In any event, it cannot be maintained that the Buddha was incapable of making a categorical statement on a self if it did really exist and it would certainly be conceded that if the Buddha had the least lurking belief in a self of any sort, he would not have hidden it from his own, only son. And, yet, this is what he taught Rāhula: "Now, Rāhula, when a monk by perfect wisdom realises with regard to the elements (which comprise the human being) 'this is not mine, this is not I, this is not my *attā,*' then does he cut himself off from craving, loosen bonds and by overcoming the vain conceit (of *attā*) makes an end of suffering." As the commentator Kumāralābha asks in desperation: "If there was an *attā,* what on earth was there to prevent the Buddha from saying so?"

In the Mahāvagga of the Vinaya (Vin I) there is a story of thirty young "bloods" (elsewhere called the Bhaddavaggiyas) who went on a picnic with their wives. One of them who had no wife had brought a courtesan and when they were not noticing her she made off with their belongings. While seeking her they came across the Buddha and asked if he had seen a woman. The Buddha replied, "Come now, which would be better for you, that you seek the woman or seek yourself (*attānaṃ gaveseyyatha*)?" The word *attānaṃ* has been interpreted (e.g., by Mrs. Rhys Davids, *Manual of Buddhism,* p. 147) as meaning "the self, the God within you," thus giving to it an import which has deeply coloured the whole of the subsequent argument. The use of the singular accusative is quite in accordance with Pali idiom and there is no need to use here any more than the reflexive sense "each one seeking himself," i.e., learning the truth about himself. In this passage and in such passages as *attā hi attano nātho* (one is lord of oneself), *attadīpā viharatha* (be a refuge unto yourselves), the word *attā* merely refers to the living individual(s) to whom the statement is made or the advice given.

To attribute to the Buddha any teaching accepting the existence of a self or soul would necessitate the supposition that his disciples who came after him had suppressed his teaching so effectually that no one remembered anything of it. Although at the time of his death his teaching was preserved in the minds of thousands of disciples, there is no trace of it even as a heresy among the Buddhists. Unprejudiced scholars have always been struck by the spirit of extreme hostility which undoubtedly reveals itself in the oldest Buddhist sects whenever the idea of a self or soul is mentioned. All Buddhist schools, without exception, have rejected the *atta-vāda* or the doctrine which teaches the idea of a surviving personality of some sort, a psychophysical entity. What, in the view of the Buddha's disciples, he did consider permanent is stated in the Sarvāstivāda version of the *Anattalakkhaṇa Sutta*, which begins: "Form has the nature of the destructible and with its cessation is Nirvāna which is of indestructible nature," and so on with each of the five *khandhas* (*Avadāna sataka*, 248).

There is a discourse in the Saṃyutta Nikāya (S III 25) called the "Burden-Sutta" (*Bhārahāra Sutta*), which speaks of the burden, the taking of the burden, the grasping of the burden and the laying down of the burden. The five *khandhas* are the burden. The grasping of the burden is the craving which tends to rebirth. The laying down of the burden is the complete cessation of this craving in all its forms. Here the word *bhara hara* is used in reference to the individual, the person (*puggala*) of such and such a clan. It has sometimes (e.g., by Keith, *Buddhist Philosophy*; p. 82) been translated as "burden-bearer," thus supporting the view that the sutta accepts a person, i.e., an *attā* or self apart from the five *khandhas.* But the word could equally well and with greater consistency be translated "burden-taking." In any case, it is not important because it would be unjustified to try to prove from a single text that the individual is to be regarded as a permanent entity.

It should be added that two Buddhist schools, the Sammitīyas and the Vajjiputtakas, held the conception of a person (*puggala*) which for all practical purposes may be regarded as an effective self. They taught that the internal *khandhas* at a given moment constitute a certain unity which is related to them as fire is to fuel. This which is called *puggala* assumes new elements at birth and casts them off at death. Since it was obviously another name for a self, this view was rejected by orthodox Buddhists and the arguments adduced are given in the *Kathāvatthu* (i,1). It is significant that the "heretics" never thought of calling this self *ātman* but used instead a new term *puggala.* The *Abhidharmakoṣa* devotes a whole chapter to its refutation.

It has been asked (e.g., by Mrs. Rhys Davids, *Buddhist Psychology* 2nd ed., p. 235) why, if *anattā* was such a fundamental tenet in Buddhism, when the Paribbājaka Vacchagotta asked the Buddha: "Is there an *attā* or is there not," the Buddha remained silent instead of saying categorically that there was no *attā.* The reason was given by the Buddha himself later to Ānanda, that if he had answered "self exists," he would have been quoted by those who held the view of a permanent soul (*sassatavādins*). Whereas if he had said "self does not exist," he would be siding with the annihilationists (*ucchedavādins*). Both were views with which he did not agree (S IV 400f). Besides, Vacchagotta was not yet ripe to understand the truth regarding *attā.* That ripeness came later and Vacchagotta became an arahant.

Buddhism has no objection to the use of the words *attā* or *satta* or *puggala* to indicate the individual as a whole or to distinguish one person from another, where such distinction is necessary, especially as regards such things as memory and *kamma,* which are private and personal, and where it is necessary to recognise the existence of separate lines of continuity (*santāna*). But, even so, these terms should be treated only as labels, binding-conceptions and conventions in language, assisting economy in thought and word and nothing more. Even the Buddha uses them sometimes: "These are worldly usages, worldly terms of communication, worldly descriptions, by which a Tathāgata communicates without misapprehending them" (D I 195f).

The doctrine of *anattā,* like all other doctrines enunciated by the Buddha, has moral perfection as its purpose. The analysis of the five *khandhas* is in order to find out the condition and causes of their existence and their functioning, which are involved in impermanence and suffering, so that the Path to their cessation may be discovered and followed. To do this effectively, according to the Buddha, all false views and misconceptions should be eliminated. Among the strongest of these views are the various beliefs about self (*attā*), particularly those that conceive it as a permanent entity. The individual being entirely phenomenal, governed by causal laws, were there to be in him a supernatural self which transcends these laws, then ethical life would lose its point. Then the Exalted One took up a pinch of dust on the tip of his nail and said: "Even if this much *rūpa* (matter) be permanent, stable, eternal, by nature unchanging, standing fast, then the living of the holy life for the utter destruction of suffering would not be set forth by me." And so on with the other *khandhas* (S III 147).

The passionate sense of egoism is regarded as the root of the world's unhappiness. For one thing, it makes the individual blind to the reality of other persons. When the notion of self disappears, the notion of "mine" also disappears and one becomes free from the idea of "I" and "mine" (*ahaṃkāra-mamaṅkāra*), and there follows a gentler, profounder sympathy with all sentient existence. The first factor of the Noble Eightfold Path is *sammā diṭṭhi,* Right View. When the path is trodden, the goal is ultimately reached, which is Nibbāna (Skt.: Nirvāṇa), complete emancipation and supreme bliss. There are four stages to this goal, the first of which is described as *sotāpatti* (entering the stream). This is reached when three of the ten *saṃyojana* (fetters) have been cast off. These three are (1) belief in a permanent individuality (*sakkāya-diṭṭhi*), (2) doubt (*vicikicchā*) and (3) belief in the efficacy of mere morality and rites and ceremonies (*sīlabbata-parāmāsa*).

It is noteworthy that *sakkāya-diṭṭhi* is the first of the fetters which hinder the attainment of that complete insight on which depends the final release from all suffering and unhappiness. It is said (e.g., in S III 131ff, S II 53) that final deliverance cannot be attained till the subtle remnant of the "I am" conceit, of the "I am" desire, of the lurking tendency to think "I am" is utterly removed. Acceptance of the doctrine of a self (*attavāda*) is one of the four kinds of graspings (*upādāna*) which attach beings to continued rebirth. Another term *atta-diṭṭhi* (the heresy of self) is also sometimes mentioned and *attagāha* (misconception of self), e.g., in the Mahāniddesa.

The individual who has attained Nibbāna is described by many names, one of them being Tathāgata. The question was asked of the Buddha himself, e.g., in the *Alagaddūpama Sutta* (M I 139f)[4] as to what happens to a Tathāgata when he dies. Would it be true to say that the Tathāgata exists after death? When the question is thus put, every possible way of asserting or denying it is stated and rejected. It is one of the "undetermined questions" (*avyākata*). It is worth noting, however, that among the statements denied is the view that a disciple in whom all the fetters have been destroyed is annihilated and destroyed with the dissolution of the body and does not exist after death (e.g., S III 109). "A Tathāgata released from what is called body, etc., is profound, immeasurable, hard to fathom, like the great ocean. It does not fit the case to say that he is reborn or not reborn, reborn and not reborn, or neither reborn nor not reborn." When dissatisfaction is expressed with this declaration the Buddha answers: "Profound is this doctrine, hard to see, hard to comprehend, calm, excellent, beyond the sphere of reasoning, subtle, intelligible only to the wise"(M I 487).

The truth of *anattā* is, according to Buddhist teaching, of all truths the most difficult to realise. Thus Buddhaghosa says (Vibh-a 49f) that the description of the characteristics of not-self is the province of none but a Buddha. It is no idle tradition which states that even the *pañcavaggiyas*, the Buddha's first five disciples, who were very nearly his peers in knowledge and wisdom, failed to realize arahantship till he preached to them the *Anattalakkhaṇa Sutta* on the characteristics of *anattā* (Vin I 13f). The belief in the categories of an abiding self with changing qualities is so deeply

4. See *The Discourse on the Snake Simile* (*Alagaddūpama Sutta*), tr. by Nyanaponika Thera (*The Wheel* No. 48/49)

rooted in our habits of thought that we are reluctant to admit the doctrine of pure and complete change.

Even among the Buddhist schools the doctrine did not hold undisputed sway. The notion of a permanent entity, constituting reality, though officially banned and repudiated, constantly tended to appear through some back door and to haunt the domain of Buddhist philosophy in various guises. Nor is this surprising, for it is only with the attainment of arahantship that the threefold illusion of self, known as the three conceits (*māna*), is destroyed. Even the *anāgāmi,* who has attained the third stage of the Path is not free from the *māna-maññanā,* the conceit of "I am" (S III 128f). Till the fetters of *avijjā* (ignorance) are completely broken and *paññā* (insight) has been attained our attempts to escape from belief in self are like those of the hare in the old Indian tale who, annoyed with the earth, jumped off it, hoping never to return, only to find that the higher he jumped the greater was the thud with which he fell. It is because of our clinging that this is so, says the Buddha (S III 182). To the herdsman who has no cows, the cry of "wolf" no longer brings any terror; to him who has no clinging the realisation of *anattā* spells the highest liberation.

Sixty Songs of Milarepa

Translated by

Garma C.C. Chang

Selected and Introduced by

Bhikkhu Khantipālo

WHEEL PUBLICATION NO. 95/96/97

Jetsun Milarepa and the Huntsman

Jetsun Milarepa is shown sitting at ease in front of the cave at Ghadaya near the Tibet-Nepal border. Above him appears the form of his Guru, Marpa the Translator, since meditations visualizing a Buddha or the Guru above the head are commonly practised in Tibet (see also the *Jinapañjara*, a Pali composition). Around him tower rocks and mountains while waterfalls cascade below. To his right sits a deer and to his left a hunting dog. Before him kneels a huntsman who has cast down his weapons as an offering to the Jetsun (see Song 14). This illustration follows the traditional iconography of Milarepa, his sitting at ease indicating that he has already experienced the state beyond striving.

"Wearing cotton from Nepal" and a meditation-belt and with his hand cupped to his ear as though listening to the "long tongue of the Dhamma," which preaches everywhere and all the time, the great yogi prepares to instruct the erstwhile hunter.

The picture on the previous page was kindly provided by the Venerable Dhardo Rinpoche of the Indo-Tibet Buddhist Cultural Institute, Kalimpong (W. Bengal).

Introduction

Outside the land of Tibet, where the stories and songs of Milarepa are very well-known and loved, far too little is known of this great Buddhist sage. In English,[1] French and German, biographies, partial or complete, have been published but a great number of Milarepa's songs have remained inaccessible, except to those reading Tibetan, until very recently. It is possible to reproduce here sixty of his songs on the Dhamma through the kind permission of the translator, Prof. C. C. Chang, and the courtesy of his publishers, University Books Inc., New York.[2]

The songs printed here all concern that Dhamma which is common to the whole Buddhist tradition. Everyone who has read some of Lord Buddha's discourses in the Pali Canon will find the subject matter here familiar to them. The nearest approach in Pali literature to these Dhamma-songs of Milarepa are the inspired utterances of Lord Buddha in the Sutta Nipāta, Udāna and Itivuttaka (and also in the Dhammapada), and the poems of gnosis spoken by the great bhikkhus and bhikkhunīs of the Noble Sangha, now collected into such books as the Theragāthā and Therīgāthā. Among the bhikkhus living in the Buddha-time, Vaṅgīsa Thera was outstanding for his inspired utterances (see SN 8; Theragāthā 395). The mind inspired and illumined with the knowledge of liberation (*vimutti*) pours forth its wisdom with ease in the shape of verses of great beauty and deep significance. Such was the case with Lord Buddha and some of his immediate disciples, and later, such was the case with Milarepa.

His songs have been arranged here according to subject, though no rigid classification is possible since many of the songs deal with more than one aspect of the Dhamma. First come Milarepa's descriptions of some of his hermitages, then songs on

---

1. See *Tibet's Great Yogi, Milarepa*, translated by Lama Kazi Dawo-Samdup, edited by Evans-Wentz, published by Oxford University Press.

2. The complete work, from which all the songs reproduced below are extracted, is the *Hundred Thousand Songs of Milarepa*, first translated from Tibetan into English by Prof. C. C. Chang, in two volumes, published by the University Books Inc., New Hyde Park, New York.

renunciation and the dangers of saṃsāra, followed by many more on impermanence. After them come songs describing different aspects of saṃsāra—such as the Six Realms of Birth; birth, old age, sickness and death; and home, relatives and wealth. Next are songs relating to practise—advice on how to practise and warnings about what not to do; then upon the Six Pāramitā and other such helpful qualities for practise as loving-kindness (*mettā*), striving (*viriya*) and mindfulness (*sati*). Last of all come songs describing aspects of Milarepa's realisation—his contentment, happiness and non-attachment—concluding with his blessings to his patrons.

It will be seen from the above sequence that the Teaching here is not at all strange to Theravāda, including as it does the impermanence (*anicca*) of all things, states, people, places; that they are impermanent since they arise dependent upon conditions (*paccaya*); that what is conditioned, and therefore relative, is also devoid of essential being (*sabbe dhammā anattā*) and void of self (*suñña*); and that by not recognising these truths and by thinking in terms of permanence, self, etc., we come to experience unending unsatisfactoriness (*dukkha*). Milarepa also points out the way to transcend *dukkha* and emphasises the keeping of precepts (*sīla*), concentrating the scattered mind (*samādhi*) and the development of wisdom (*paññā*).

In making comparisons of different Buddhist traditions many similarities are apt to come to light. One that might be mentioned here is the immense respect and honour paid to Enlightened Teachers in any Buddhist tradition, quite regardless of the differences of time and place. One who has seen and known the Way from his own experience has always been lauded as worthy of the highest honour and the greatest devotion, as in Pāli: *āhuneyyo, pāhuneyyo, dakkhiṇeyyo, añjalikaraṇīyo*. Indeed, we find this as much in the pages of the Pāli Canon as from the *Hundred Thousand Songs*. It is heard as much in the exalted devotion of Pingiya (Sutta Nipāta 1131ff) as in the paeans of praise uttered by the principle disciples of Milarepa, Rechungpa and Gambopa. It is found in modern times in seemingly diverse surroundings—whether in a jungle monastery in Thailand, where a *thudong* (*dhutaṅga*) bhikkhu is respecting his teacher; or whether it is Tibetan bhikkhus or laymen receiving a meditation transmission from their lama. The same devotion here finds expression; it is called saddha or bhatti (*bhakti*—a word first occurring in Indian literature in the Pāli Canon), for this is the act by one still unenlightened, of setting his heart upon Enlightenment in the presence of one who is Enlightened.

Then again, the Hundred Thousand Songs many times mention the "Whispered Transmission" of meditation instructions which are imparted by the teacher, here Milarepa, to his disciples. By some this is contrasted with the statement of Lord Buddha that he was not a teacher who had a "closed fist", that is, one who keeps some Teaching secret or esoteric. Nonetheless, he is well-known for his remarkable ability in preaching exactly the right Dhamma to fit the situation and meet the understanding of those who listened. He did not teach the deep truths of Dhamma to those who were not prepared as yet to receive them and in a like fashion Milarepa graded his teachings for varying circumstances and intelligences.

Meditation instructions given by Lord Buddha to his disciples were also fitted to their temperaments and abilities. It is true that one may now read books explaining the principles of meditation in Theravāda Buddhism, but with books alone, even if one reads all the Pāli Canon, the disadvantage remaining is very great. In all Buddhist countries, it is always assumed that one must have a teacher if meditation practise is to be really successful. It is this teacher who, like Lord Buddha in past times, imparts to one the *details* of the practice and *how*, moreover, it applies to one's special problems and circumstances. As Bhadanta Nyanaponika Mahathera has written in his "*heart of Buddhist Meditation*: "A brief statement on practical meditation, even if limited to the very first steps as is done here, cannot replace personal guidance by an experienced teacher who alone can give due consideration to the requirements and rate of progress of the individual disciple." This is, if not a "Whispered Transmission," at least an oral instruction.

The "grace" of the teacher (*guru*) consists of those merits which he has gathered by his own practice and which, it is believed, may be transferred to the disciple, thus "blessing" him. This can only happen, however, provided that the conditions (of spiritual purity, faith, concentration, etc.) exist between that master and disciple. It is a great mistake to suppose that the disciple is getting something for nothing, for in the absence of these conditions he will experience no "help" from the teacher.

For the dramatic and very inspiring life-story of Jetsun Milarepa as written down by a great-grand-disciple in his tradition, we have but little space here. Those interested in reading it may consult the book mentioned in the footnotes above. Suffice to say here that the Jetsun was born in 1596 (CE 1052) into a wealthy merchant family. As a boy he was known as Tubhaga (delightful-to-hear), a name which people said was particularly appropriate since he had a fine voice and frequently sang the local ballads. His voice was later to be used for spreading the Dhamma, and those who heard it were deeply moved.

Fortunately, Milarepa has given an outline of his life in one of the songs he later sang for his disciples and we cannot do better than introduce an extract of it here.

1

I am Milarepa blessed by his (Marpa's) mercy.
My father was Mila Shirab Jhantsan,
My mother was Nyantsa Karjan.
And I was called Tubhaga ("Delightful-to-hear").

Because our merits and virtues were of small account,
And the Cause-Effect Karma of the past spares no one,
My father Mila passed away (too early in his life).
The deceiving goods and belongings of our household
Were plundered by my aunt and uncle,
Whom I and my mother had to serve.
They gave us food fit only for the dogs;
The cold wind pierced our ragged clothing;
Our skin froze and our bodies were benumbed.
Often I was beaten by my uncle,
And endured his cruel punishment.
Hard was it to avoid my aunt's ill temper.

I lived as best I could, a lowly servant,
And shrugged my shoulders (in bitter resignation).
Misfortunes descended one after the other;
We suffered so, our hearts despaired.

In desperation, I went to Lamas[3] *Yundun and Rondunlaga,*
From whom I mastered the magic arts of Tu, Ser and Ded. [4]
Witnessed by my aunt and uncle, I brought
Great disaster on their villages and kinsmen,
For which, later, I suffered deep remorse.
Then I heard the fame of Marpa, the renowned Translator,
Who, blessed by the saints Naropa and Medripa,
Was living in the upper village of the South River.
After a hard journey I arrived there.
For six years and eight months (I stayed)
With him, my gracious Father Guru, Marpa.
For him I built many houses,
One with courtyards and nine storeys;
Only after this did he accept me.

(Page numbers in the complete translation: pp. 267–268)

Then Milarepa lists the meditation instructions which he was given by his Guru Marpa after he had thus served a long period of hard probation and tells how by their practise he reached Enlightenment (see conclusion of this Introduction).

The name by which he is known in Tibet is Jetsun Milarepa. "Jetsun" is an honorific meaning "holy", while "Repa" means "clad in cotton". Mila was a family name. Hence, in English he may be called Holy Mila the Cotton-clad. He earned the latter name by his power to live throughout the bitter Tibetan winter with only one length of cotton cloth. Where others would have died, he lived happily immersed in the various states of samādhi producing, by his control of them, sufficient body heat. After twelve years of intense meditations in remote mountain caves far from the haunts of men in the valleys below, he succeeded in winning Enlightenment. After this time, disciples gradually gathered around him, the first being Rechungpa, his "moon-like" disciple, while later came his

3. Lama = Ācariya or Teacher. It is not the Tibetan equivalent of "bhikkhu" (which is "gelong"). Thus in Tibet not all bhikkhus are therefore lamas.

4. "Three different arts of black magic." Notes in parentheses are quoted from the translation of the *Hundred Thousand Songs*.

"sun-like" disciple Gambopa.[5] His closest disciples went forth from their homes to take up homeless life with him. Gambopa and some others were already bhikkhus, while many more such as Rechungpa were called "Repa", that is, yogis clad in one piece of cotton.

Like Lord Buddha, the Jetsun taught Dhamma to all—to the emissary of a king and to shepherds, to nuns and wealthy ladies, to bhikkhus and yogis, to bandits and merchants. His conversion of the hunter, Chirawa Gwumbo Dorje, is as popular a story in Tibet as is the pacifying of Angulimala by Lord Buddha, in southern Buddhist lands.

At the age of eighty, Jetsun Milarepa relinquished the body, passing away surrounded by disciples both human and celestial. For 900 years the traditions of meditation in which he trained his disciples have been handed down in Tibet. It has come to be known as the Ghagyupa (sometimes seen as Kargyutpa), which is translated as the "Whispered Transmission." This school of Buddhist practice has, of course, its own special emphasis upon certain doctrines but songs concerned with them are not included in this booklet and the interested reader is requested to consult the *Hundred Thousand Songs of Milarepa*.

In the time of Milarepa, as is evident from these songs, many bhikkhus spent long years in study but never gave much heed to practise. Thus is the divorce of *paṭipatti-dhamma* or *sīla* (moral precepts) and samādhi (meditation), from pariyatti-dhamma or simply learning. Scholar-bhikkhus of Tibet were evidently, at that time, very able in arguing the finer points of Buddhist philosophy and well-equipped with logic to worst outsiders as well as fellow Buddhists in debates. Somehow, in the welter of this study (and the Tibetan Canon and its Commentaries are considerably more extensive than their lengthy Pāli counterparts), the urge to practise meditation, many of its foremost exponents were masters not possessing the monk's robes. This was true of the spiritual forebears of Milarepa (his immediate Guru, Marpa, and the Indian yogis, Naropa and Tilopa). In several places he criticises those bhikkhus, and indeed anyone, who studies the Dhamma just for intellectual

5. In English, we have his *Jewel Ornament of Liberation*, translated by H. V. Guenther, Rider & Co., London.

satisfaction or even for worldly advantage. Many sincere bhikkhus did approach him for meditation instructions and, thereafter, practised with him as their Teacher. He was, therefore, a source for the spiritual regeneration of the Sangha in Tibet.

With his insistence upon the *practice* of Dhamma, Milarepa's life and teaching present striking similarities in many respects to the Way as practised by the *thudong* (*dhutaṅga*) bhikkhu. The greatest difference is that a bhikkhu in any country is bound to observe his Fundamental Precepts (*Pātimokkha*), which, as Milarepa did not have the bhikkhu ordination (*upasampadā*), he did not have to keep. Nevertheless, even a quick look at his life after he began his practice would reveal that he maintained scrupulously those injunctions given him by his Teacher, Marpa the Translator, as well as cultivating those twin bases of moral conduct in the Dhamma, wisdom and compassion (*paññā-karuṇā*). Far greater than this are the resemblances between him and the *thudong* bhikkhu. For instance, both praise contentment with little, living remotely with utter detachment from worldly affairs, great ability in meditation, and so on.

Though he had not the formal ordination of a bhikkhu and wore not the monks' robes, yet Milarepa was truly one gone forth (*pabbajita*). No one reading of his life and some of the songs included here can possibly doubt this. According to definitions given in the Dhammapada, he was indeed a true bhikkhu:

> *"Not by adopting the outward form does one become a bhikkhu"* (266).
>
> *"He who has no attachment whatsoever towards the 'mind-and-body' and who does not grieve for what he has not—he, indeed, is called a bhikkhu"* (367).
>
> *"Whoso herein has abandoned both merit and demerit, he who is holy, he who walks with understanding in this world—he, indeed, is called a bhikkhu"* (267). [6]

These various points, and perhaps others, could be raised to point out that it is in the practice of Dhamma (*paṭipatti*) that different schools of Buddhist thought are shown to have many

6. Translated by Buddharakkhita Thera of Bangalore, India.

similarities. Finally, it is in realisation of the Dhamma (*paṭivedha*) where all divergence ceases, since all the methods practised by all the schools are without exception aimed at the experience of Bodhi, or Enlightenment. If the Dhamma is only studied from books, then many differences are seen separating the many Buddhist traditions but in *practice* there is very much in common. Since all Buddhists are urged to *practise* their Teachings, it is through this that harmony between the divergent traditions of Dhamma may be discovered.

This little introduction may be concluded with a stanza drawn from the autobiographical song, part of which is quoted above. More than this need not be said here, for it is better that the Jetsun sings to you his inspiring and wisdom-inspired songs of the Dhamma.

"I renounced all affairs of this life;
And, no longer lazy, devoted myself to Dharma.
Thus I have reached the State of Eternal Bliss.
Such is the story of my life."

Bhikkhu Khantipālo,
Wat Bovoranives Vihāra,
Bangkok, Thailand.
6th of the Waning Moon of Citta 2508
(22nd April 1965)

In the following text, the writer of this introduction is responsible for the precis stories and the notes, except where matter is found in parentheses. The latter has been drawn from the *Hundred Thousand Songs*.

2

One day, after leaving his cave to collect firewood, Milarepa returned "to find five Indian demons with eyes as large as saucers" whom he thought to be apparitions of the deities who disliked him. As he had never given them any offering, he then began to sing a...

Complimentary Song to the Deities of Red Rock Jewel Valley

This lonely spot where stands my hut
Is a place pleasing to the Buddhas,
A place where accomplished beings dwell,
A refuge where I dwell alone.

Above Red Rock Jewel Valley
White clouds are gliding;
Below, the Tsang River gently flows;
Wild vultures wheel between.

Bees are humming among the flowers,
Intoxicated by their fragrance;
In the trees, birds swoop and dart,
Filling the air with their song.

In Red Rock Jewel Valley
Young sparrows learn to fly
Monkeys love to leap and swing,
And beasts to run and race,
While I practise the Two Bodhi-minds[7] *and love to meditate.*

Ye local demons, ghosts and gods,
All friends of Milarepa,
Drink the nectar of kindness and compassion,
Then return to your abodes.

(p. 5)

7. The Bodhisatta's Vow and Practice to save all sentient beings either in mundane respect when voidness has not been realised, or as transcendental when suññata has been experienced. His practice includes the perfections, or those qualities which help one in "crossing over" from saṃsāra to Nibbāna—the Pārami(tā).

3

One day, Milarepa's patrons from Dro Tang came to visit him. They asked him what benefits Junpan Nanka Tsang had to offer. In reply, Milarepa sang:

I pray to my Guru, the Holy One.
Listen, my patrons, and I will tell you
the merits of this place.

In the goodly quiet of this Sky Castle of Junpan
High above, dark clouds gather;
Deep blue and far below flows the River Tsang.

At my back the Red Rock of Heaven rises;
At my feet, wild flowers bloom, vibrant and profuse;
At my cave's edge (wild) beasts roam, roar and grunt;
In the sky vultures and eagles circle freely,
While from heaven drifts the drizzling rain.
Bees hum and buzz with their chanting;
Mares and foals gambol and gallop wildly;
The brook chatters past pebbles and rocks;
Through the trees monkeys leap and swing;
And larks carol in sweet song.

The timely sounds I hear are all my fellows.
The merits of this place are inconceivable—
I now relate them to you in this song.

Oh, good patrons,
Pray follow my Path and my example;
Abandon evil, and practise good deeds.
Spontaneously from my heart
I give you this instruction.

(pp. 68–69)

4

One day, some villagers from Ragma came to see the Jetsun. They asked him, "Why do you like this place so much? Why is it that you are so happy here? Pray, tell us what you think of all these things!" In answer, Milarepa sang:

Here is the Bodhi-Place, quiet and peaceful.
The snow-mountain, the dwelling-place of deities,
stands high above;
Below, far from here in the village, my faithful patrons live;
Surrounding it are mountains nestling in white snow.

In the foreground stand the wish-granting trees;
In the valley lie vast meadows, blooming wild.
Around the pleasant, sweet-scented lotus, insects hum;
Along the banks of the stream
And in the middle of the lake,
Cranes bend their necks, enjoying the scene,
and are content.

On the branches of the trees, the wild birds sing;
When the wind blows gently, slowly dances the weeping willow;
In the treetops monkeys bound and leap for joy;
In the wild green pastures graze the scattered herds,
And merry shepherds, gay and free from worry,
Sing cheerful songs and play upon their reeds.
The people of the world, with burning desires and craving,
Distracted by affairs, become the slaves of earth.

From the top of the Resplendent Gem Rock,
I, the yogi, see these things.
Observing them, I know that they are fleeting and transient;
Contemplating them, I realise that comforts and pleasure
Are merely mirages and water-reflections.

I see this life as a conjuration and a dream.
Great compassion rises in my heart
For those without a knowledge of this truth.
The food I eat is the Space-Void;
My meditation is Dhyāna—beyond distraction.

Myriad visions and various feelings all appear before me—
Strange indeed are samsaric phenomena!
Truly amazing are the dharmas in the Three Worlds,[8]
Oh, what a wonder, what a marvel!
Void is their nature, yet everything is manifested.

(pp. 64–65)

5

This song was sung to a young, well-dressed girl who after asking Milarepa about his father and mother, brothers and sisters, further enquired: "But do you also have any Samsaric companions, sons and belongings?" Milarepa then sang in reply:

At first, my experiences in saṃsāra[9]
Seemed most pleasant and delightful;
Later, I learned about its lessons;
In the end, I found a Devil's Prison.
These are my thoughts and feelings on saṃsāra.
So I made up my mind to renounce it.

At first, one's friend is like a smiling angel;
Later, she turns into a fierce exasperated woman;
But in the end a demoness is she.
These are my thoughts and feelings on companions.
So I made up my mind to renounce a friend.

At first, the sweet boy smiles, a Babe of Heaven;
Later, he makes trouble with the neighbours;
In the end, he is my creditor and foe.
These are my thoughts and feelings about children.
So I renounced both sons and nephews.

At first, money is like the Wish-fulfilling Gem;
Later, one cannot do without it;
In the end, one feels a penniless beggar.

8. Or Three Realms—of Desire, of Form and of Non-Form. "They include all sentient beings in the various Realms of Samsaric existence."

9. The realm of repeated birth-and-deaths brought into experience by the mistaken conceptions of 'I', 'self', 'ego', and 'soul' as abiding entities.

These are my thoughts and feelings about money.
So I renounced both wealth and goods.

When I think of these experiences,
I cannot help but practise Dharma;
When I think of Dharma,
I cannot help but offer it to others.
When death approaches,
I shall then have no regret.

(p. 209)

6

On his way to Shri Ri to meditate, Milarepa lodged at an inn where a merchant, Dhawa Norbu (the Moon Jewel), was also staying with a great retinue. Milarepa begged alms from him, upon which the merchant remarked that it would be better for him to work to support himself. Milarepa pointed out that enjoying pleasures now is the source for more suffering in the future. Then he said: "Now listen to my song."

The Eight Reminders

Castles and crowded cities are the places
Where now you love to stay;
But remember that they will fall to ruins
After you have departed from this earth!

Pride and vain glory are the lure
Which now you love to follow;
But remember, when you are about to die
They offer you no shelter and no refuge!

Kinsmen and relatives are the people now
With whom you love to live;
But remember that you must leave them all behind
When from this world you pass away!

Servants, wealth and children
Are things you love to hold;
But remember, at the time of your death
Your empty hands can take nothing with you!

Vigour and health
Are dearest to you now;
But remember, at the moment of your death
Your corpse will be bundled up and borne away!

Now your organs are clear,
Your flesh and blood are strong and vigourous;
But remember, at the moment of your death
They will no longer be at your disposal!

Sweet and delicious foods are things
That now you love to eat;
But remember, at the moment of your death
Your mouth will let the spittle flow!

When of all this I think,
I cannot help but seek the Buddha's Teachings!
The enjoyments and the pleasures of this world
For me have no attraction.

I, Milarepa, sing of the Eight Reminders,
At the Guest House in Garakhache of Tsang.
With these clear words I give this helpful warning;
I urge you to observe and practise them!

(pp. 150–151)

7

Milarepa once said to Shindormo, his patroness: "But if you have a precious human body and have been born at a time and place in which the Buddhist religion prevails, it is very foolish indeed not to practise the Dharma." Milarepa thus sang:

At the feet of the Translator Marpa, I prostrate myself,
And sing to you, my faithful patrons.

How stupid it is to sin[10] *with recklessness*
While the pure Dharma spreads all about you.

---

10. Used throughout to express the Buddhist teaching of deeds which bring harm on others (and ruin to oneself). This action is "unskilful" (*akusala*) and "sin" here must be understood in thus sense.

How foolish to spend your lifetime without meaning,
When a precious human body is so rare a gift.

How ridiculous to cling to prison-like cities
and remain there.
How laughable to fight and quarrel
with your wives and relatives,
Who do but visit you.
How senseless to cherish sweet and tender words
Which are but empty echoes in a dream.
How silly to disregard one's life by fighting foes
Who are but frail flowers.

How foolish it is when dying
to torment oneself with thoughts of family,
Which bind one to Maya's[11] *mansion.*
How stupid to stint on property and money,
Which are a debt on loan from others.
How ridiculous it is to beautify and deck the body
Which is a vessel full of filth.
How silly to strain each nerve for wealth and goods,
And neglect the nectar of the inner teachings!

In a crowd of fools, the clear and sensible
Should practise the Dharma, as do I.

(pp. 33–34)

8

A yogi who had great faith in Milarepa came with other patrons, bringing copious offerings, and they asked Milarepa "how he had managed to undergo the trials of his probationship and had exerted himself..." Milarepa answered with...

The Six Resolutions

When one has lost interest in this world,
His faith and longing for the Dharma is confirmed.

11. Delusion; illusory nature of saṃsāra.

To relinquish one's home ties is very hard;
Only by leaving one's native land
Can one be immune from anger.

It is hard to conquer burning passions
Towards relatives and close friends;
The best way to quench them
Is to break all associations.

One never feels that one is rich enough;
Contented, he should wear humble cotton clothes.
He may thus conquer much desire and craving.

It is hard to avoid worldly attractions;
By adhering to humbleness,
Longing for vain, glory is subdued.

It is hard to conquer pride and egotism;
So, like the animals,
Live in the mountains.

My dear and faithful patrons!
Such is the real understanding
That stems from perseverance.

I wish you all to practise deeds that are meaningful,[12]
And amass all merits!

(pp. 100–101)

9

Milarepa went out one day for alms and coming to a meeting of Dharma-followers, was ridiculed. One of them, however, recognised him and said: "To inspire those attending this meeting, therefore, please now sing for us." In response, Milarepa sang a song...

The Ocean of Saṃsāra

Alas, is not saṃsāra like the sea?
Drawing as much water as one pleases,

12. Virtuous deeds that lead one to Enlightenment.

It remains the same without abating.
Are not the Three Precious Ones like Mount Sumeru,
That never can be shaken by anyone?

Are there Mongol bandits invading yogis' cells?
Why, then, do great yogis stay in towns and villages?
Are not people craving for rebirth and Bardo?[13]
Why, then, do they cling so much to their disciples?
Are woollen clothes in the next life more expensive?
Why, then, do women make so much of them here?
Do people fear that saṃsāra may be emptied?
Why, then, do priests and laymen hanker after children?
Are you reserving food and drink for your next life?
Why, then, do men and women not give to charity?
Is there any misery in Heaven above?
Why, then, do so few plan to go there?
Is there any joy below in Hell?

Why, then, do so many prepare to visit there?
Do you not know that all sufferings
And Lower Realms are the result of sins?
Surely you know that if you now practise virtue,
When death comes you will have peace of mind
and no regrets.

(*pp. 538–539; extract*)

10

Upon the arrival of autumn, Milarepa decided to leave Upper Lowo, where he had been preaching the Dharma during the summer, and go to Di Se Snow Mountain. His patrons gave him a farewell party, circling round him, and made him offerings and

13. The intermediate state of existence between death and rebirth (Skt.: *antarabhava*, *sambhavesi*), but its existence is disputed in Theravāda, where rebirth is said to be immediate. The question is complicated by the fact that time is a relative concept (*paññatti*) and its perception dependent upon the possession of certain senses. Bardo, according to Tibetan Buddhism, is a very important state, like crossroads, and the fate and fortune of one's rebirth depends much upon it.

obeisance. They said: "Be kind enough to give us, your disciples, some instructions and advice." The Jetsun then emphasised the transiency of all beings, admonishing them to practise Dharma earnestly. And he sang...

The Song of Transience with Eight Similes

Faithful disciples here assembled (ask yourselves):
"Have I practised Dharma with great earnestness?
Has the deepest faith arisen in my heart?"
He who wants to practise Dharma and gain
non-regressive faith,
Should listen to this exposition of the Mundane Truths
And ponder well their meaning.
Listen to these parables and metaphors:

A painting in gold,
Flowers of turquoise blue,
Floods in the vale above,
Rice in the vale below,
Abundance of silk,
A jewel of value,
The crescent moon,
And a precious son—
These are the eight similes.

No one has sung before
Such casual words (on this),
No one can understand their meaning
If he heeds not the whole song.

The gold painting fades when it is completed—
This shows the illusory nature of all beings,
This proves the transient nature of all things.
Think, then, you will practise Dharma.

The lovely flowers of turquoise blue
Are destroyed in time by frost—
This shows the illusory nature of all beings,
This proves the transient nature of all things.
Think, then, you will practise Dharma.

The flood sweeps strongly down the vale above,
Soon becoming weak and tame in the plain below—
This shows the illusory nature of all beings,
This proves the transient nature of all things.
Think, then, you will practise Dharma.

Rice grows in the vale below;
Soon with a sickle it is reaped
This shows the illusory nature of all beings,
This proves the transient nature of all things.
Think, then, you will practise Dharma.

Elegant silken cloth
Soon with a knife is cut—
This shows the illusory nature of all beings,
This proves the transient nature of all things.
Think, then, you will practise Dharma.

The precious jewel that you cherish
Soon will belong to others—
This shows the illusory nature of all beings,
This proves the transient nature of all things.
Think, then, you will practise Dharma.

The pale moonbeams soon will fade and vanish—
This shows the illusory nature of all beings,
This proves the transient nature of all things.
Think, then, you will practise Dharma.

A precious son is born;
Soon he is lost and gone—
This shows the illusory nature of all beings,
This proves the transient nature of all things.
Think, then, you will practise Dharma.

These are the eight similes I sing.
I hope you will remember and practise them.

Affairs and business will drag on forever,
So lay them down and practise now the Dharma.
If you think tomorrow is the time to practise,
Suddenly you find that life has slipped away.
Who can tell when death will come?

Ever think of this,
And devote yourselves to Dharma practise.

(pp. 203–205)

11

Travelling with his disciples, Milarepa came to Din Ri Namar, where he enquired for the name of the outstanding patron. Learning that the physician Yang Nge was a devoted Buddhist, he proceeded to his house, where the physician said, "It is said that Jetsun Milarepa can use anything at hand as a metaphor for preaching. Now please use the bubbles of water in this ditch before us as a metaphor and give us a discourse." In response, Jetsun sang a song...

The Fleeting Bubbles

I pay homage to my gracious Guru—
Pray make everyone here think of the Dharma!
As he said once, "Like bubbles is
This life, transient and fleeting—
In it no assurance can be found."
A layman's life is like a thief
Who sneaks into an empty house.
Know you not the folly of it?

Youth is like a summer flower—
Suddenly it fades away.
Old age is like a fire spreading
Through the fields—suddenly 'tis at your heels.
The Buddha once said, "Birth and death
Are like sunrise and sunset—
Now come, now go."
Sickness is like a little bird
Wounded by a sling.
Know you not, health and strength
Will in time desert you?
Death is like an oil-dry lamp
(After its last flicker).
Nothing, I assure you,

In this world is permanent.
Evil Karma is like a waterfall,
Which I have never seen flow upward.
A sinful man is like a poisonous tree—
If you lean on it, you will injured be.
Transgressors are like frost-bitten peas—
Like spoiled fat, they ruin everything.
Dharma-practisers are like peasants in the field—
With caution and vigour they will be successful.
The Guru is like medicine and nectar—
Relying on him, one will win success.
Discipline is like a watchman's tower—
Observing it, one will attain Accomplishment.
The Law of Karma is like saṃsāra's wheel—
Whoever breaks it will suffer a great loss.
Saṃsāra is like a poisonous thorn
In the flesh—if not pulled out,
The poison will increase and spread.
The coming of death is like the shadow
Of a tree at sunset—
It runs fast and none can halt it.
When that time comes,
What else can help but Holy Dharma?
Though Dharma is the fount of victory,
Those who aspire to it are rare.
Scores of men are tangled in
The miseries of saṃsāra;
Into this misfortune born,
They strive by plunder and theft for gain.

He who talks on Dharma
With elation is inspired,
But when a task is set him,
He is wrecked and lost.

Dear patrons, do not talk too much,
But practise the Holy Dharma.

(pp. 632–633)

12

"This is indeed very helpful to my mind," commented the physician, "but please preach still further for me on the truth of Karma and the suffering of birth, old age, illness and death, thus enabling me to gain a deeper conviction in Buddhadharma." In response, the Jetsun sang:

Please listen to these words,
Dear friends here assembled.

When you are young and vigourous
You ne'er think of old age coming,
But it approaches slow and sure
Like a seed growing underground.

When you are strong and healthy
You ne'er think of sickness coming,
But it descends with sudden force
Like a stroke of lightning.

When involved in worldly things
You ne'er think of death's approach
Quick it comes like thunder
Crashing 'round your head.

Sickness, old age and death
Ever meet each other
As do hands and mouth.
Waiting for his prey in ambush,
Yama [14] is ready for his victim,
When disaster catches him.

Sparrows fly in single file. Like them,
Life, Death and Bardo follow one another.
Never apart from you
Are these three "visitors".

---

14. The Lord of Hell before whom, according to some accounts, evildoers are dragged and tried. Such visions seen by one arising in the Hells are often explained as mental projections appearing very real to those who see them. They are, of course, the fruit (*phala*, *vipāka*) of unskilful action (*akusala kamma*).

Thus thinking, fear you not
Your sinful deeds?

Like strong arrows in ambush waiting,
Rebirth in Hell, as Hungry Ghost, or Beast
Is (the destiny) waiting to catch you.
If once into their traps you fall,
Hard will you find it to escape.

Do you not fear the miseries
You experienced in the past?
Surely you will feel much pain
If misfortunes attack you?
The woes of life succeed one another
Like the sea's incessant waves
One has barely passed, before
The next one takes its place.
Until you are liberated, pain
and pleasure come and go at random
Like passers-by encountered in the street.

Pleasures are precarious,
Like bathing in the sun;
Transient, too, as snowstorms
Which come without warning.
Remembering these things,
Why not practise the Dharma?

(pp. 634–635)

13

Rechungpa, after returning from India, had contracted the disease of pride and in various ways Milarepa tried to cure him. As his disciple required food, they went for alms but were abused by an old woman who declared that she had no food. The next morning they found her dead and Milarepa said: "Rechungpa, like this woman, every sentient being is destined to die, but seldom do people think of this fact. So they lose many opportunities to practise the Dharma. Both you and I should remember this incident and learn a lesson from it." Whereupon, he sang...

The Song of Transiency and Delusion

When the transiency of life strikes deeply into one's heart
One's thoughts and deeds will naturally accord with Dharma.
If repeatedly and continuously one thinks about death,
One can easily conquer the demons of laziness.
No one knows when death will descend upon him—
Just as this woman last night!

Rechungpa, do not be harsh, and listen to your Guru!
Behold, all manifestations in the outer world
Are ephemeral like a dream last night!
One feels utterly lost in sadness
When one thinks of this passing dream.
Rechungpa, have you completely wakened
From this great puzzlement?
Oh, the more I think of this,
The more I aspire to Buddha and the Dharma.

The pleasure-yearning human body is an ungrateful creditor.
Whatever good you do to it,
It always plants the seeds of pain.

This human body is a bag of filth and dirt;
Never be proud of it, Rechungpa,
But listen to my song!

When I look back at my body,
I see it as a mirage-city;
Though I may sustain it for a while,
It is doomed to extinction.
When I think of this,
My heart is filled with grief!
Rechungpa, would you not cut off saṃsāra?
Oh, the more I think of this,
The more I think of Buddha and the Dharma!

A vicious person can never attain happiness.
Errant thoughts are the cause of all regrets,
Bad dispositions are the cause of all miseries,
Never be voracious, oh Rechungpa,
But listen to my song!

When I look back at my clinging mind,
It appears like a short-lived sparrow in the woods—
Homeless, and with nowhere to sleep;
When I think of this, my heart is filled with grief.
Rechungpa, will you let yourself indulge in ill-will?
Oh, the more I think of this,
The more I aspire to Buddha and the Dharma!

Human life is as precarious
As a single slim hair of a horse's tail
Hanging on the verge of breaking;
It may be snuffed out at anytime
Like this old woman was last night!
Do not cling to this life, Rechungpa,
But listen to my song!

When I observe inwardly my breathings
I see they are transient, like the fog;
They may vanish any moment into nought.
When I think of this, my heart is filled with grief.
Rechungpa, do you not want to conquer
That insecurity now?
Oh, the more I think of this,
The more I aspire to Buddha and the Dharma.

To be close to wicked kinsmen only causes hatred.
The case of this old woman is a very good lesson.
Rechungpa, stop your wishful-thinking
And listen to my song!

When I look at friends and consorts
They appear as passers-by in the bazaar;
Meeting with them is only temporary,
But separation is forever!
When I think of this, my heart is filled with grief.
Rechungpa, do you not want to cast aside
All worldly associations?
Oh, the more I think of this,
The more I think of Buddha and the Dharma.

A rich man seldom enjoys
The wealth that he has earned;

This is the mockery of Karma and saṃsāra,
Money and jewels gained through stinginess and toil
Are like this old woman's bag of food.
Do not be covetous, Rechungpa,
But listen to my song!

When I look at the fortunes of the rich,
They appear to me like honey to the bees—
Hard work, serving only for others' enjoyment,
Is the fruit of their labour.
When I think of this, my heart is filled with grief.
Rechungpa, do you not want to open
The treasury within your mind?
Oh, the more I think of this,
The more I aspire to Buddha and his Teachings.

(pp. 433–435)

14

When Milarepa was sitting in meditation, a frightened deer dashed by, followed by a ravening hound. By the power of his loving-kindness and compassion (*mettā-karuṇā*), Milarepa made them lie down, one on either side of him, and then preached to them. Then came the fierce and proud huntsman, Chirawa Gwunbo Dorje, who was enraged by the sight of the Jetsun and shot an arrow at him, but missed. Milarepa sang to him and his heart began to turn to the Dharma. Then the hunter saw that Milarepa was living an austere life and great faith arose in him. He wished then to practise Dharma after talking with his family but the Jetsun warned him that his present meritorious thought might change and he sang:

Hearken, hearken, huntsman!
Though the thunder crashes,
It is but empty sound;
Though the rainbow is richly-coloured,
It will soon fade away.
The pleasures of this world are like dream-visions;
Though one enjoys them, they are the source of sin.
Though all we see may seem to be eternal,
It will soon fall to pieces and will disappear.

Yesterday perhaps one had enough or more,
All today is gone and nothing's left;
Last year one was alive, this year one dies.
Good food turns into poison,
And the beloved companion turns into a foe.

Harsh words and complaints requite
Good-will and gratitude.
Your sins hurt no one but yourself.
Among one hundred heads, you value most your own.
In all ten fingers, if one is cut, you feel the pain.
Among all things you value, yourself is valued most.
The time has come for you to help yourself.

Life flees fast. Soon death
Will knock upon your door.
It is foolish, therefore, one's devotion to postpone.
What else can loving kinsmen do
But throw one into saṃsāra?
To strive for happiness hereafter
Is more important than to seek it now.
The time has come for you to rely upon a Guru,
The time has come to practise Dharma.

(p. 284)

15

Milarepa: "If one is really determined to free oneself from the sufferings of saṃsāra, such as birth, old age, illness, death, and so on, he will have peace of mind all the time and will not need to make any effort. Otherwise, he should bear in mind that the sufferings in a future life could be much more durable and longer-lasting than those in this life, and the burden could also be much heavier. It is, therefore, of paramount importance to take steps to prepare for the next life (p.114)". This was said to some young men from his native country, who asked how they could extricate themselves from worldly affairs. Then, Milarepa said: "Please hearken, and I will sing a song for you."

We sentient beings moving in the world

Float down the flowing stream
Of the Four Sufferings.[15]
Compared to this, how much more formidable
Are the unceasing future lives in saṃsāra
Why not, then, prepare a boat for the "crossing"?

The state of our future lives is far more fearful
And deserving of far more concern
Than are the dreadful demons, ghosts and Yama,
So why not prepare for yourself a guide?

Even the dread passions—craving, hatred and blindness—
Are not so fearful
As the state of our (unknown) future,
So why not prepare for yourself an antidote?

Great is the Kingdom of the Three Realms of Saṃsāra,
But greater is the endless road of birth-and-death,
So why not prepare for yourself provisions?
It will be better if you practise Dharma
If you have no assurance in yourselves.

(pp. 114–115)

Milarepa said: "A human body, free and opportune, is as precious as a jewel, and to have a chance to practise the Dharma is likewise very rare. Also, to find one serious Buddhist in a hundred is difficult! Considering the difficulties of meeting the right Gurus, and other necessary favourable conditions for practising Buddhism, you should deem yourselves very fortunate that you have now met all these requirements. Do not, therefore (waste them), but practise the Dharma."

(p. 116)

16

Shiwa Aui, a leading disciple of Milarepa, once asked his Master, when the latter was nearing the end of his life: "Please tell us what are the joys and miseries that sentient beings experience in the

15. Of birth, old age, sickness and death.

Six Realms? Especially, please tell us what are the pleasures *devas* enjoy?" The Jetsun replied: Do not be fascinated by the pleasures of heavenly beings; they also have miseries—like this:

The pleasures enjoyed by men and devas
Are like the amusements of the Heavenly Yak:[16]
It may low like thunder
But what good can it do?

(Swooning in a state of trance),
The devas in the four Formless Heavens[17]
Cannot distinguish good from evil.
Because their minds are dull and callous,
Insensible, they have no feeling.
In unconscious stupefaction,

They live many kalpas in a second.
What a pity that they know it not!
Alas, these heavenly births
Have neither sense nor value.
When they think vicious thoughts
They start to fall again.
As to the reason for their fall
(Scholars), with empty words,
Have dried their mouths in explanations.

In the Heavens of Form,[18]
The devas of the five higher and twelve lower realms
Can only live until their merits are exhausted.
Their virtues are essentially conditional,
And their Karma basically Saṃsāric.

Those Dharma-practicers subject to worldly desires,
And those "great yogis" wrapped in stillness,
Have yet to purify their minds;
Huge may be their claims and boasts,
But habitual thought-seeds

16. A legendary yak ox said to dwell in Heaven.
17. Gained by the practice of the four *arūpa jhānas*: infinity of space, of consciousness, of no-thingness and of neither-perception-nor-non-perception.
18. Gained by the practice of the four *rūpa jhānas*.

In their minds are deeply rooted.
After a long dormant time,
Evil thoughts again will rise.
When their merits and fortunes are consumed;
They to the Lower Realms[19] *will go once more!*

If I explain the horror of a deva's death,
You will be disheartened and perplexed.
Bear this in your mind and ever meditate!

(pp.662– 663)

17

In a sad mood the disciples then asked the Jetsun to preach to them of the sufferings of the *asuras*. In response, he sang:

Great are asuras' sufferings.
Misled by malignant thoughts,
To all they bring misfortunes
Knowing not their true Self-mind[20]
Their deeds are self-deceiving,
Their feelings coarse, their senses crude,
Deeming all to be their foes,
Not even for a moment
Can they know the truth.
Evil by nature, they can hardly bear a loss;
Harder is benevolence for them to cherish.
Blinded by the Karma-of-Belligerence,
Never can they take good counsel.

All nature such as this is caused
By seeking pleasures for oneself
And bearing harmful thoughts towards others.
Pride, favouritism, vanity and hatred
Are the evil Karmic forces
That drag one to a lower birth,

19. Of titans (*asuras*), hungry ghosts (*petas*), animals, and hell-wraiths.

20. This is the true nature of mind (*citta-sabhava*) which is *anattā, suñña*, etc., but is not recognised due to holding ideas of permanence, happiness, ego, etc.

Making sinful deeds more easy.

Ripening Karma brings (to them)
An instinctive hatred;
Failing to distinguish right from wrong,
They can hardly be helped by any means.
Bear, oh my disciples, this in your minds
And meditate with perseverance all your lives!

(p. 664)

18

Shiwa Aui said, "Now please tell us about the sufferings of *human beings.*" In answer, Milarepa sang:

We human beings are endowed with power
To do good or evil deeds;
This is because our body (personality)
Is made of all Six Elements.[21]

You junior Repas who desire to be great scholars
Should know the "kernel and shell" of Buddhism.
Lest learning lead you only to confusion.

Knowing not the root of mind,
Useless is it to meditate for years.
Without sincerity and willingness,
Rich offerings have no real meaning.

Without giving impartial aid to all,
Patronage of one's favourite is wrong.

---

21. The reason why a personality endowed with all the six elements (earth, water, fire, air, space and consciousness) can commit all good and evil deeds is implicitly given in the *Abhidharmakoṣa*. Sentient beings in the *rūpa*- and *arūpa*-realms are not endowed with all six elements, some of them having only two elements or one, thus being incapable of the commission of great evil deeds such as killing, sexual perversion, etc. This is why it is often said that here in this world is the best place either to attain Nirvana or to fall into Realms of Woe, since human beings are endowed with great mental and physical powers partly dependent on the possession of the six elements.

Knowing not the right counsel for each man,
Blunt talk will only bring trouble and discord.

He who knows the appropriate way
To help men of diverse dispositions,
Can use expedient words[22] *for kind and fruitful purposes.*
He who knows but little of himself
Can harm many by his ignorance.
When good-will arises in one's mind,
Stones, trees and earth all become seeds of virtue.

Again, an over-punctilious person
Knows not how to relax;
A gluttonous dog knows not what is hunger;
A brazen Guru knows not what is fear.

Rich men are wretched creatures with their money,
Poor men are wretched creatures without money.
Alas, with or without money, both are miserable!
Happiness will come, dear children,
If you can practise the Dharma.
Remember, then, my words and practise with perseverance.

(pp. 664–665)

19

"It is very true that human beings suffer like this," agreed the disciples. "Now please tell us about the sufferings in the three miserable realms, even though just to mention them may be distressing. Also, to spur our spiritual efforts, please preach to us of the causes of *Hell* and its woe." In response, Jetsun sang:

Those who, for meat and blood
Slaughter living beings,
Will in the Eight Hot Hells be burned.
But if they can remember the Good Teachings,
Soon will they be emancipated.

22. As for instance, did Lord Buddha to Nanda when leading him to practise the true Dhamma, by first promising him rewards of exquisite pleasures in the heavens of desire.

Ruthless robbers who strike and kill,
Wrongly eating others' food
While clinging to their own with greed,
Will fall into the Eight Cold Hells.
Yet if they do not hold wrong views against the Dharma
It is said that their time for deliverance will come.
(The Holy Scriptures) also say
Whene'er the denizens of hell
Recall the name of Buddha,
Delivered will they be immediately.

Ever repeating sinful deeds means
Dominance by vice and evil Karma.
Fiends filled with the craving for pleasures,
Murder even their parents and Gurus,
Rob the Three Gems of their treasure,
Revile and accuse falsely the Precious Ones,
And condemn the Dharma as untrue;
In the Hell-of-unceasing-torment[23]
These evil-doers will be burned;
Far from them, alas, is Liberation.
This, my sons, will certainly distress you,
So into Dharma throw your hearts
And devote yourselves to meditation!

(p. 666)

20

"For the benefit of sentient beings, please tell us now about the sufferings of the *Hungry Ghosts.*" In reply, Milarepa sang:

Hungry Ghosts, seeing all forms as foes,
Run from each successive terror.
Wild beasts fight and eat each other.
Who of them is to blame?

23. It is said that the denizens of this hell suffer unceasing torment, whereas in other hells, temporary relief of pain is possible. Those who now afflict the Dharma in Tibet should take notice of the inevitable fate in store for persecutors of the Dharma!

The sufferings of the Hungry Ghosts
Grow from their stinginess.
Like a rat is he who fails
To give alms when he is rich,
Begrudges food when he has plenty,
Gives no food to others, but checks
Them over, counts and stores them—
Discontented day and night.
At the time of death he sees
That his hard-earned wealth
Will be enjoyed by others.

Caught in Bardo[24] *by the agony of loss,*
As a Hungry Ghost he lives his life.
Due to his delusive thoughts
He suffers thirst and hunger.
When he sees his goods enjoyed by others
He is tormented by avarice and hate.
Again and again will he thus fall down (to Hell).
I, the great Yogi of Strength,
Now sing for you the woes
Of Hungry Ghosts. Dear sons
And disciples here assembled, think on
My words and meditate with perseverance!

(p. 667)

21

Shiwa Aui then requested, "Now please tell us of the sufferings of *animals*." Whereupon Milarepa sang:

Animals, alas, are ignorant and benighted;
Most stupid men will incarnate amongst them.
Blind and enslaved by evil Karma,
The ignorant know not Dharma's Truth.
Blind both to evil and to virtue,
They quickly waste their lives away.

---

24. See note 13.

Unable to reason and use symbols,
They act like blind automatons;
Unable to distinguish wrong from right,
Like maniacs, they do much wrong.
Some people even say 'tis good
(To be an animal);
Since it does neither regret nor repent,
Alas! How foolish is this thought!
Then, all stupid life-takers
Will incarnate as beasts;
The fools who know not right from wrong,
And those who harbour vicious thoughts,
Will incarnate as common brutes.
Hard it is for me to describe
Their Karmas, but think on my words
And cultivate your minds.

(pp. 667–668)

22

Milarepa once took Rechungpa to the market of Nya Non in order to further his spirit of renunciation. Many butchers had gathered there. The meat was piled up like walls, animals' heads were stacked in huge heaps, skins were scattered over the ground, and blood ran together like water in a pond. In addition, rows of livestock were fastened to the stakes for slaughtering.... Whereupon with overwhelming compassion, Milarepa sang:

How pitiful are sentient beings in saṃsāra!
Looking upward to the Path of Liberation,
How can one feel aught but sorrow for these sinful men.
How foolish and sad it is to indulge in killing,
When by good luck and Karma one has a human form.
How sad it is to do an act
That in the end will hurt oneself.
How sad it is to build a sinful wall
Of meat made of one's dying parents' flesh?[25]

25. All beings have been one's parents at some time or other.

How sad it is to see
Meat eaten and blood flowing.
How sad it is to know confusions
And delusions fill the minds of men.

How sad it is to find but vice,
Not love, in peoples' hearts.
How sad it is to see
That blindness veils all men
Who cherish sinful deeds.

Craving causes misery,
While worldly deeds bring pain.
With this in mind one feels sorrowful,
Thinking thus, one searches for a cure.
When I think of those who never
Take heed for their future lives,
But indulge in evil deeds,
I feel most disturbed and sad,
And deeply fearful for them.
Rechungpa, seeing all these things,
Don't you remember Holy Dharma?
Don't you in saṃsāra lose all heart?
Rouse the spirit of renunciation,
Go, Rechungpa, to the cave to meditate!

Heed the bounty of your Guru
And avoid all sinful deeds,
Casting worldly things aside
Stay firm in your practice
Keep your good vows
And devote your life to meditation.

(pp. 566–567)

23

A very beautiful girl of about fifteen years of age, whose name was Bardarbom, said to Milarepa: "By merely meeting you I shall have accumulated a great deal of merit" and begged to be taken as his servant and disciple. Milarepa replied, "If you seriously want to practise the Dhamma, you must learn that worldly affairs are your enemies and renounce them." And he sang a song called...

The Four Renunciations

Listen, you fortunate girl,
You who have wealth and faith!

Future lives last longer than this life—
Do you know how to make provision?
Giving with niggardly heart
As if feeding a strange watchdog,
Only brings more harm than good—
Bringing nothing in return but a vicious bite,
Renounce parsimony, now that you know its evil.

Listen, you fortunate girl!
We know less of this life than the next one.
Have you prepared and lit your lamp?
Should it not be ready,
Meditate on the "Great Light."
If you choose to help an ungrateful foe,
You will gain not a friend, but damage.
Beware of acting blindly:
Beware of this evil and discard it.

Listen, you fortunate girl.
Future lives are worse than this life—
Have you a guide or escort for your journey?
If you have not the right companion,
Rely on the holy Dharma.
Beware of relatives and kinsmen;
They hinder and oppose (the Dharma).
They never help but only harm one.

Did you know that your kinsmen are your foes?
If this be true, surely you should leave them.

Listen, you fortunate girl.
The journey in the future life
is more hazardous than this one—
Have you prepared a fine horse of perseverance for it?

If not, you should strive hard and work with diligence.
The excitement of the start will soon diminish;
Beware the foe, "Inertness,"[26] *which makes one go astray.*
Of no avail are hurry and excitement, which only harm one.
Do you yet know that your enemies are laziness and caprice?
If you understand my words,
you should cast them both away.

(pp. 145–146)

24

Going to Bardarbom's house for alms, Milarepa encountered "an ugly old woman with a handful of ashes." She rushed at him, shouting, "You miserable yogi-beggars! I never see you in one place! In the summer you all show up begging for milk and butter! In the winter you all come for grain! I'll wager you wanted to sneak in to steal my daughter's and daughter-in-law's jewellery!" Grumbling and trembling with rage, she was about to throw the ashes at Milarepa, when he said, "Wait a minute, grandmother! Please listen to me!" He then sang...

A Song with Nine Meanings

Above is the auspicious Heaven,
Below are the Three Paths of Misery,
In between, are those who are not free
to choose their birth.[27]

These three all converge on you.
Grandmother, you are an angry woman,
And dislike the Dharma!
Question your own thoughts and your mind examine.
You should practise the Buddha's Teaching,
You need a qualified and dependable Guru.

---

26. In Pāli, *arati* = accidie, spiritual boredom, indifference to what is spiritually skilful.

27. Man is not free to choose where he will be reborn, this being a process depending upon what karma he has made for himself.

Think carefully, dear lady;
When you were first sent here,
Did you dream that you would become an old nanny-goat?

In the morning you get up from bed,
In the evening you go to sleep,
In between, you do the endless housework;
You are engrossed in these three things.
Grandmother, you are an unpaid maid.
Question your own thoughts and your mind examine.
You should practise the Buddha's Teaching,
You need a qualified and dependable Guru,
And then things may be different for you.

The head of the family is the most important one,
Income and earnings are the next most longed-for things,
Then sons and nephews are wanted most.
By these three you are bound.
Grandmother, for yourself you have no share.
Question your own thoughts and your mind examine.
You should practise the Buddha's Teaching,
You need a qualified and dependable Guru,
And then things may be different for you.

Attaining what you want even though you steal,
Getting what you desire even though you rob,
Fighting your foe without regard to death and wounds,
To these three things you are subjected.

Grandmother, you are burned up with fury
When you come upon your foe.
Question your own thoughts and your mind examine.
You should practise the Buddha's Teaching,
You need a qualified and dependable Guru,
And then things may be different for you.

Gossip about other women and their manners
Is what interests you;
To the affairs of your own son and nephew
You pay attention,
To talk of widows and relatives is your delight.

These three things enchant you.
Grandmother, are you so gentle when you gossip?
Question your own thoughts and your mind examine.
You should practise the Buddha's Teaching,
You need a qualified and dependable Guru,
And then things may be different for you.

To lift you from a chair is like pulling out a peg;
With feeble legs you waddle like a thieving goose;
Earth and stone seem to shatter when you drop into a seat;
Senile and clumsy is your body.
Grandmother, you have no choice but to obey.
Question your own thoughts and your mind examine.
You should practise the Buddha's Teaching,
What you require is a qualified and dependable Guru,
And from that you may find out how you have changed.
Your skin is creased with wrinkles;
Your bones stand out sharply from your shrunken flesh,
You are deaf, dumb, imbecile, eccentric and tottering;
You are thrice deformed.
Grandmother, your ugly face is wrapped in wrinkles.
Question your own thoughts and your mind examine.
You should practise the Buddha's Teaching,
You need a qualified and dependable Guru,
And then things may be different for you.

Your food and drink are cold and foul;
Your coat is heavy and in rags;
Your bed so rough it tears the skin;
These three are your constant companions.
Grandmother, you are now a wretch,
half woman and half bitch!
Question your own thoughts and your mind examine!
You should practise the Buddha's Teaching,
What you need is a qualified and dependable Guru,
And then things may be different for you.

To attain higher birth and Liberation
Is harder than to see a star in daytime;
To fall into saṃsāra's wretched path

Is easy and often happens.
Now, with fear and grief at heart,
You watch the time of death draw nigh.
Grandmother, can you face death with confidence?
Question your own mind and your thoughts examine!
What you need is to practise the Teaching of the Buddha,
What you need is a qualified and dependable Guru.

(pp. 136–139)

25

Milarepa said to his faithful patroness, Shindormo, "My dear patroness, except for advanced Dharma practitioners, the pains of birth, decay, illness and death descend upon everyone. It is good to think about and fear them, because this enables one to practise the Dharma when death is approaching." Whereupon he sang:

In the river of birth, decay, illness,
And death we worldly beings are submerged;
Who can escape these pains on earth?
We drift on with the tide.
Amidst waves of misery and darkness
We flow on and on.
Seldom in saṃsāra can one find joy.

More miseries come by trying to avoid them;
Through pursuing pleasures one's sins increase.
To be free from pain,
Wrong deeds should be shunned.
When death draws near, the wise
Always practise Dharma.

(p. 552)

26

"I do not know how to observe the suffering of *birth*," said Shindormo. "Please instruct me how to meditate upon it." In answer, the Jetsun sang:

My faithful patroness, I will

Explain the suffering of birth.
The wanderer in the Bardo plane
Is the Ālaya Consciousness.[28]
Driven by lust and hatred,
It enters a mother's womb

Wherein it feels like a fish
In a rock's crevice caught.
Sleeping in blood and yellow fluid,
It is pillowed in discharges,
Crammed in filth, it suffers pain.
A bad body from a bad Karma is born.

Though remembering past lives,
It cannot say a single word.
Now scorched by heat,
Now frozen by the cold,
In nine months it emerges
From the womb in pain excruciating,
As if pulled out gripped by pliers.
When from the womb its head is squeezed,
The pain is like being thrown into a bramble pit.
The tiny body on the mother's lap,
Feels like a sparrow grappled by a hawk.
When from the baby's tender body
The blood and filth are being cleansed,
The pain is like being flayed alive.
When the umbilical cord is cut,
It feels as though the spine was severed.
When wrapped in the cradle it feels bound
By chains, imprisoned in a dungeon.

He who realises not the truth of No-arising[29]
Never can escape from the dread pangs of birth.

---

28. The "Store" Consciousness, the function of which is to preserve the "seeds" of mental impressions. Memory and learning are made possible because of this consciousness.

29. "There is a realm, O bhikkhus... (where) there is no coming or going or remaining, or deceasing or arising ... thus is the end of suffering." (Udāna 80–81)

There is no time to postpone devotion:
When one dies one's greatest need
is the divine Dharma.
You should then exert yourself
To practise Buddha's Teaching.

(pp. 553–554)

27

Shindormo asked again, "Please preach for us the sufferings of *old age*." In response, the Jetsun sang:

Listen, my good patrons, listen
To the sufferings of old age.

Painful is it to see one's body
Becoming frail and quite worn out.
Who can help but feel dismayed
At the threat of growing old?
When old age descends upon one,
One's straight body becomes bent;
When one tries to step firmly,
One staggers against one's will;
One's black hairs turn white.
One's clear eyes grow dim;
One's head shakes with dizziness,
And one's keen ears turn deaf,
One's ruddy cheeks grow pale,
And one's blood dries up.

One's nose—the pillar of one's face—sinks in;
One's teeth—the essence of one's bones—protrude.
Losing control of tongue, one stammers.
On the approach of death,
one's anguish and debts grow.
One gathers food and friends,
But one cannot keep them;
Trying not to suffer,
One only suffers more;
When one tells the truth to people,

Seldom is one believed;
The sons and nephews one has raised
And cherished, often become one's foes.
One gives away one's savings,
But wins no gratitude.
Unless you realise the truth of Non-decay,[30]
You will suffer misery in old age.
He who when old neglects the Dharma,
Should know that he is bound by Karma.
It is good to practise
The divine Dharma while you can still breathe.

(pp. 554–555)

28

Shindormo then said, "What you have just told us is very true; I have experienced these things myself. Now please preach for us the sufferings of *sickness.*" In reply, Milarepa sang:

Dear patrons, you who know grief and sorrow,
Listen to the miseries of sickness.

This frail body is subject e'er to sickness,
So that one suffers excruciating pain.
The illnesses of Prāna (mind), gall and phlegm[31]
Constantly invade this frail human body,
Causing its blood and matter to be heated;
The organs are thus gripped by pain.
In a safe and easy bed
The sick man feels no comfort,
But turns and tosses, groaning in lament.
Through the Karma of (past) meanness,
Though with best of food you feed him,
He vomits all that he can take.
When you lay him in the cool,

30. See note 29.

31. According to Tibetan pathology, these are the three major sicknesses of man.

He still feels hot and burning;
When you wrap him in warm cloth,
He feels cold as though soaked in sleet.
Though friends and kinsmen gather round,
None can relieve or share his pains.
Though warlocks and physicians are proficient,
They cannot help cases caused by Ripening Karma.

He who has not realised the truth of No-illness[32]
Much suffering must undergo.

Since we know not when sickness will strike,
It is wise to practise Holy Dharma—
The sure conqueror of illness!

(p. 555)

29

"I hope to practise (more) Dharma when death draws near," said Shindormo. "Now please preach for me the suffering of *death.*" In answer, Milarepa sang:

Listen, my disheartened patroness:
Like the pain of repaying compound debts,
One must undergo the suffering of death,
Yama's guards catch and carry one
When the time of death arrives.
The rich man cannot buy it off with money,
With his sword the hero cannot conquer it,
Nor can the clever woman outwit it by a trick.
Even the learned scholar cannot
Postpone it with his eloquence.
Here, the unlucky cannot make appeal,
Nor can a brave man here display his valour.

When all the Nadis[33] *converge in the body,*
One is crushed as if between two mountains—

32. See note 29.
33. Channels of spiritual force in the body.

All vision and sensation become dim.
When Bon[34] *priests and diviners become useless,*
The trusted physician yields to his despair.
None can communicate with the dying man,
Protecting guards and devas vanish into nought.
Though the breath has not completely stopped,
One can all but smell the stale odour of dead flesh.
Like a lump of coal in chilly ashes
One approaches to the brink of death.

When dying, some still count the dates and stars;
Others cry and shout and groan;
Some think of worldly goods;
Some, that their hard-earned wealth
Will be enjoyed by others.

However deep one's love, or great one's sympathy,
He can but depart and journey on alone.
His good friend and consort
Can only leave him there;
In a bundle his beloved body
Will be folded[35] *and carried off,*
Then thrown in water, burned in fire,
Or simply cast off in a desolate land.
Faithful patrons, what in the end can we retain?
Must we sit idly by and let all things go?
When your breath stops tomorrow
No wealth on earth can help you.
Why, then, should one be mean?
Kind kinsmen circle round
The bed of the dying,
But none can help him for a moment.
Knowing that all must be left behind,
One realises that all great love
And attachment must be futile
When that final moment comes,

34. The ancient, pre-Buddhist religion of Tibet.
35. It is Tibetan custom to fold the body at the waist and make it into a bundle to be borne away.

Only Holy Dharma helps.

You should strive, dear patroness,
For a readiness to die!
Be certain and ready and when the time comes,
You will have no fear and no regret.

(pp. 555–557)

30

A married couple of the village of Mang Yul who had no children invited Milarepa to their house when he came that way for alms. They sought to adopt him into their family and said: "We have a good strip of land which we can give you; you can then marry an attractive woman, and soon you will have relatives." Milarepa replied, "I have no need of these things and I will tell you why":

Home and land at first seem pleasant;
But they are like a rasp filing away
one's body, word and mind!
How toilsome ploughing and digging can become!
And when the seeds you planted never sprout,
You have worked for nought!
In the end it becomes a land of misery—
Desolate and unprotected—
A place for hungry spirits, and of haunting ghosts!
When I think of the warehouse
For storing sinful deeds,
It gnaws at my heart,
In such a prison of transiency I will not stay,
I have no wish to join your family!

(pp. 119–120)

31

At first, when a man greets his relatives,
He is happy and joyful; with enthusiasm
He serves, entertains and talks to them.

Later, they share his meat and wine.
He offers something to them once, they may reciprocate.

In the end, they cause anger, craving and bitterness;
They are a fountain of regret and unhappiness.
With this in mind, I renounce pleasant and sociable friends;
For kinsmen and neighbours, I have no appetite.

(pp. 121–122)

32

Wealth, at first, leads to self-enjoyment,
Making other people envious.
However much one has, one never feels it is enough,
Until one is bound by the miser's demon;
Hard it is then to spend it on virtuous deeds.

Wealth provokes enemies and stirs up ghosts.
One works hard to gather riches which others will spend;
In the end, one struggles for life and death,
To amass wealth and money invites enemies;
So I renounce the delusions of saṃsāra.
To become the victim of deceitful devils,
I have no appetite.

(p. 122)

33

The Jetsun was about to leave Nya Non for other hermitages, but the patrons of that place besought him to stay with the utmost earnestness. The Jetsun replied: "If I do not die, I shall try to come back to your village. If for some time we cannot see each other, try at times to remember and practise these things." Whereupon he sang:

Alas, how pitiful are worldly things!
Like precious jade they cherish
Their bodies, yet like ancient trees
They are doomed in the end to fall.

Sometimes bridle your wild thoughts
And pay heed to the Dharma.

Though you gather wealth
As hard as bees collect their honey,
The ills that upon you may fall
Can never be foretold,
Sometimes bridle your wild thoughts
And pay heed to the Dharma.

One may offer to a Lama[36]
Loads of silk for many years;
But when an ill-fortune descends,
Like a fading rainbow
One's faith at once dissolves.
Sometimes bridle your wild thoughts
And pay heed to the Dharma.

Like a pair of mated beasts,
Lovers live together,
But calamity by the wolf's attack
May fall on you at any time.
Sometimes bridle your wild thoughts
And pay heed to the Dharma.

You may cherish your dear son,
Like a hen hatching her egg;
But a falling rock may crush it at any time.
Sometimes bridle your wild thoughts
And pay heed to the Dharma.

A face may be as pretty as a flower,
Yet at any time it can be spoiled by violent hail.
Think at times of how this world
Is sorry, transient and futile.

Though son and mother have affection
For each other, when discords arise,
Like foes they clash and quarrel,
Sometimes towards all sentient beings

36. See note 3.

You should feel compassion.

Basking in the warm sunlight
May be pleasant and a comfort,
But a storm of woe may rise
And choke you at any time,
Remember sometimes the deprived,
And give alms to those in need.

Oh, dear men and women patrons,
For him who cannot practise Dharma,
All his life will be meaningless,
All his acts wrong-doings!

(pp. 627–628)

34

"When the Jetsun Milarepa was staying in the Stone House of Drin, Tsese, Ku Ju, and many other patrons came to him for the Dharma. Tsese said, "Please give us some Buddhist teaching that is easy for us to understand." Milarepa replied, "Very well, lend your ears and listen carefully to this song."

Dear patrons, with care listen
For a moment to my words.

Superior men have need of Dharma;
Without it, they are like eagles—
Even though perched on high,
They have but little meaning.

Average men have need of Dharma;
Without it, they are like tigers—
Though possessing greatest strength,
They are of little value.

Inferior men have need of Dharma;
Without it, they are like a peddler's asses—
Though they carry a big load,
It does them but little good.

Superior women need the Dharma;

Without it, they are like pictures on a wall—
Though they look very pretty,
They have no use or meaning.

Average women need the Dharma;
Without it, they are like little rats—
Though they are clever at getting food,
Their lives have but little meaning.

Inferior women need the Dharma;
Without it, they are just like vixens—
Though they be deft and cunning,
Their deeds have little value.

Old men need the Dharma;
Without it, they are like decaying trees.
Growing youths the Dharma need;
Without it, they are like yoked bulls.
Young maidens need the Dharma,
Without it, they are but decorated cows.
All young people need the Dharma;
Without it, they are as blossoms
Shut within a shell.
All children need the Dharma;
Without it, they are as robbers possessed by demons.
Without the Dharma, all one does
Lacks meaning and purpose.
Those who want to live with meaning
Should practise the Buddha's teaching.

(pp. 653–654)

35

The King of Ye Rang and Ko Kom (in Nepal) had heard of Milarepa and sent his envoy to invite the Jetsun to Nepal. As he declined to go, the envoy expostulated that then his king would get nothing except the envoy's empty hands and thorn-pricked feet. To this the Jetsun replied, "I am the great Universal Emperor. There is no other emperor who is happier, richer or more powerful than I." The envoy retorted, "If you claim that you are the great Universal Emperor himself, then you must have Seven Precious Articles of Royalty.[37] Please show me one of them." The Jetsun replied, "If you worldly kings and officers will follow my Royal Way, each of you may also become the Supreme Emperor, and thus be rich and noble." Whereupon he sang:

If you kings and courtiers who seek pleasures,
Follow the Royal Succession of Milarepa,
Eventually you will obtain them.

This is the Royal Succession of Milarepa:
My faith is the Royal Precious Wheel
Revolving 'round the virtues day and night.
My wisdom is the Royal Precious Gem
Fulfiling all the wishes of myself and others.

The discipline's observance is my Royal Precious Queen;
She is my adornment, one most beautiful.
Meditation is my Royal Precious Minister;
With him I accumulate the Two Provisions.[38]
Self-inspection is my Royal Precious Elephant,
Which takes responsibility for Buddhist Dharma.

Diligence is my Royal Precious Horse,
Which bears the Klesas to Non-ego Land.
Study and contemplation is my Royal Precious General
Who destroys the enemy of vicious thoughts.

If you have these Royal Precious Trappings,
You will gain a king's fame and prosperity,
And conquer all your foes.
You may then spread the Ten Virtues[39] *in your dominion,*

---

37. For these seven Possessions of a Righteous Emperor, see *Mahāsudassana Sutta*, Dīgha Nikāya.
38. Spiritual provisions for Buddhahood: *ñāṇa-sambhāra* (*paññāpāramī*) = Provision of Wisdom; *puñña-sambhāra* (the other *pāramī*) = Provision of Merits accumulated by way of Compassion.
39. Antithesis of killing, stealing, sexual misconduct, lying, backbiting, harsh speech, nonsensical talk, covetousness, anger and perverted views.

And urge all mother-like[40] sentient beings
To follow my noble teachings.

(p. 290)

36

At Gung Tang Castle, some men were building a house and Milarepa approached them for alms. Saying that they had no time and were busy while he appeared to be idle, they invited him to join in their house construction. But Milarepa declined to work upon worldly building, for he said his house was already constructed in his own way. The men asked him, "How did you build your house, and why do you spurn our work so strongly?" Milarepa sang in reply:

Faith is the firm foundation of my house,
Diligence forms the high walls,
Meditation makes the huge bricks,
And Wisdom is the great corner stone.
With these four things I build my castle,
And it will last as long as the Truth eternal!
Your worldly houses are delusions,
Mere prisons for the demons,
And so I would abandon and desert them.

(p. 106)

37

Some demons had come to afflict Milarepa, but after he had sung two songs to them they began to turn towards the Dharma. They said: "We are most grateful for your preaching on the truth of Karma. In all frankness, we are of limited intelligence and limitless ignorance. Our minds are steeped in a morass of stubborn habitual

40. All sentient beings may be regarded as one's mothers since as Lord Buddha says: "I see no beginning to beings who, blinded by ignorance and impelled by craving, are hurrying through the round of birth." In this way, we have a relationship with all living creatures as they have all been our mothers.

thoughts. Pray, therefore, teach us a lesson profound in meaning, great in profit, and simple in comprehension and observation." Milarepa then sang...

The Song of the Seven Truths

However beautiful a song's words may be,
It is but a tune to those
Who grasp not the words of Truth.
If a parable agrees not with the Buddha's Teaching,
However eloquent it may sound,
'Tis but a booming echo.
If one does not practise Dharma,
However learned in the Doctrines one may claim to be,
One is only self-deceived.
Living in solitude is self-imprisonment,
If one practises not the instruction
of the Oral Transmission.[41]
Labour on the farm is but self-punishment,
If one neglects the teaching of the Buddha.

For those who do not guard their morals,
Prayers are but wishful thinking.
For those who do not practise what they preach,
Oratory is but faithless lying.
Wrong-doing shunned, sins of themselves diminish;
Good deeds done and merit will be gained.
Remain in solitude, and meditate alone,
Much talking is of no avail,
Follow what I sing, and practise Dharma!

(pp. 16–17)

38

The people of Nya Non, hearing that Milarepa had decided to go, brought him good offerings and besought him to stay. However,

41. Or Whispered Transmission: the Ghagvupa School of Buddhist Practice—See Introduction, p. 531

Milarepa replied, "I am going to another place to await the coming of my death. If I do not die soon, there will always be a chance for us to meet again. In the meantime, you should all try to practise these things," and he sang to them of the Six Pāramitā[42] and their applications:

Property and possessions
Are like dew on the grass—
Give them away without avarice.

A human body that can practise Dharma
is most precious—
(To attain it again), you should keep the precepts well
As if protecting your own eyes!

Anger brings one to the Lower Realms,
So, never lose your temper,
Even though your life be forfeit.

Inertia and slackness
Never bring accomplishment—
Exert yourself therefore in devotion.

Through distractions Mahāyāna[43]
Can never be understood—
Practise therefore concentration.

Since Buddhahood cannot be won without,
Watch the nature of your mind within.

Like fog is faith unstable—
When it starts to fade, you should
Strengthen it more than ever.

(pp. 626–627)

42. Or "Perfections." In Northern Buddhist tradition these are six (Giving, Moral Conduct, Patience, Diligence, Meditation, Wisdom) with another four added occasionally. Apart from Meditation the other five are counted among the Perfections in Theravāda, which lists ten. Two of these are of Loving-kindness and Equanimity, which would of course fall under Meditation.
43. See note 50.

39

Milarepa cautioned his disciple Rechungpa to live as he had lived, saying, "You also should renounce all Eight Worldly Desires (or Winds)[44] and meditate hard while you still have the chance. Now hearken to my song:"

Remember how your Guru lived
And bear in mind his honeyed words.
He who wastes a chance for Dharma,
Will never have another.

Bear, then, in mind the Buddha's Teaching
And practise it with perseverance,
By clinging to things of this life,
In the next, one suffers more.
If you crave for pleasures
Your troubles but increase.

One is indeed most foolish
To miss a chance for Dharma.
Practise hard in fear of death!
Committing sins will draw
You to the Lower Realms.
By pretending and deceiving,
You cheat and mislead yourself.
Merits diminish
With the growth of evil thoughts.
If you are concerned with future life,
Diligently practise your devotions.
A yogi longing for good clothes
Will soon lose his mind;
A yogi yearning for good food
Will soon do bad deeds;
A yogi loving pleasant words
Will not gain, but lose.
Renounce worldly pursuits, Rechungpa,
Devote yourself to meditation.

44. See note 63.

If you try to get a patron
Who is rich, you will meet a foe.
He who likes to be surrounded
By crowds, will soon be disappointed.
He who hoards much wealth and money,
Soon is filled with vicious thoughts.

Meditate, my son Rechungpa,
And put your mind into the Dharma.

Realisation will be won
At last by him who practises;
He who cannot practise
But only talks and brags,
Is always telling lies.
Alas, how hard it is to find
The chance and time to practise long.
Rechungpa, try to meditate without diversions.

If you merge your mind with Dharma,
You will e'er be gay and joyful;
You will always find it better
If oft you dwell in solitude.
Son Rechungpa, may the precious
Illuminating-Void samādhi
Remain forever in your mind!

(pp. 564–566)

40

Rechungpa had a wish to visit Central Tibet (Weu) but Milarepa tried to dissuade him from going by saying that it was not yet the right time for him to leave his Guru. But Rechungpa still kept pressing his request. Whereupon the Jetsun sang:

It is good for you, the white lion on the mountain,
To stay high, and never go deep into the valley,
Lest your beautiful mane be sullied!
To keep it in good order,
You should remain on the high snow mountain.
Rechungpa, hearken to my words today!

It is good for you, the great eagle, on high rocks
To perch, and never fall into a pit,
Lest your mighty wings be damaged!
To keep them in good order,
You should remain in the high hills.
Rechungpa, hearken to your Guru's words!

It is good for you, the jungle tiger,
To stay in the deep forest: if you rove
About the plain, you will lose your dignity!
To keep your splendour in perfection,
In the forest you should remain.
Rechungpa, hearken to your Guru's words!

It is good for you, the golden-eyed fish,
To swim in the central sea;
If you swim too close to the shore,
You will in a net be caught.
You should remain in the deep waters.
Rechungpa, hearken to your Guru's words!

It is good for you, Rechungdordra of Gung Tang,
For you to stay in hermitages;
If you wander in different places,
Your experience and realisation will dim.
To protect and cultivate devotion
You should remain in the mountains.
Rechungpa, hearken to your Guru's words!

(p. 587)

41

Drashi Tse, a patron, once asked Milarepa: "Do you think I should concentrate my effort on meditation alone or not?" The Jetsun replied, "It is for the very sake of practise that the Dharma is preached and studied. If one does not practise or meditate, both studying and preaching will be meaningless."

Hearken, my faithful patrons!
Even sinful persons,

Not knowing the great power of Karma,
Dream of achieving Liberation.
Life wears out as days and years go by,
Yet in pursuing pleasures
People spend their lives.
They ask, "Will this month or year be good?"
Blind to life's speedy passing,
Fools cherish foolish questions.
He who truly wants to practise Dharma
Should make offerings to the Holy Ones,
Take Refuge in the Triple Gem,
Give service to the Jetsun Guru,
Pay respect to his parents,
Give alms without hoping for reward.
He should offer help to those in need,
He should live and act up to
The Dharma's principles.
Not much is needed for Buddhist practise;
Too many vows lead to self-cheating.
Dear patrons, try to practise what I say.

(pp. 650–651)

Milarepa said: "Many people think that they will have ample time to practise the Dharma, but without their notice or expectation, death suddenly descends upon them and they lose forever the chance to practise. What then can they do? One should turn all one's Buddhist knowledge inside one's mouth, and then meditate. If one does not further one's studies and meditation at the same time, but thinks that one should first learn a great deal before starting the actual practise (one will be completely lost) because knowledge is infinite, and there is no possibility of mastering it all."

(p. 650)

42

Some patrons had made copious offerings to the young and handsome Rechungpa before his departure for Weu but had offered his old Teacher, the Jetsun, only third-rate provisions.

Milarepa came to know of this and shamed them to their faces, whereupon they felt guilt and deep regret. One day they came again and brought excessive offerings, saying, "Please sing for us to awaken our insight into the transiency of beings." Milarepa would not accept their offerings but he sang this for them:

Hearken, you mean patrons!
For the sake of fame, to do
Meritorious deeds—
For this life's sake to seek
The protection of Buddha—
To give alms for the sake
Of returns and dividends—
To serve and offer for the sake
Of vanity and pride—
These four ways will never requite one!

For the sake of gluttony
To hold a sacramental feast—[45]
For the sake of egotism
To strive for Sutra-learning—
For distraction and amusement
To indulge in foolish talk and song—
For vainglory's sake
To give the Initiations—[46]
These four ways will never bring one blessings!

If for love of preaching one expounds
Without the backing of scripture,
If through self-conceit,
One accepts obeisance;
If like a bungling, fumbling fool one teaches,
Not knowing the disciple's capacity,
If to gather money one behaves
Like a Dharma practiser—
These four ways can never help the welfare of sentient beings!

To prefer diversions to solitude,

45. Offerings made to the Buddhas, Bodhisattvas and deities.

46. Instructions for the practice of meditation.

To love pleasures and hate hardship,
To crave for talk when urged to meditate,
To wallow arrogantly in the world—
These four ways will never bring one to Liberation!

This is the song of Fourfold Warning
Dear patrons, bear it in your minds!

(pp. 601–602)

43

Rechungpa had just returned from India complete with new learning, instructions in various meditations, skill in logic, and a swollen head. In order to clear up Rechungpa's pride and arrogance, Milarepa sang:

...Oh, my son, your pride in what you learned
Will lead you well astray!

To preach a lot, with empty words,
Ruins your good experience and meditation.
To be swollen with pride and arrogance
Proves you have betrayed the Guru's precepts.
Nothing gives cause for more regret
Than disobedience to the Guru.
No one is more distracted and confused
Than he who ceases to meditate in solitude.
Nothing is more fruitless
Than a Buddhist[47] *who renounces not his kin.*
Nothing is more shameful
Than a learned Buddhist who neglects his meditation.
Nothing is more disgraceful
Than a monk who violates the rules.

(pp. 424–425 extract)

47. A Buddhist bhikkhu or yogi is meant here.

44

More advice sung by Milarepa to try to cure Rechungpa's pride:

It is fine that father and son are in harmony—
Maintaining harmony with people is a great merit;
But the best merit is to keep in harmony
with one's father.
If one is discordant with all the people he knows
He must be a person ominous or obnoxious.
Yet even more ominous is discord between father and son.

Good it is to maintain harmony with one's
father by right deeds,
Good it is to repay one's mother's kindness and bounties,
Good it is to act in concord with all.

One's wish can be fulfiled
If one is on good terms with one's brothers;
To please one's Guru
Is to gain his blessings;
To be humble is to succeed.
A good Buddhist is one who conquers all bad dispositions.

Kindness is toleration of slanders;
To be modest is to gain fame and popularity;
To maintain pure discipline
Is to do away with pretence and concealment;
To live with a sage is to gain improvement;
To be indifferent is to stop all gossip;
To be good and compassionate is to advance
one's Bodhi-mind.
These are things that a wise man should do,
But a fool can never distinguish friend from foe.

(pp. 426–427 extract)

45

Another exhortation to Rechungpa not to go as yet to Weu:

Listen, Rechung Dorjedrapa,
The well-learned Buddhist scholar.
Listen, and think with care on what I say.
Before faith and yearning arise for Dharma,
Beg not alms for mere enjoyment.
Before you have realised primordial Truth,
Boast not of your sublime philosophy.
Before you have fully mastered the Awareness within,
Engage not in blind and foolish acts.
Before you can feed on the Instructions,
Involve yourself not in wicked occultism.[48]
Before you can explain the profound Teaching,
Be not beguiled by partial knowledge.
Before you can increase your merits,
Dispute not over others' goods.
Before you can destroy your inner cravings,
Treat not charity as if it were your right.
Before you can stop projecting habitual thoughts,
Guess not when you make predictions.
Before you have gained Supreme Enlightenment,
Assume not that you are a venerable Lama.
Before you can master all virtues and practices,
Consider not leaving your Guru.
Son Rechungpa, it is better not to go, but stay!

(pp. 588–589)

46

A yogi of Gu Tang, who had great faith in the Jetsun, requested meditation instructions. After these had been given he said: "To help ignorant men like us, pray now, instruct us in the practice of

48. As with the other couplets, when one can "feed on the Instructions," has "mastered the Awareness within," etc., one will naturally not be involved in evil and unskilful acts.

the Six Pāramitās."[49] Milarepa sang in reply:

Property and wealth are like dew on grass;
Knowing this, gladly should one give them away. (*charity*)

It is most precious to be born a leisured and
worthy human being;
Knowing this, one should with care observe the precepts
As if protecting one's own eyes. (*moral discipline*)

Anger is the cause of falling to the Realms Below;
Knowing this, one should refrain from wrath,
Even at the risk of life. (*patience*)

Benefit to oneself and to others
Can never be achieved through sloth;
Strive, therefore, to do good deeds. (*diligence*)

A perturbed, wandering mind
Never sees the truth of Mahāyāna;[50]
Practise, therefore, concentration. (*meditation*)

The Buddha cannot be found through searching;
So contemplate your own mind. (*wisdom*)

Until the autumn mists dissolve into the sky,
Strive on with faith and determination.

(p. 100)

47

Two scholar-bhikkhus came to argue about the Dharma with Milarepa but the discussion (which was a demonstration of his mastery of meditation) turned against them. Upon which, one of them asked for his instruction in the Six Pāramitās. In answer, Milarepa sang:

---

49. See note 53.

50. Mahāyāna here need not be understood in any sectarian sense but means rather the Buddha's Great Way of Wisdom-Compassion, transcending narrow sectarian dogmatism. In contrast to the latter, the Jetsun taught essentially a Way of Practice and Realisation.

If from parsimony one cannot free oneself,
What is the use of discussing charity? (dāna)
If one does not forswear hypocrisy and pretence,
What is the use of keeping discipline? (sīla)
If one abjures not malicious revilings,
What is the use of exercising
pretentious "patience"? (khanti)
If one abandons not indifference and inertness,
What is the use of swearing to be Moral? (viriya)
If one conquers not the errant thoughts within,
What is the use of toiling in meditation? (samādhi)
If one does not see all forms as helpful,
What is the use of practising the Wisdom (paññā)
If one knows not the profound teaching
Of forbidding and allowing,
What is the use of learning?

If one knows not the art of taking and rejecting,
What is the use of speaking on Karma-causation?
If one's mind does not accord with the Dharma,
What is the use of joining the Order?
If the poisonous snake of Klesa[51] *is not killed,*
The yearning for wisdom only leads to fallacy.
If venomous jealousy is not overcome,
One's yearning for the Bodhi-mind will be an illusion.
If one refrains not from hurting people,
One's longing for respect and honour
Is merely wishful thinking.
If one cannot conquer ego-clinging and prejudice,
One's craving for the Equality of Dharma[52]
Only brings wrong views.
If one cannot subdue the demon, clinging-ego,
One's Klesas will be great and his Yoga bound to fail.
If one's actions conform not with the Dharma,

51. *Klesa, Kilesa* = Defilement; poison of mind, such as lust, hatred and delusion.

52. Freedom from "all thoughts and conceptualizations, be they simple or complex, good or evil, monistic or dualistic... then one is said to have acquired the wisdom of Equality or Non-discrimination."

One will always hinder the good deeds of others.
If one has not yet absorbed one's mind in Dharma,
One's babbling and prattling will only disturb others' minds.
Therefore, do not waste your life in words and chatter
But try to gain the assurance of no-regret
And the confidence of facing death!

(pp. 387–388 extract)

Milarepa said: "Dear teachers, the proverb says: 'Judging from the complexion of his face, one knows whether a man has eaten or not.' In the same light, the fact that one knows or knows not the Dharma, can easily be detected by whether or not one can conquer one's own ego-clinging desires. If he can, that proves that one knows and practises the Buddhist teachings. One may be very eloquent talking about the Dharma and win all the debates, but if one cannot subdue even a fraction of one's ego-clinging and desires, but merely indulges oneself in words and talk, one's victories in debate will never bring one any profit but will only increase one's egotism and pride."

(p. 384)

48

One of the scholar-bhikkhus who had previously been opposed to the Jetsun gradually acquired faith in him and eventually came to him for the Dharma, requesting, "Now please be kind enough to instruct me in the essence of the Six Pāramitās." In response, the Jetsun sang:

I am not well-versed in words,
Being no scholar-preacher,
Yet this petitioner is sincere and good.

The Six Pāramitās [53] *contain all Buddhist teachings.*
To those who practise Dharma,
Wealth is but a cause of diversion.
He who gives his (wealth) all away,

53. Sometimes translated 'perfections' but in Chinese and Tibetan as "Reaching-the-other-shore," meaning reaching Nirvana beyond saṃsāra.

Will be born a Prince of Heaven.
Noble is it to practise charity!
Moral discipline is a ladder to Liberation
Which neither monks nor laymen can discard.
All Buddhist followers should practise it!
Buddhist patience, by the Patience-preacher[54]
exemplified,
Is the virtue which the Buddha cherished most.
It is a garment difficult to wear,
Yet all merits grow when it is worn.

Diligence is the short path to freedom
And a necessity for Dharma-practice.
Without it nothing can be done.
Ride then upon the horse of diligence!

These four Dharmas bring merit to men,
Being indispensable for all.
Now I will speak of Wisdom.
Meditation is a teaching between these two,
As it applies both to Wisdom and Merit practice,
By it all distractions are overcome,
For all Buddhist practice, it is most important.

Wisdom-Pāramitā is the teaching of Final Truth,
The dearest treasure of all Buddhas.
Enjoy it then without exhaustion;
it is the Wish-fulfiling Gem of Heaven,
Fulfiling the hopes of all sentient beings.
To those who can renounce activities,
Wisdom-Pāramitā will bring final rest.
This provision of Wisdom is most precious;
Whereby one will reach perfection step by step.

This is my reply, Venerable Monk,
Remember and practise it with joy!

(pp. 501–502)

54. See *Khantivādi Jātaka*—No. 313.

49

Upon Mount Bonbo, Milarepa instructed many Repas who were preparing to depart for meditation in distant hermitages. Those junior Repas who wanted to stay with the Jetsun then said to him, "We are now in an age of defilement. For the sake of inferior and slow-witted persons like us, please preach something appropriate to our needs." In response, Milarepa sang:

Hearken further, my Son-disciples!
At this time of defilement
That shadows the Dharma of Sakyamuni,
One should strive with perseverance,
And carve upon one's mind-stone
The word, "Diligence."
When you feel sleepy during meditation, try
To pray[55] *hard with your awakened body, mouth and mind.*
When the fire-spark of Wisdom dims, try
To inflame it with the wind of mindfulness.
If you want to be freed from saṃsāra's prison,
Practise hard without diversion.
If to Nirvana you aspire,
Abandon then this world.
If from the depths of your heart
You want to practise Dharma,
Listen to my words and follow in my footsteps.
If you want to consummate the (Supreme)
Accomplishment,
Never forget that death will come.
If hard and long you meditate, all Buddhas
In the past, the present and the future
Will be well-pleased.
If you are ever straightforward and upright in the Dharma,
You will receive the grace of your Guru.
If without error you understand these words,
You can be sure that more happiness
And joy will come your way,

55. Using body, mouth and mind in some devotional exercise, such as the "Long Prostrations" so often and vigorously practised by Tibetans.

For such is my experience.

(pp. 547–548)

50

Some devas invited Milarepa to preach the Dharma in Heaven but he cautioned them, saying, "You must know that Heaven is far from dependable; it is not eternal, and one should not rely on it. To be born in heaven is not necessarily a wonderful thing." The Devas of Heaven said, "In ignorant beings like us, the Klesas always follow the mind. Pray give us a teaching with which we can correct this fault, so that we may depend upon it and practise it frequently." In response to their request, Milarepa sang:

Should you, oh faithful lady Devas,
intend to practise the Dharma often,
Inwardly you should practise concentration
and contemplation.
The renunciation of external affairs is your adornment.
Oh, bear in mind this remedy for external involvement!
With self-composure and mindfulness,
you should remain serene.
Glory is the equanimity of your mind and speech!
Glory is the resignation from many actions!

Should you meet disagreeable conditions,
Disturbing to your mind,
Keep watch upon yourself and be alert;
Keep warning yourself:
"The danger of anger is on its way."

When you meet with enticing wealth,
Keep watch upon yourself and be alert;
Keep a check upon yourself:
"The danger of craving is on its way."

Should hurtful, insulting words come to your ears,
Keep watch upon yourself and be alert,
And so remind yourself:
"Hurtful sounds are but delusions of the ear".

When you associate with your friends,
Watch carefully and warn yourself:
"Let not jealousy in my heart arise!"

When you are plied with services and offerings,
Be alert and warn yourself:
"Let me beware lest pride should spring up in my heart!"

At all times, in every way, keep watch upon yourself.
At all times try to conquer evil thoughts within you!
Whatever you may meet in your daily doings,
You should contemplate its void and illusory nature.

Were even one hundred saints and scholars gathered here,
More than this they could not say.
May you all be happy and prosperous!
May you all, with joyful hearts,
Devote yourselves to the practice of the Dharma!

(pp. 92–93)

51

A young shepherd by the name of Sanje Jhap, who was sixteen years old, became interested in knowing what his mind really was. Milarepa tested his ability by instructing him to go for Refuge to the Three Precious Ones and then to visualise a Buddha-image in front of his nose. The boy was not seen for seven days and his father feared that he was dead. They found him in a clay pit sitting upright and asked him why he had not returned home for seven days. The boy said that they must be joking for he had only been there a short time—but it was seven days. While giving him instructions Milarepa sang to him about his mind:

Listen to me, dear shepherd, the protector (of sheep)!
By merely hearing of the taste of sugar,
Sweetness cannot be experienced;
Though one's mind may understand
What sweetness is,
It cannot experience it directly;
Only the tongue can know it.

In the same way, one cannot see in full the nature of mind,
Though he may have a glimpse of it
If it has been pointed out by others.[56]
If one relies not on this one glimpse,
But continues searching for the nature of mind,
He will see it fully in the end.
Dear shepherd, in this way you should observe your mind.

(pp. 123–124)

52

Listen to me, young shepherd.
The body is between the conscious and unconscious state,
While the mind is the crucial and decisive factor!
He who feels sufferings in the Lower Realms,
Is the prisoner of saṃsāra,
Yet it is the mind that can free you from saṃsāra.
Surely you want to reach the other shore?
Surely you long for the City of Well-being and Liberation?
If you desire to go, dear child,
I can show the Way to you
And give you the instructions.

(pp. 124–125)

53

Upon Rechungpa's return from India, with books on logic, incantations from outsiders and much pride, as well as genuine meditation instructions, Milarepa decided to rescue him from this evil and so to welcome him, he sang:

I am a yogi who lives on snow mountain peak.
With a healthy a body I glorify the Mandala of the Whole.[57]

---

56. Sudden insight experienced through the action of the Teacher, either verbally or physically—many well-known cases in Zen Buddhism.
57. It is significant that the words "holy" and "whole" are etymologically related.

Cleansed of vanity from the Five Poisons,
I am not unhappy;
I feel nought but joy!
Renouncing all turmoil
And fondness for diversion,
I reside alone in perfect ease.
Forswearing the bustle of this world,
Joyfully I stay in no-man's land.
Since I have left embittered family life,
I no longer have to earn and save;
Since I want no books,
I do not intend to be a learned man;
Since I practise virtuous deeds,
I feel no shame of heart.
Since I have no pride or vanity,
I renounce with joy the saliva-splashing debate!
Hypocrisy I have not, nor pretension.
Happy and natural I live
Without forethought or adjustment.
Since I want no fame nor glory,
Rumours and accusations disappear.
Where'er I go, I feel happy,
Whate'er I wear, I feel joyful,
Whatever food I eat, I am satisfied.
I am always happy.
Through Marpa's grace,
I, your old father, Milarepa,
Have realised saṃsāra and Nirvana.
The Yoga of joy ever fills my hermitage.
Your Repa brothers are well;
On hills remote they make progress in their meditations.
Oh, my son Rechung Dorje Draugpa,
Have you returned from India?
Did you feel tired and weary on the journey?
Has your mind been sharpened and refreshed?
Has your voice been good for singing?
Did you practise and follow your Guru's instructions?
Did you secure the teachings that you wanted?
Did you obtain all the various instructions?

Have you gained much knowledge and much learning?
Have you noticed your pride and egotism?
Are you altruistic in your thoughts and actions?
This is my song of welcoming for you,
On your return.

(pp. 422–423)

54

Five young nuns from Mon had become Milarepa's disciples. Having dwelt with him for some time, they decided to invite him to their village (whence they thought of returning). They said to him: "Revered One, since your mind no longer changes, there is no need for you to practise meditation. Therefore, for the sake of sentient beings please come to our village and preach the Dharma for us." Milarepa replied, "Practising meditation in solitude is, in itself, a service to the people. Although my mind no longer changes, it is still a good tradition for a great yogi to remain in solitude." He then sang:

Through the practice (of meditation)
I show gratitude to my Guru.
Pray grant me your grace, ripen and liberate me.

You, gifted disciples, followers of Dharma,
Heed carefully, with all attention,
While I sing of the profound Essential Teaching.

The Great Lioness of the upper snow mountain
Poses proudly on the summit of the peak;
She is not afraid—
Proudly dwelling on the mountain
Is the snow lion's way.

The Queen Vulture on Red Rock
Stretches her wings in the wide sky;
She is not afraid of falling—
Flying through the sky is the vulture's way.

In the depths of the great ocean
Darts the Queen of Fish, glittering;

She is not afraid (of drowning)—
Swimming is the fish's way.

On the branches of the oak trees,
Agile monkeys swing and leap;
They are not afraid of falling—
Such is the wild monkey's way.

Under the leafy canopy of the dense wood,
The striped tiger roams and swiftly runs,
Not because of fear or worry—
This shows her haughty pride,
And is the mighty tiger's way.

In the wood on Singa Mountain,
I, Milarepa, meditate on voidness,
Not because I fear to lose my understanding—
Constant meditation is the yogi's way.

Those great yogis who have mastered the Practice
Never desire anything in this world.
It is not because they want fame
That they remain in solitude;
It is the natural sign springing from their hearts—
The true feeling of non-attachment and renunciation.

Yogis who practise the teaching of the Path Profound,
Dwell always in caves and on mountains;
Not that they are cynical or pompous,
But to concentrate on meditation is their self-willing.

I, the cotton-clad, have sung many songs,
Not to amuse myself by singing sophistries,
But for your sake, faithful followers who assemble here,
From my heart I have spoken words helpful and profound.

(pp. 81–83 extract)

55

A monk-disciple of Milarepa, Ligor Sharu, wanted the Jetsun to adapt himself somewhat to worldly conventions, so as to win the interest and following of great scholars. Milarepa refused this idea, saying that he would ever follow his Guru's instructions to live remotely, and he sang to Ligor Sharu:

I bow down to Marpa, the Translator.
Realising that fame is as unreal as an echo,
I abandon not the ascetic way of life,
Throwing away all cares and preparations.
Whatever reputation I may have,
I shall always be happy and contented.
Realising that all things are illusion,
I cast away possessions;
For wealth obtained by strife I have not the least desire!
Whatever my means and prestige,
I shall always be happy and contented.
Realising that all followers are phantoms,
I have no concern for human relationship
And travel where I please—
Unlike those artificial scholar-priests
Who act with discretion and restraint.[58]
Whatever the status I may have
I shall always be happy and contented.

Realising that desires and sufferings
Are themselves the Great Equality,[59]
I cut the rope of passion and of hatred.
With or without associates,
I shall always be happy and contented.

58. "Artificial" because their scholarship was combined only with a morality of restrictions, thus lacking the essential practice of Dharma.

59. Unenlightened worldly beings discriminate between likes and dislikes, etc., but with Transcendent wisdom (*paññā*) this is seen to be a false process, for where there is no discrimination, there is no desire or suffering.

The nature of being is beyond play-words;[60]
Attachments to any doctrine or concept
Is merely a matter of self-confusion.
Unshackling the fetter of the knower-and-the-known,
Whatever I become and wherever I remain,
I shall always be happy and contented.

In the great Illuminating Mind itself,
I see no pollution by wandering thoughts.
Throwing away all reasonings and observations,
Whatever words I hear and say,
I shall always be happy and contented.

(pp. 517–518)

56

Rechungpa first went to India to be cured of leprosy, and before he went he sealed up with clay the mouth of the cave where the Jetsun was meditating. When he returned, having been cured, people said that the yogi Mila had not been seen for some time. Rechungpa went to the cave and broke down the wall, which was still intact. Milarepa was still in meditation and then sang to him as a greeting:

I bow down at the feet of Marpa, the Gracious One.

Because I have left my kinsmen, I am happy;
Because I have abandoned attachment to my country,
I am happy;
Since I disregard this place,
I am happy;
As I do not wear the lofty garb of priesthood,[61]
I am happy;
Because I cling not to house and family, I am happy;
I need not this or that, so I am happy.

60. Words are learned, concepts are formed, and through confusion with them one assumes that even ultimate Truth can be expressed by words; but Nibbāna is beyond such "play-words."
61. The allusion is to the Sangha's degeneracy in Mila's days and to the pride in scholarship which strangled Dhamma practice.

Because I possess the great wealth of Dharma, I am happy;
Because I worry not about property, I am happy;
Because I have no fear of losing anything, I am happy;
Since I never dread exhaustion, I am happy;
Having fully realised Mind-Essence,[62] *I am happy;*
As I need not force myself to please my patrons,
I am happy;
Having no fatigue or weariness, I am happy;
As I need prepare for nothing, I am happy;
Since all I do complies with Dharma, I am happy,
Never desiring to move, I am happy;
As the thought of death brings me no fear, I am happy;
Bandits, thieves and robbers never molest me,
So at all times I am happy!
Having won the best conditions for Dharma-practice,
I am happy;
Having ceased from evil deeds and left off sinning,
I am happy;
Treading the Path of Merits, I am happy;
Divorced from hate and injury, I am happy,
Having lost all pride and jealousy, I am happy;
Understanding the wrongness of the Eight Worldly Winds,[63]
I am happy;
Absorbed in quiet and even-mindedness, I am happy;
Using the mind to watch the mind, I am happy;
Without hope or fear, I am happy.

In the sphere of Non-clinging Illuminations[64]
I am happy;
The Non-distinguishing Wisdom of Dharmadhātu[65]
is itself happy;
Poised in the natural realm of Immanence[66]
I am happy;

62. Mind-essence is the true nature of mind.
63. Gain, loss, praise, blame, honour, ridicule, joy, sorrow.
64. 4 and 5 are 3 different aspects or descriptions of Enlightenment.
65. They are 3 different aspects or descriptions of Enlightenment.
66. They are 3 different aspects or descriptions of Enlightenment.

In letting the Six Groups of Consciousness go by
To return to their original nature,[67] *I am happy.*

The five radiant gates of sense all make me happy;
To stop the mind that comes and goes is happy;
Oh, I have so much of happiness and joy!
This is a song of gaiety I sing,
This is a song of gratitude to my Guru and the
Three Precious Ones—
I want no other happiness.

Through the grace of Buddha and the Gurus,
Food and clothes are provided by my patrons.
With no bad deeds and sins,
I shall be joyful when I die;
With all good deeds and virtues,
I am happy while alive.
Enjoying yoga, I am indeed most happy.
But how are you, Rechungpa?
Is your wish fulfiled?

(pp. 110–112)

57

The envoy of the Nepali King, upon meeting him for the first time, was wonderstruck at Milarepa's lack of material possessions and asked him: "Don't you find it hard to live thus without taking nourishing food? Why is it necessary to abandon all belongings?" Milarepa then answered the envoy: "I am the Tibetan yogi, Milarepa. 'Without belongings' means 'without sufferings.'" Now listen to my song:

I bow down to all holy Gurus.
I am the man called Milarepa.
For possessions I have no desire.
Since I never strive to make money,
First I do not suffer
Because of making it;

67. Realising their nature to be void (*suññа*).

Then I do not suffer
Because of keeping it;
In the end I do not suffer
Because of hoarding it.
Better far and happier is it
Not to have possessions.

Without attachment to kinsmen and companions,
I do not seek affection in companionship,
First I do not suffer
Because of heart-clinging;
Then I do not suffer
From any quarrelling;
In the end I do not suffer
Because of separation.
It is far better to have no affectionate companions.

Since I have no pride and egotism,
I do not look for fame and glory.
First I do not suffer
Because of seeking them;
Then I do not suffer
In trying to preserve them;
In the end I do not suffer
For fear of losing them.
It is far better to have neither fame nor glory.

Since I have no desire for any place,
I crave not to be here, nor there.
First I do not worry
About my home's protection;
Then I do not suffer
From a fervent passion for it;
In the end I am not anxious to defend it.
It is far better to have neither home nor land.

(pp. 288–289)

58

This is the song of Milarepa to some patrons from Drin who were ashamed because of the Jetsun's lack of conventional behaviour:

Through wandering long in many places,
I have forgotten my native land.
Staying long with my Holy Jetsun,
I have forgotten all my kinsmen.
Keeping for long the Buddha's Teaching,
I have forgotten worldly things.
Staying for long in hermitages,
I have forgotten all diversions.
Through long watching of monkeys' play,
I have forgotten sheep and cattle.
Long accustomed to a tinder-box,
I have forgotten all household chores.
Long used to solitude without servant or master,
I have forgotten courteous manners.
Long accustomed to be carefree,
I have forgotten worldly shame.
Long accustomed to the mind coming and going
By itself, I have forgotten how to hide things.
Long used to burning Duma-heat,[68]
I have forgotten clothing.

Long accustomed to practising Non-discriminating Wisdom,
I have forgotten all distracting thoughts.
Long used to practising the Two-in-One Illumination,[69]
I have forgotten all nonsensical ideas.
These twelve 'oblivions' are the teachings of this yogi.
Why, dear patrons, do you not also follow them?
I have untied the knot of dualism;
What need have I to follow your customs.
To me, Bodhi is spontaneity itself!

---

68. A heat produced in the body by means of meditation, thus enabling a yogi to live high in the snow mountains. Milarepa wore only one piece of cotton cloth.

69. Non-distinction between means (the first five *pāramī*) and wisdom (the sixth one).

The Dharma of you worldly people
Is too difficult to practise.
Caring for nought, I live the way I please.
Your so-called 'shame' only brings deceit
And fraud; How to pretend I know not.

(pp. 579–580)

59

In a gathering of patrons, a young man said to Milarepa: "We would like to come to you for instructions; please tell us where your temple is and who provides your sustenance." In answer Milarepa sang:

My temple is an unnamed hermitage,
My patrons are men and women everywhere,
No one can tell where I go or stay.
In the caves where no man comes
I, the yogi, am lost to view.
(When I travel) I carry
Only my Guru's Instructions—lighter
Than feathers, I shoulder them with ease;
More handy than gold, I conceal them where I please;
Stronger than a solid castle,
In all perils they stand firm.
In the three winters I dwell happily in forests;
In the three summers I stay cheerfully on snow mountains;
In the three springs I live with pleasure in the marshes;
In the three autumns I wander joyfully for alms.
In the teaching of my Guru, my mind is always happy;
Singing songs of inspiration, my mouth is always happy,
Wearing cotton from Nepal, my body's always happy.
In delight I accomplish all and everything—
To me there is but cheer and joy.

(pp. 537–538)

60

The patrons of Nya Non wished Milarepa to stay with them permanently. Milarepa replied, "I cannot stay here long, but I will bestow the blessing of long life and good health upon all of you. Also I will make a wish that we meet again under auspicious circumstances conducive to the Dharma." Then he sang:

In the immense blue sky above
Roll on the sun and moon.
Their courses mark the change of time.
Blue sky, I wish you health and fortune,
For I, the moon-and-sun, am leaving
To visit the Four Continents for pleasure.

On the mountain peak is a great rock
'Round which circles oft the vulture,
The King of birds.
Their meeting
And their parting mark the change of time.
Dear rock, be well and healthy, for I,
The vulture, now will fly away
Into the vast space for pleasure.
May lightnings never strike you,
May I not be caught by snares.
Inspired by the Dharma,
May we soon meet again,
In prosperity and boon.

Below in the Tsang River,
Swim fish with golden eyes;
Their meeting and their parting
Mark the change of time.
Dear stream, be well and healthy, for I,
The fish, am going to the Ganges for diversion.
May irrigators never drain you,
May fishermen ne'er net me.
Inspired by the Dharma,
May we soon meet again
In prosperity and boon.

In the fair garden blooms the flower, Halo;
Circling round it is the Persian bee.
Their meeting and their parting
Mark the change of time.
Dear flower, be well and healthy, for I
Will see the Ganges' blooms for pleasure.
May hail not beat down upon you,
May winds blow me not away.
Inspired by the Dharma,
May we soon meet again
In prosperity and boon.

Circling round the Yogi Milarepa
Are the faithful patrons from Nya Non;
Their meeting and their parting
Mark the change of time.
Be well and healthy, dear patrons, as I
Leave for the far mountains for diversion.
May I, the yogi, make good progress,
And you, my patrons, all live long.
Inspired by the Dharma,
May we soon meet again
In prosperity and boon!

(pp. 602–604)

Apaṇṇaka Sutta
Cūla Māluṅkya Sutta
Upāli Sutta

Three Discourses
from the Majjhima Nikāya

Translated by

Nārada Thera & Mahinda Thera

WHEEL PUBLICATION NO. 98/99

Introduction to the Apaṇṇaka Sutta (Majjhima Nikāya No. 60)

During his uninterrupted ministry of forty-five years, the Blessed One had occasion to address all sorts and conditions of people, from the humble outcast to the boastful *Brahmin* and arrogant *Kshatriya*. And the Buddha adapted each discourse to the needs of the people immediately concerned and to the occasion. Each sermon is a special prescription, intended to meet the requirements of a particular disease.

To us, who today read these "prescriptions" of the Great Physician, it sometimes seems that contradictory remedies are advised and sometimes that a certain inconstancy of behaviour characterised the Master.

Why does the Buddha at times exalt the household life, calling it "a high blessing," and again stigmatize it as "a den of strife"? Why to the self-same question does the Master sometimes vouchsafe an answer, sometimes remain silent, and sometimes even administer a rebuke?

The solution to these puzzles is clear only to him who sees the whole picture of the Buddha *Dhamma*. To one who studies that Dhamma sympathetically, earnestly and deeply, never forgetting that the *Suttas* are but prescriptions for diverse maladies, there comes the understanding to patch up the immense picture, putting each seemingly irregular fragment in its proper place till a vast panorama of harmonious adjustment rewards the patient toil.

In this Discourse the Blessed One reveals the Incontrovertible Doctrine to the *Brahmins* of a Kosalan township who come to him for instruction. It is a most interesting sermon in that it deals with the five popular philosophical opinions of that time:

1. The annihilationist doctrine taught by Ajita of the hair-blanket (*Ajita Kesakambalī*), which denied that action, good or evil, brought about any result or fruit. "Do as you please," said Ajita, in effect, "for there is no happiness to be derived by being virtuous, and no pain to fear through being evil." According to this belief man is built up of the four elements. When he dies, what in him is earthy returns to earth, fluid returns to water, heat

to fire, gases to air, and his six senses (with mind as sixth) vanish in space—and there is an end of the matter.

2. The school of *Purāṇa Kassapa* believed in non-action. Kassapa held that no special merit resulted from liberality, meditation, self-control and truth on the one hand, or demerit from robbery, rape and murder on the other. Action was to him a thing which was, far from being meritorious or de-meritorious, empty and void, for the good reason that there was no such thing as action, though people imagined they acted in this way or that.

3. *Makkhali Gosāla* preached a variety of fatalism. Everything that happened was independent of a cause, here or elsewhere, present, past or future. We go blundering through existence and as a ball of string will one day somehow unwind itself, so someday "fools and wise alike, wandering in existence for an allotted space, shall make an end of pain." There is no hurrying or delaying of an inexorable fate. All action, one way or another, is vain, for action has no result and fate rules our wanderings and the termination.

4. Then there was a school which denied that such a state as a "formless realm" existed, on the ground that they had no proof of it.

5. The last class denied such a thing as a final salvation, a *Nibbāna,* when ceases all life's turmoil and woe.

The whole discourse is extremely interesting and should be read in conjunction with the *Kandaraka Sutta*, which was published in Wheel Publication No. 79. Particularly would we draw the reader's attention to the Buddha's earnest affirmation, as one who knows, from first-hand knowledge: "Indeed there is a world beyond; another world exists, that there is none is to speak falsely and deny the word of those worthy ones who know there is another world." May the reader profit by this assurance, for it is certain that, more than our acts of foolish commission or omission is the mental attitude of scoffing scepticism, and mulish refusal to face unpalatable facts, that sways the minds of this generation.

Apaṇṇaka Sutta

The Incontrovertible Doctrine

Thus have I heard:

Once, when the Blessed One was wandering from place to place in the land of Kosala, accompanied by a large company of bhikkhus, he arrived at a Brahmin village named Sālā.

Now the Brahmin householders of Sālā heard, "Verily, the Venerable Samaṇa Gotama, scion of the Sākyas, ordained from a Sākya family, is wandering from place to place in the land of Kosala with a large company of bhikkhus, and has arrived at Sālā. Thus have the good tidings of the fame of that glorious Gotama gone forth: 'Such indeed is that Blessed One. Holy, fully enlightened, endowed with knowledge and virtue, who has achieved the Goal, Knower of the worlds, an incomparable Guide for the training of men, a Teacher of gods and humans, enlightened and blessed. He has fathomed by his own intuitive wisdom, this world together with the worlds of the gods, of the *Māras* and the *Brahmas*, including the communities of recluses and Brahmins, gods and men, and makes known the same. He expounds the Truth, excellent in the beginning, excellent in the middle, excellent in the end, both in the spirit and the letter. He proclaims the Holy Life, altogether perfect and pure.' Blessed indeed is the sight of such an Exalted One."

Thereupon the Brahmin householders of Sālā went to the Blessed One, and, drawing near, some respectfully saluted him and sat on one side; some exchanged friendly greetings with the Blessed One and after the customary words of friendship and civility sat aside; some before taking their seats extended their hands with palms together towards the Blessed One; some announced their names and families to him before sitting down whilst others sat down in silence.

And when they were seated, the Blessed One addressed those Brahmin householders of Sālā as follows: "Is there, householders, any inspiring teacher in whom you have acquired a reasonable faith?"[1]

"No, Venerable Sir, there is no inspiring teacher in whom we have acquired a reasonable faith."

"Not having found an inspiring teacher, householders, this incontrovertible[2] doctrine should be observed and practised by you. For, householders, this incontrovertible doctrine, perfected and observed, will long conduce to your well-being and happiness. And which, householders, is the incontrovertible doctrine? There are, householders, some ascetics and Brahmins who expound and hold such views as these:

- There is no such thing as alms or sacrifice or offering.[3]
- Neither is there fruit nor result of good or evil deeds.
- There is no such thing as this world or a world beyond.[4]
- There is neither mother nor father,[5] nor beings of spontaneous birth.
- Neither are there in the world any ascetics and brahmins (*samaṇa-brāhmaṇā*) who walk rightly (i.e. live a blameless life),

---

1. The Commentator states that the village of Sālā was situated at the entrance to a forest where various sects of ascetics and Brahmins, who hold diverse beliefs, resort in the evening after wandering throughout the day. The villagers accord to them a warm welcome and the guests instruct them with their respective religious beliefs. Today they are given to understand by some that the world is eternal, tomorrow they are taught by some others that the world is non-eternal. Their minds were in this unsettled state when the Buddha put this question to them.
2. *Apaṇṇaka*—Explained in the Commentary as *aviruddho, advejjhagāmi, ekaṃsgāhako,* i.e., not contrary (non-contradictable), doubtless, definitely acceptable. The Commentary to the *Apaṇṇaka Jātaka* (J 1) adds *niyyānika,* "leading out (of *saṃsāra*), leading to salvation." As further meaning of this difficult and important term we prefer "incontrovertible," both because it fits the trend of this discourse and agrees with the equivalent, *aviruddha,* of the old Commentary. The term also occurs at A I 113; II 76.
3. That is, they deny the effects that necessarily follow from them.
4. That is, there is no "this world" to those who live in another and no world beyond to those who live here. They declare that all beings perish utterly just where they are.
5. They deny the consequences that result from acting rightly or wrongly towards parents.

conduct themselves well, and who, having comprehended both this world and the next by their own intuitive wisdom, make known the same.[6]

"Yet, amongst these same ascetics and Brahmins, O householders, there are some who hold directly opposite views. They say thus:

- There is such a thing as alms, as sacrifice, as offering.
- There is the fruit, the result, of good and evil deeds.
- There exists both this world and a world beyond.
- There is a mother and a father.
- There are beings of spontaneous birth.
- Also, there are in the world Samaṇas and Brāhmaṇas who walk rightly, conduct themselves well, and who, having comprehended both this world and the world beyond by their own intuitive wisdom, make known the same."

"What do you think of this, householders? Do not these ascetics and Brahmins hold views in direct opposition to each other?"

"Certainly, Venerable Sir."

"Therefore, householders, of those ascetics and Brahmins who expound and hold such views as these: 'There is no such thing as alms or sacrifice or offering ... Neither are there in the world any Samaṇas or Brāhmaṇas who walk rightly, conduct themselves well, and who, having comprehended both this world and the next by their own intuitive wisdom, make known the same,' this is to be expected: whatever bodily, verbal and mental evil actions there be, these three meritorious conditions they will entirely avoid; whatever bodily, verbal and mental evil actions there be, these three de-meritorious conditions they will observe and practise.

"And for what reason? Because, these good ascetics and Brahmins do not see the evils, vanity and depravity of immoral conditions nor the advantages and the pure side of moral

---

6. That is, they deny the existence of omniscient Buddhas. The above list of ten constitutes the "ten bases of heretical beliefs." Ajita of the Hair Garment (Ajita Kesakambalī), one of the six heretical teachers, was the greatest exponent of this doctrine of nihilism (*natthika-vādo*). See the *Sāmaññaphala Sutta* (*Dīgha -Nikāya* No. 2).

conditions found in renunciation. Assuredly there really is a world beyond. The belief that there is no such world, that is a false view.[7] Undoubtedly, a world beyond really exists. One hopes that there is no such world: that is a false hope.[8] One states that there is no world beyond: that is a false statement.[9] To say of the world beyond, which really exists, that there is no such world beyond, is to contradict those Exalted Ones (*arahanta*) who actually know the world beyond. To make known to others (concerning the world beyond, which assuredly exists) that there is no such world, that is the teaching of a wicked doctrine; and by such wicked doctrine one exalts oneself and despises others.

"Thus, because of the aforesaid (wrong views) one's morality is abandoned, and immorality is imminent; for this is a false belief, a false speculation, a false statement, a contradiction of the Noble Ones, the teaching of a wicked doctrine, the exalting of self and the despising of others. Thus, these various evil and unwholesome states arise as a result of false belief.

"Therefore, householders, a wise person reflects thus: If there is really no world beyond, then this good individual, upon the dissolution of the body, after death will be safe;[10] if however there is a world beyond, then this good individual, upon the dissolution of the body, after death, will be reborn in a state of sorrow, of evil, of torment, and of misery.

"Well (for argument's sake), let there be no world beyond, and let the words of those good ascetics and Brahmins be true! But even so this good individual, in this life itself, is contemptible to the wise who hold him to be 'an immoral person, a heretic, an annihilationist!'

"Therefore, if there really exists a world beyond, then this good individual is defeated in both worlds; for in this present life he is contemptible to the wise, and upon the dissolution of the body, after death, he will be reborn in a state of sorrow, of

7. *Micchā-diṭṭhi.*

8. *Micchā-saṅkappo.*

9. *Micchā-vācā.*

10. *Safe,* that is, with regard to the next world, which, if not existent, has no pains in store for him. But in this world, such a being through his evil action is liable to all kinds of misery.

evil, of torment, and of misery. Thus would the Incontrovertible Doctrine be unskilfully observed; he embraces one aspect (i.e., his own nihilistic view),[11] but misses the skilful attitude.

"Therefore, householders, of those ascetics and Brahmins who expound and hold such views as these: 'There is such a thing as alms, as sacrifice, as offering, ... also, there are in the world ascetics and Brahmaṇas who walk rightly, conduct themselves well, and who, having comprehended both this world and the world beyond by their own intuitive wisdom, make known the same,' this is to be expected: whatever bodily, verbal and mental evil actions there be, these three de-meritorious conditions they will entirely omit; whatever bodily, verbal and mental good actions there be, these three meritorious conditions they will observe and practise.

"For what reason? Because, these good ascetics and Brahmins see the evils, vanity and depravity of immoral conditions, and the advantages and the pure side of moral conditions (to be found) in renunciation.

"Certainly there really is a world beyond, the belief that there is such a world is a right view. Assuredly, a world beyond really exists. One hopes that there is such a world: that is a right hope. One states that there is a world beyond: that is a right statement. To say—of the world beyond which really exists—that there is such a world beyond, is not to contradict those Exalted Ones (*arahanta*) who know the world beyond. To make known to others (concerning the world beyond which assuredly exists) that there is such a world, that is the teaching of a sound doctrine. And by such sound doctrine, indeed, one neither exalts oneself nor despises others.

"Thus, because of the aforesaid (right views) one's immorality is abandoned, and morality is imminent; for this is a right belief, a right aspiration, a right statement, a confirmation of the Noble Ones, the teaching of a sound doctrine, the non-exalting of self and not despising of others. Thus, these various wholesome states arise as a result of right belief.

---

11. *Ekaṃsaṃ pharitvā tiṭṭhati:* Commentary: he adheres to one side, namely, only to his own doctrine (*ekantaṃ ekakoṭṭhāsaṃ sakavādaṃ eva pharitvā adhimuccitvā titthati*). Sub Commentary: "He insists (*avadhārento*) on his own nihilistic view, thinking, 'This only is true, everything else is false,' and does not give room for another view"—Editor.

"Therefore, householders, a wise person reflects thus: If, indeed, there is a world beyond, then this good individual upon the dissolution of the body, after death, will be reborn in a happy heavenly world.

"Well (for argument's sake), let there be no world beyond, and let the words of those good ascetics and Brahmins be true! But even so this good individual, in this life itself, is praised by the wise who hold him to be 'a virtuous person, one having right belief, one who maintains that something is.'[12] Therefore, if there really exists a world beyond, then this good individual is victorious in both worlds; for, in this present life, he is praised by the wise, and upon the dissolution of the body, after death, he will be reborn in a happy heavenly world. Thus would the Incontrovertible Doctrine be skilfully observed; one embraces both aspects,[13] and avoids an unskilful attitude.

"There are, householders, some ascetics and Brahmins who expound and hold such views as these: 'No evil is done by him who acts or causes others to act; who mutilates or causes others to mutilate; who torments or causes others to torment; who causes others to grieve; who causes others to suffer; who trembles or causes others to tremble; who kills living creatures; who steals; who breaks into houses; who seizes plunder; who commits burglary; who lies in ambush; who commits adultery; or who lies.

"Even if with a wheel edged with razors he should make a shambles, one single mass of flesh, of all the living creatures of this earth, no evil results thereby, there is no acquisition of evil. Even should he go along the southern bank of the Ganges beating, killing, mutilating and causing others to mutilate, tormenting and causing others to torment, no evil results thereby, there is no acquisition of evil. Or should he go along the northern bank of the Ganges giving alms and causing others to give alms, worshipping and causing others to worship, no merit results thereby, there is no acquisition of merit. Neither by giving, by

12. *Atthika-vādo,* an affirmationist, one who believes in the existence of a world beyond (*atthi paraloko*) and of positive moral values (*atthi dānaṃ,* etc.) as opposed to the *natthika-vādo,* the nihilist or annihilationist—Editor.

13. That is, he takes into account both possibilities, the existence or non-existence of a world beyond—Editor.

self-control, by asceticism nor by truthfulness, is there merit or acquisition of merit.'

"Yet, amongst these same ascetics and Brahmins, householders, there are some who hold directly opposite views. They say thus: 'Evil is done by him who acts or causes others to act; who mutilates or causes others to mutilate; who torments or causes others to torment; who causes others to grieve; who causes others to suffer; who trembles or causes others to tremble; who kills living creatures; who steals; who breaks into houses; who seizes plunder; who commits burglary; who lies in ambush; who commits adultery; or who lies. ...

"By giving, by self-control, by asceticism and by truthfulness, there is merit; there is acquisition of merit.'

"What do you think of this, householders? Do not these ascetics and Brahmins hold doctrines in direct opposition to each other?"

"Certainly, Venerable Sir."

"Therefore, householders, of those ascetics and Brahmins who expound and hold such views as these: 'No evil is done by him who acts or causes others to act. ... Neither by giving, by self-control, by asceticism nor by truthfulness, is there merit or acquisition of merit,' this is to be expected: whatever bodily, verbal and mental good actions there be, these three meritorious conditions they will entirely avoid; whatever bodily, verbal and mental evil actions there be, these three de-meritorious conditions they will observe and practise.

"And for what reason? Because these good ascetics and Brahmins do not see the evils, vanity and depravity of immoral conditions, or the advantages and the pure side of moral conditions (to be found) in renunciation.

"Assuredly, there really is action;[14] the belief that there is no action—that is a false belief. Undoubtedly, there is action. One hopes there is no action—that is a false hope. One states that there is no action—that is a false statement. To say of action, which really is, that there is no such action is to contradict those Exalted Ones who assert that there is action.

14. That is, morally efficacious action (*kamma*)—Editor.

"To make known to others, concerning action, which assuredly is, that there is no such action, that is the teaching of a wicked doctrine; and by such wicked propagation one exalts oneself and despises others.

"Thus, because of the aforesaid (wrong views) one's morality is abandoned, and immorality is imminent; for this is a false belief, a false speculation, a false statement, a contradiction of the Noble Ones, the teaching of a wicked doctrine, the exalting of self and the despising of others. Thus these various evil unwholesome states arise as a result of false belief.

"Therefore, householders, a wise person reflects thus: 'If there is really no action, then this good individual, upon the dissolution of the body, after death, will be safe; if, however, there is action, then this good individual upon the dissolution of the body, after death, will be reborn in a state of sorrow, of evil, of torment and of misery.'

"Well (for argument's sake), let there be no action, and let the words of those good ascetics and Brahmins be true! But even so this good individual, in this life itself, is despised by the wise who hold him to be 'an immoral person, a heretic, a denier of action.'[15]

"Therefore, if there really is action, then this good individual is defeated in both worlds; for in this present life he is despised by the wise, and upon the dissolution of the body, after death, he will be reborn in a state of sorrow, of evil, of torment and of misery. Thus would the Incontrovertible Doctrine be unskilfully observed; he embraces one aspect but misses the skilful attitude.

"Therefore, householders, of those ascetics and Brahmins who expound and hold such views as these: 'Evil is done by him who acts or causes others to act. ... By giving, by self-control, by asceticism and by truthfulness, there is merit, there is acquisition of merit,' this is to be expected: Evil actions they will entirely avoid; good actions they will observe and practise, because they see the evils of immoral, and the advantages of moral conditions.

"Assuredly, there really is action. The belief that there is action is a right view. Such hope is a right aspiration. Such statement is

15. *Akiriyavādo,* a denier of the moral efficacy of action. In DN 2 this view is ascribed to the heretical teacher Pūraṇa Kassapa.

a right statement. What he says does not contradict those Exalted Ones who assert that there is action. His teaching is a sound doctrine by which he neither exalts himself nor despises others.

"Thus, because of the aforesaid (right views) immorality is abandoned, and morality is imminent. ... Hence, these various wholesome states arise as a result of right belief.

"Therefore, householders, a wise person reflects thus: 'If there really is action, then this good individual will be reborn in a happy heavenly world.' Supposing there be no action, even so he is praised, in this life itself, by the wise, who say, 'a virtuous person; one having right belief; who maintains the view that there is action.' ... Thus would the Incontrovertible Doctrine be skilfully observed; one embraces both aspects and avoids an unskilful attitude.

"There are, householders, some ascetics and Brahmins who expound and hold such views as these: 'There is no cause or reason for the depravity of beings. Without reason and without cause they are defiled. Neither is there a cause or reason for the rectitude of beings. Without reason and without cause they are pure. There is no strength, no energy, no manly vigour, no virile might.[16] All animals, all that breathe, all beings, all living things, are powerless, without strength or energy; they are shaped by fate, association and nature[17] and in accordance with the six species of (human) existence[18] they experience happiness and pain.'

Yet, amongst these same ascetics and Brahmins, householders,

16.Commentary: "There is no strength, no energy ... capable of making beings defiled or pure."—The views in this section are ascribed to Makkhali Gosāla.

17.*Niyati-saṅgati-sabhāva.—Saṅgati* also means "chance," "coincidence," but the Commentary explains it here as the "coming together," the contact, between the six species of people (see Note 18), that is, the influence of the human environment, the milieu—Editor.

18. The six species are named according to colour. They are black, dark blue, red, yellow, fair and extremely fair (Commentary). These six colours are supposed, according to Makkhali Gosāla's theory, to personify beings as they evolve higher and higher. As a "heretic," of course, he placed his own sect of Ājīvakas, naked ascetics, highest of all. See Aṅguttara Nikāya, *Chakka Nipāta*, No. 57.

there are some who hold directly opposite views. They say thus: 'There is a cause and a reason for the depravity of beings. With reason and with cause are they defiled. There is a cause and a reason for the rectitude of beings. With reason and with cause are they pure. There is strength, there is energy, there is manly vigour there is virile might. All animals, all that breathe, all beings, all living things are not powerless, are not without strength or energy; they are not shaped by fate, association and nature and do not experience happiness and pain in accordance with the six species of (human) existence.'

"What do you think of this, householders? Do not these ascetics and Brahmins hold doctrines in direct opposition to each other?"

"Certainly, Venerable Sir."

"Therefore, householders, of those ascetics and Brahmins who expound and hold such views as these: There is no cause or reason for the depravity of beings ... they are shaped by fate, association and nature and in accordance with the six species of (human) existence they experience happiness and pain', this is to be expected: Good actions they will entirely avoid; evil actions they will observe and practise because they do not see the evils of immoral, and the advantages of moral conditions.

"Assuredly, there really is a cause. The belief that there is no cause is a false view; such aspiration is false aspiration; such statement is false statement and it contradicts those Exalted Ones (*arahanta*) who assert that there is a cause. Such teaching is a wicked doctrine by which one exalts oneself and despises others.

"Thus, because of the aforesaid (wrong views) one's morality is abandoned and immorality is imminent.... Hence, these various evil, unwholesome states arise as a result of false belief.

"Therefore, householders, a wise person reflects thus: 'If there is really no cause, then this good individual will be safe; otherwise he will be reborn in a state of sorrow, evil, torment and misery.'

"Supposing there be no cause, even so he is despised, in this life itself, by the wise who say, 'an immoral person, a heretic, one who denies that there is cause.'[19]

19. *Ahetukavādo:* a denier of moral causation; a doctrine attributed to Makkhali Gosāla. The preceding three views are called wrong views with mixed results (*niyatā-micchā-diṭṭhi*), i.e. (1) nihilism (*natthika-diṭṭhi*), (2)

"Thus would the Incontrovertible Doctrine be unskilfully observed; he embraces one aspect, but misses the skilful attitude.

"Therefore, householders, of those ascetics and Brahmins who expound and hold such views as these: 'There is a cause and a reason for the depravity of beings. ... They are not shaped by fate, association and nature and do not merely experience happiness and pain in accordance with the six species of (human) existence,' this is to be expected: Evil actions they will entirely avoid, good actions they will observe and practise, because they see the evils of immoral and the advantages of moral conditions.

"Assuredly, there really is a cause. The belief that there is cause is a right view; such aspiration is right aspiration; such statement is right statement and does not contradict those Exalted Ones who assert that there is a cause. Such teaching is sound doctrine by which one neither exalts oneself nor despises others.

"Thus, because of the aforesaid (right views), immorality is abandoned, and morality is imminent.... Hence, these various wholesome states arise as a result of right belief.

"Therefore, householders, a wise person reflects thus: 'If there really is a cause, then this good individual will be reborn in happy heavenly world. Supposing there be no cause, even then he is praised, in this life itself, by the wise, who say a virtuous person is, one having right belief, who maintains the view that there is cause.' Thus would the Incontrovertible Doctrine be skilfully observed, embracing both aspects and avoiding an unskilful attitude.

"There are, householders, some ascetics and Brahmins who expound and hold such a view as this: 'There is no realm that is formless throughout.'

"Yet amongst these same ascetics and Brahmins, householders, there are some who hold a directly opposite view. They say thus: 'There is undoubtedly a realm that is formless throughout.'[20]

---

moral inefficacy of action (*akiriya-diṭṭhi*), (3) denial of moral causality (*ahetuka-diṭṭhi*). The tenacious holding of these views excludes, at least for the next existence (but probably for longer), rebirth in a heavenly world and attainment of liberation. See Appendix—Editor.

20. *Āruppa*—Buddhists maintain that there are realms where mind exists without matter. Is this possible? Is it possible for an iron bar to float in the air? The reply to both questions is "Yes." The iron bar "floats" in the air

"What then do you think, O householders? Do not these ascetics and Brahmins hold doctrines in direct opposition to each other?"

"Certainly, Venerable Sir."

"Therefore, householders, a wise person reflects thus: There are those good ascetics and Brahmins who expound and hold this view: 'There is no realm that is formless throughout. We have not perceived it!' There are also others who expound and hold this view: 'There is undoubtedly a realm that is formless throughout. This, we have not discerned!' Indeed, though I also neither know nor perceive, ought I to take one side and say 'This alone is true; the other is foolish?' That would not be proper of me.

"If the words of those good ascetics and Brahmins who expound and hold this view: 'There is no realm that is formless throughout, be true; there is this possibility. My rebirth amongst those deities possessed of forms created by mind,[21] will be certain.'

"But if the words of those good ascetics and Brahmins who expound and hold this view: 'There is undoubtedly a realm that is formless throughout be true; there is this possibility: Verily my rebirth amongst those formless deities created by perception will be certain.[22] Truly, on account of form, there is manifested the using of sticks and weapons, quarrels, strife, reviling, recrimination, slandering, and lying; but there is naught of this in the formless realm.'

"Reflecting thus, he sets himself to the practice which leads to disgust for, to no desire for, to the cessation of forms themselves.

---

because it has been flung there, and there it will remain so long as it retains any unexpended momentum. The "formless" being appears through being flung into that state by powerful mind-force, and there it will remain till that momentum is expended. It is a temporary separation of mind from matter, which normally co-exist.

21. *Mano-maya.* This refers to *jhāna*-consciousness—Commentary.

22. The perception is the one arising in the formless meditations (Commentary). This person entertains doubts as to the existence of the formless realm because he hears contradictory views regarding the existence of such a realm. He, however, develops the jhānas and, attaining the fourth jhāna, endeavours to develop the formless absorptions (*arūpa-jhāna*) with the object of gaining life in a formless realm. If he fails, he is certain of the "form sphere" (*rūpa-loka*); if he succeeds he is certain of the "formless realm." This is the significance of the phrase "My rebirth there will be certain."

"There are, householders, some ascetics and Brahmins who expound and hold such a view as this: 'There is never a cessation of existence.'[23]

"Yet amongst these same ascetics and Brahmins, householders, there are some who hold a directly opposite doctrine. They say thus: 'There is an entire cessation of existence.'

"What then do you think, O householders? Do not these ascetics and Brahmins hold doctrines in direct opposition to each other?"

"Certainly, Venerable Sir."

"Therefore, O householders, a wise person reflects thus: 'There are those good ascetics and Brahmins who argue and contend thus: There is never a cessation of existence. We have not perceived it!'

"There are also others who expound and hold this view: 'There is an entire cessation of existence. This, we have not discerned!'

"Indeed, though I also neither know nor perceive, should I take one side and say 'This alone is true; the other is foolish?' That would not be proper of me.

"If the words of those good ascetics and Brahmins who argue and contend thus, that there is never a cessation of existence, be true, there is this possibility: My rebirth amongst those formless deities created by perception will be certain.

"But, if the words of those good ascetics and Brahmins who argue and contend thus, that 'there is an entire cessation of existence,' be true, there is this possibility: That I shall attain Nibbāna in this life itself!

"This belief of those good ascetics and Brahmins who argue and contend thus that 'there is never a cessation of existence' is close to craving, close to the fetters, close to delight, close to cleaving, close to clinging.

"But this belief of those good ascetics and Brahmins who argue and contend thus that 'there is an entire cessation of existence' is close to the freedom from craving, from fetters, from delight, from cleaving and from clinging.

"Reflecting thus, he sets himself to the practice which leads to disgust for, to no desire for, to the cessation of existence itself.[24]

23. *Bhava-nirodho,* a synonym for Nibbāna

24. This wise person has developed the eight (meditative) attainments (*attha-*

"These four individuals exist, O householders; they are found in the world. Who are the four? Here, O householders, a certain individual is a tormentor of self, is addicted to the practice of self-torment. Here, householders, a certain individual is a tormentor of others, is addicted to the practice of tormenting others. Here, householders, a certain individual is a tormentor of self and others, is addicted to the practice of tormenting self and others. Here, householders, a certain individual is neither a tormentor of self nor of others, is not addicted to the practice of tormenting self or others; he neither torments self nor others; in this life itself he is desireless, quenched (of passions), cool, experiences happiness, lives nobly.

"And which individual, O householders, is a tormentor of self, is addicted to the practice of self torment?

"Here, O householders, a certain individual is naked; is devoid of social habits; licks his hands (after eating).[25] Thus, in this manner, he lives addicted, in various ways, to the practice of mortifying and tormenting the body. This individual, householders, is said to be a tormentor of self, addicted to the practice of self-torment.

"And which individual, O householders, torments others and is addicted to the practice of tormenting others? Here, householders, a certain individual is a butcher; is a pig-killer; or follows any other cruel occupation whatsoever. This individual, householders, is said to be a tormentor of others, addicted to the practice of tormenting others.

"And which individual, O householders, is a tormentor of self and others and is addicted to the practice of tormenting self and others? Here householders, a certain individual is an anointed king of the warrior caste. (He fasts and practises austerities himself,

---

samāpatti) and as such he entertains no doubt with regard to the formless realm. (The eight attainments are the four *rūpa-jhānas* and the four *arūpa-jhānas*). Nevertheless, he doubts that there is a "cessation of existence" (Nibbāna) because he has not personally experienced it and because he hears others expressing contrary views with regard to it. He however cultivates insight (*vipassanā*) with the object of realising Nibbāna. If he fails, he is certain of being reborn in the formless realm as he possesses the *arūpa-jhānas*. Should he succeed he will attain the arahant stage and Nibbāna in this life itself.

25. The details of these practices of self-torment are exactly as in the *Kandaraka Sutta* (see *The Wheel* No. 79, p. 8 ff).

and worries his slaves, servants and workmen who, terrified with sticks, driven by fear, with woeful faces and in tears, do the work).[26] This individual, householders, is said to be a tormentor of self and others, addicted to the practice of tormenting self and others.

"And which individual, O householders, is neither a tormentor of self nor of others, is not addicted to the practice of tormenting self or others; who, neither tormenting himself nor others, in this life itself is desireless, quenched (of passions), cool, experiences happiness, lives nobly?

"Here, householders, an Accomplished One appears in the world, an Exalted One, an Omniscient One. (He expounds the Truth, hearing which a householder acquires confidence in this Blessed One and abandoning his home, goes forth to homelessness. He observes the bhikkhu life, abstains from evil, and practises meditation.)

"Abandoning the five hindrances and by wisdom, having weakened the corruptions of the mind, remote indeed from sense-desires and unskilful conditions, but exercising reflection and investigation, in the joy and happiness born of seclusion, he lives abiding in the first ecstasy ... in the second ecstasy ... in the third ecstasy ... in the fourth ecstasy.

"Thus with thoughts tranquilised, purified, cleansed, free from lust and impurity, pliable, alert, steady and unshakable, he directs his mind to the recollection and cognition of former existences. He recalls his varied lot in former existences, as follows: First one life, then two lives. ... Thus he recalls the mode and details of his varied lot in former existences.

"Thus with thoughts tranquillized, purified, cleansed, free from lust and impurity, pliable, alert, steady and unshakable, he directs his mind to the perception of the disappearing and reappearing of beings.

"With clairvoyant vision, purified and supernormal, he perceives beings disappearing from one state of existence and reappearing in another; he beholds the base and the noble, the beautiful and the ugly; the happy and the miserable, and beings passing on in accordance with their deeds.

"Thus with thoughts tranquillised, purified, cleansed, free from lust and impurity, pliable, alert, steady and unshakable,

26. For details see *The Wheel* No. 79, pp. 9 ff.

he directs his mind to the comprehension of the cessation of the corruptions. He realises, in accordance with fact, 'This is Sorrow.' 'This, the Arising of Sorrow.' 'This, the Ceasing of Sorrow.' 'This, the Path leading to the Cessation of Sorrow.'

"Likewise, in accordance with fact, he realises, 'These are the Corruptions.' 'This, the Arising of the Corruptions.' 'This, the Ceasing of the Corruptions.' 'This, the Path leading to the Cessation of the Corruptions.'

"Thus cognising, thus perceiving, his mind is delivered from the Corruption of Sensual Craving, from the Corruption of Craving for Existence, from the Corruption of Ignorance.

"Being delivered, he knows: 'Delivered am I' and he realises: 'Rebirth is ended; fulfiled the holy life; done, what was to be done; there is none other beyond this life.'

"This individual, O householders, is said to be neither a tormentor of self nor of others, addicted neither to the practice of tormenting self nor others; he neither tormenting himself nor others, in this life itself is desireless, quenched (of passions), cool, experiences happiness, lives nobly."

When the Blessed One had thus spoken, the Brahmin householders of Sālā said, "Excellent, happy Gotama, excellent! It is as if, O happy Gotama, a man were to set upright that which was overturned. ... We too, take refuge in the noble Gotama, the Doctrine, and the Order. May the noble Gotama receive us as followers who have taken refuge from this very day to life's end."

Appendix to the Apaṇṇaka Sutta

Wrong Views with Fixed Result (niyatā-micchā-diṭṭhi)

It is the program of the sutta editions in this series to furnish, along with faithful translations, relevant exegetical material from the commentarial tradition, which generally will not be accessible to readers unfamiliar with the original Pali. Hence a longer disquisition on Wrong Views with Fixed Results (see above Footnote 19) has been supplied here from the old Commentary to the *Apaṇṇaka Sutta*, supplemented by extracts from the Sub-commentaries to a parallel passage in the *Sāmaññaphala Sutta* (DN 2).—Editor, The Wheel.

Comy: Commentary to the *Apaṇṇaka Sutta*;

DCy : Commentary to Dīgha No. 2;

SCy : Sub-commentary to Dīgha;

NSCy: New Sub-commentary to Dīgha (*Abhinava-ṭīkā*).

Comy: Of these three views:

- The nihilistic view (*natthika-diṭṭhi*) rejects the result of kamma (*vipāka*) (*SCy:*) because, by asserting that "there is no such thing as alms" any fruit of alms-giving is denied (*DCy:*) and because this view holds that "on the dissolution of the body there is annihilation" (*SCy:*), by which any future rebirth is entirely denied.
- The view of the moral inefficacy of action (*akiriya-diṭṭhi*) rejects kamma (*DCy:*), because it asserts that "no evil is done by him who acts. ..."
- The view denying moral causality (*ahetuka-diṭṭhi*) rejects both kamma and its result (*DCy, SCy:*), because, by asserting that "there is no cause," any effect of a cause is also denied.

DCy: Here, by rejecting kamma (as in the second view), its result is likewise rejected; and by excluding kamma-result (as in the first view), kamma itself is excluded (*SCy:*) because the assumption of kamma is useless if there is no result from it.

Comy: Hence, as all these three doctrines, in fact, reject both kamma and its result, all of them are nihilistic as well as deniers of moral causation and of morally significant action (*iti sabbe p'ete... natthikavādā ceva ahetukavādā ca akiriyavādā ca honti*).

But in the case of those who accept their opinions and sit down day and night to study and explore those views, in them wrong mindfulness (*micchā-sati*) becomes established, taking as object one of those three views; their mind is concentrated on them, the (active) impulsions (of the perceptual series) impel (the thought process in that very direction; *javanāni javanti*).[27] At the first moment of impulsion, they are still curable, and so up to the sixth moment; but at the seventh, not even the Buddhas can cure them or turn them back; in that they are similar to the monk Ariṭṭha and the novice Kaṇṭaka (see *vinaya*).

One person may fall into a single one of the three views, another into two or three. But whether he falls into one or two or all three of them, he becomes a "believer in false views with fixed result" (*niyatā-micchā-diṭṭhika*). He has thereby come to the point where the way to heavenly rebirth and the way to liberation are closed to him. In his next existence he is unable to reach a heavenly world, to say nothing about his attaining liberation. Such a being is called a "stump in *saṃsāra*" (*vaṭṭa-khaṇuka*),[28] a "watcher of the earth" (*pathavī-gopaka*).[29]

One may question here: How is it? Is he (in his future destiny) "fixed" (*niyata*) only for one single existence (the next one), or also for other (lives)? The result is fixed only for one existence. But due to habit, that person will approve of his respective view also in another existence (*āsevanavasena pana bhavantare pi taṃ taṃ diṭṭhihi roceti evā'ti*). Hence, for such a person, there is generally no transcending of existence.

---

27. Within a complete series of 17 thought-moments required for an act of perception, it is the phase of impulsion (*javana*) where kamma is performed. This phase of impulsion normally consists of seven moments of consciousness to which the text above refers.

28. This figurative expression may refer to one who remains firmly rooted in *samsāric* existence.

29. This may mean that, like a watcher, he remains when others have left.

"Therefore a discerning monk, wishing for progress, should shun ignoble people from afar, like vipers."

[The following are further glosses from the Sub-commentaries to phrases in the above commentarial passage.]

NSCy: "*Wrong mindfulness becomes established.*" It is "craving (*taṇhā*)," associated with that erroneous opinion which is called here "wrong mindfulness". That opinion, for instance, "He who acts thus, does not do anything evil," is first accepted in its general meaning as a tradition; later, by reasoning and reflecting about it, it appears to the mind as vividly as if it had assumed visible form; then, by getting familiar with these ideas for a long time, one derives satisfaction from contemplating them (*nijjhānakkhamabhāvūpagamena*). Through the wrong way of thinking, which is formed in one who habitually and repeatedly conceives things in that light, and by thus gaining support from preceding "wrong effort" (*micchā-vāyāma*) it finally becomes an avowed opinion by which one takes to be true what is actually false. It is "craving," associated with such opinionatedness (*laddhi*) that, under the name of "wrong mindfulness", is spoken of here as becoming established in the mind of such a person.

NSCy: "*The mind is concentrated on them.*" Under the key word "mind" "wrong concentration" (*micchā-samādhi*) is spoken of here. Under the conditions described, this "wrong concentration" obtains "strength-by-development" (*laddha-bhāvanā-balo*) and fulfils the function of concentrating the mind as applicable in this case, just as (concentration is required for instance) when shooting game.

"*The impulsions impel.*" (*SCy*:) When preceding serial processes of impulsion have occurred many times in the same way, then in the very last series of impulsion (*NSCy*: where a definite conclusion is formed), seven thought moments of impulsion impel (the mind process).

"*At the first, up to the sixth, moment of impulsion they are still curable.*" (*SCy*:) This passage is merely for showing the characteristic nature of the *dhammas* (i.e., thought processes; *dhamma-sabhāvadassanam-ev'etaṃ*), (*NSCy*:) It shows that at that (sixth) moment, impulsion on one can effect a "cure" of these (thought moments) because one cannot, stopping at that stage, prevent the arising of the seventh moment of impulsion which must arise by necessity; also, because a cure by way of advice or instruction is impossible in a thought series of such fast movement.

"A stump in saṃsāra." NSCy: This is a figurative expression (for "fixation" in *saṃsāra*).

"Karmically," unwholesome consciousness (*akusala*) is weak, is without strength; it is not powerful and strong like *"karmically"* wholesome consciousness (*kusala*). Hence it is said that there is fixity (of result) for one existence only. Otherwise the result, fixation of "wrongfulness" (*micchatta-niyāma*), would be as final (*accantika*) as that of righteousness (*sammatta-niyāma;* i.e., the four Paths of Sanctity); but the former is *not* final.

If this is so how does the expression "*saṃsāra*-stump" fit (which signifies, as it were, a permanent "fixture")? Answering that, it was said above (in the Commentary): *"But due to habit, that person will approve of his respective view also in another existence."* Just as (in the Sevens of the Aṅguttara-Nikāya), the fool is spoken of as "once submerged he remains submerged" (*sakiṃ nimuggo pi nimuggo eva bālo*), in the same way the expression "*saṃsāra* stump" has to be understood. If someone has fallen into those views influenced by certain conditions, one cannot say that he will never be able to raise his head above them, under different conditions. Therefore, in the commentarial passage, the word "generally" (*yebhuyyena*) was inserted: "For such there is generally no transcending of existence." But as, on account of habituation, he will indulge in the respective wrong view also in another existence, it has been said that "generally there is no transcending (of *saṃsāra*) for him," and he has been called a "stump in *saṃsāra*," but not on account of any finality in the fixed results of the states of wrongfulness (*micchatta*).

Introduction to the Cūla Māluṅkya Sutta

(Majjhima Nikāya No. 63)

Buddhism does not profess to provide an explanation of each and every problem that perplexes the human mind. It has a practical and specific purpose—the cessation of sorrow. With that Supreme Goal kept constantly in view, all sideissues that tend to obscure or hinder the attainment of the main object are completely ignored. Nevertheless it undoubtedly encourages—no, most emphatically insists upon—keen personal investigation into the real nature of life, while strongly deprecating idle speculation and mere theorising.

The profound insight of wisdom is not the outcome of vain excogitation but of realisation; and for realization is required a special line of penetrative thought that is more than a mere ratiocinative process. A brilliant intellect is not uncommonly combined with a bad character, but true wisdom cannot be found apart from morality. For this reason Buddhism demands, together with a life of purity, a ruthless analysis of facts, and the consequent discarding of all fond fancies and illusions. Morality, to be genuine, must be based on fact, not fiction, no matter how pious or consoling the latter may be.

In the following sutta, a certain bhikkhu, Māluṅkyaputta, not content to tread the Path patiently in accordance with the Buddha's instructions and thus attain by degrees the perfect wisdom, desires, impatiently desires, an immediate solution of certain speculative problems, on the threat of discarding the robe forthwith.

Calmly, and in a few words, the Buddha elicits from the bhikkhu that his adoption of the holy life was in no way conditional upon the solution of such problems. Proceeding, the Buddha points out that to waste time over such idle speculations is not merely a hindrance to progress on the Path, but is actually inimical to the very existence of the holy life.

Finally, he lays emphasis on what has really been revealed by him, and why: the Four Noble Truths, encompassing that sorrow which life brings home, sooner or later, to every living creature; and, likewise, making possible the cessation of that sorrow, even in this life itself.

Cūla Māluṅkya Sutta

The Short Discourse to Māluṅkyaputta

Thus have I heard. On one occasion the Blessed One was dwelling at the monastery of Anāthapiṇḍika in the Jeta Grove, near Sāvatthī, when the following thought arose in the mind of the Venerable Māluṅkyaputta whilst meditating in solitude:

"These theories have not been elucidated and/or have been set aside and/or rejected by the Blessed One—whether

- the world is eternal or not eternal;
- the world is finite or infinite;
- the life principle[30] and the body are identical;
- the life principle is one thing and the body another;
- the Tathāgata[31] exists or does not exist after death;
- the Tathāgata both exists and does not exist after death; and/or
- the Tathāgata neither exists nor does not exist after death[32]— these the Blessed One does not elucidate to me.

"The fact that he does not elucidate these to me does not please me, nor do I approve of it. Therefore I will go to the Blessed One and inquire after this matter. If the Blessed One will elucidate these questions to me, then I will lead the holy life under him. If he will not, then I will abandon the precepts[33] and return to the lay life."

---

30. *Jīva*, "life."

31. According to the Commentary to Majjhima Nikāya 22, "the term *tathāgato* (lit.: 'thus-gone" or "thus-come") may refer either to a being in general *(satto)*, or to the Greatest Man (*uttamo puriso*, i.e., the Buddha), and/or to a taint-free saint (*khiṇāsavo*, i.e. an Arahant)." The term is often translated as "the Perfect One." See the Wheel 48/49 *Snake Simile*, Majjhima Nikāya 22, p. 35—Editor.

32. The Arahant Nāgasena's explanation as to why these were not elucidated by the Buddha will be found in *Questions of Milinda*, translated by T. W. Rhys Davids, Part I, p. 204, *Milinda's Questions*, translated by I. B. Horner, Vol. I, p. 201—Translators.

33. *Sikkhaṃ paccakkhāya*—the formal renunciation of the Order. See *Vinaya*, S.B.E., Vol. XIII, p. 275, notes 2 and 3—Translators.

And at eventide the Venerable Māluṅkyaputta, having risen from meditation, approached the Blessed One, and respectfully saluting him sat on one side. Seated thus, the Venerable Māluṅkyaputta addressed the Blessed One as follows:

"Behold, Venerable Sir, whilst meditating in solitude, the following thought occurred to me. These theories have not been elucidated, set aside and/or rejected by the Blessed One, i.e., whether the world is eternal or not eternal and/or the Tathāgata neither exists nor does not exist after death. These the Blessed One does not elucidate to me. The fact that he does not elucidate these to me does not please me, nor do I approve of it. Therefore I will go to the Blessed One and inquire after this matter. If the Blessed One will elucidate these questions to me, then I will lead the holy life under him. If he will not, then I will abandon the precepts and return to the lay life. If the Blessed One knows that the world is eternal, let the Blessed One elucidate to me that the world is eternal. If the Blessed One knows that the world is not eternal, let the Blessed One elucidate to me that it is not eternal. If the Blessed One does not know whether the world is eternal or not—in that case, certainly, for one who does not know and lacks the insight, the only upright thing is to say, 'I do not know. I do not have the insight.' If the Blessed One knows, that the world is finite, ... that the life principle and the body are identical, ... that the Tathāgata exists after death, ... whether the Tathāgata does not exist after death, ... whether the Tathāgata both exists and does not exist after death, ... whether the Tathāgata neither exists nor does not exist after death, let the Blessed One elucidate to me that the Tathāgata neither exists nor does not exist after death, if the Blessed One does not know whether the Tathāgata neither exists nor does not exist after death—in that case, certainly, for one who does not know and lacks the insight, the only upright thing is to say: 'I do not know; I do not have the insight.'"

"What, Māluṅkyaputta, did I say to you, 'Come, Māluṅkyaputta, lead the holy life under me. I will elucidate to you whether the world is eternal or not eternal, the world is finite or infinite, the life principle and the body are identical, and/or the life principle is one thing and the body another, the Tathāgata exists or does not exist after death, the Tathāgata both exists and does not exist after death and/or the Tathāgata neither exists nor does not exist after death'?"

"Certainly not, Venerable Sir."

"Or else did you say to me, 'Venerable Sir, I will lead the holy life under the Blessed One (on condition that) the Blessed One will elucidate to me whether, the world is eternal or not eternal, ... and/or the Tathāgata neither exists nor does not after death'?"

"Certainly not, Venerable Sir."

"So you admit, Māluṅkyaputta, that neither did I say, 'Come, Māluṅkyaputta, lead the holy life under me and I will elucidate these questions to you'; nor did you say, 'Venerable Sir, I will lead the holy life under the Blessed One, because he will elucidate these questions to me.'

"Such being the case, foolish one, what is your position, and what do you repudiate?[34]

"Whoever, Māluṅkyaputta, should say: 'I will not lead the holy life under the Blessed One until the Blessed One elucidates these questions to me,' that person would die before these questions had ever been elucidated by the Accomplished One.

"It is as if, Māluṅkyaputta, a person was pierced by an arrow thickly smeared with poison, and his friends and companions, relatives and kinsmen, were to procure a physician and surgeon and then he were to say, 'I will not have this arrow taken out until I know whether that person by whom I was wounded is of the warrior caste, or the Brahmin, or the merchant, or of the menial caste.'

"Or again he were to say: 'I will not have this arrow taken out until I know the name and family of that person by whom I was wounded, ... or until I know whether he is tall, or short, or of medium height or until I know whether he is black, or dusky, or of golden-brown[35] skin, ... or until I know whether he is from

---

34. *Ko santo kaṃ paccācikkhasi? Santo* is the present participle of the root *asa*—"to be." The Buddha did not promise to elucidate such questions, nor did Māluṅkyaputta make their elucidation a condition of his joining the Order. Under these circumstances, the Buddha asks *Ko santo*?— which might be freely translated as "What is your grievance?" or "Where do you stand?"—Translators.

35. *Maṅguracchavi*—P.T.S. Dictionary, gives "of golden colour"; Warren "of a yellow skin". Rhys Davids renders it "golden in colour", and, in a note, adds "perhaps of a sallow complexion" (see Dialogues, p. 258, note 2). According to the commentary on the *Mahā-Saccaka Sutta,* Majjhima Nikāya 36, it is the colour of the fish *maṅgura* (a freshwater fish having whiskers)—Translators.

such and such a village, town, or city.'

"Or again he were to say: 'I will not have this arrow taken out until I know whether the bow with which I was wounded is a long-bow or a cross-bow, ... or until I know whether the bow-string with which I was wounded is of swallow-won, bamboo-strips, sinew, *māruvā*-hemp, or milk-weed, ... or until I know whether the shaft with which I was wounded is a marsh reed or a cultivated reed, ... or until I know whether the shaft is feathered from the wings of a vulture, heron, hawk, peacock, or "loose-jaw" bird, ... or until I know whether the shaft is wound round with the sinews of an ox, buffalo, Ruru deer, or monkey.'

"Or again he were to say: 'I will not have this arrow taken out until I know whether the arrow with which I was wounded is an ordinary arrow, a claw-headed arrow, a *vekaṇḍa*-arrow, an iron arrow, a calf-tooth arrow, or a "*karavīra*-leaf" arrow.'

"That person would die, Māluṅkyaputta, before this would ever be known by him.

"In exactly the same way, Māluṅkyaputta, whoever should say 'I will not lead the holy life under the Blessed One until the Blessed One elucidates to me whether the world is eternal or not eternal, ... the Tathāgata neither exists nor does not exist after death,' that person would die, Māluṅkyaputta, before these questions had ever been elucidated by the Accomplished One.

"If it be the belief, Māluṅkyaputta, that the world is eternal, will there be observance of the holy life? In such a case—No.

"If it be the belief, Māluṅkyaputta, that the world is not eternal, will there be observance of the holy life? In that case also—No.

"But, Māluṅkyaputta, whether the belief be that the world is eternal or that it is not eternal, undoubtedly there is birth, there is old age, there is death and there are sorrow, lamentation, pain, grief and despair, the extinction of which, in this life itself, I make known.

"If it be the belief, Māluṅkyaputta, that the world is finite, ... that the life principle and the body are identical, ... if it be the belief that the Tathāgata exists after death, does not exist after death, both exists and does not exist after death, will there be observance of the holy life? In such a case—No!

"If it be the belief that the Tathāgata neither exists nor does not exist after death, will there be observance of the holy life? In that case also—No!

"But, Māluṅkyaputta, whether the belief be that the Tathāgata both exists and does not exist after death, or that he neither exists nor does not exist after death, undoubtedly there is birth, there is old age, there is death and there are sorrow, lamentation, pain, grief and despair, the extinction of which, in this life itself, I make known.

"Accordingly, Māluṅkyaputta, that which has not been revealed by me accept as unrevealed, and consider only that revealed which had been revealed by me.

"And what, Māluṅkyaputta, has not been revealed by me?

"I have not revealed whether the world is external or not external, the world is finite or infinite, the life principle and the body are identical, the life principle is one thing and the body another, the Tathāgata exists or does not exist after death, the Tathāgata both exists and does not exist after death and/or the Tathāgata neither exists nor does not exist after death.

"And why, Māluṅkyaputta, have I not revealed these? Because, Māluṅkyaputta, these are not profitable, do not concern the bases of holiness and are not conducive to aversion, to passionlessness, to cessation, to tranquillity, to intuitive wisdom, to enlightenment, or to Nibbāna.

"Therefore, I have not revealed these.

"And what, Māluṅkyaputta, has been revealed by me? Sorrow. This, Māluṅkyaputta has been revealed by me. The Cause of Sorrow. This has been revealed by me. The Cessation of Sorrow. This has been revealed by me. The Path leading to the Cessation of Sorrow. This has been revealed by me.

"And why, Māluṅkyaputta, have I revealed this? Because, Māluṅkyaputta, these are profitable, comprise the bases of holiness and are conducive to aversion, to passionlessness, to cessation, to tranquillity, to intuitive wisdom, to enlightenment and to Nibbāna. Therefore have I revealed them.

"Accordingly, Māluṅkyaputta, that which has not been revealed by me accept as unrevealed, and consider only that revealed which has been revealed by me."

Thus spoke the Blessed One. The Venerable Māluṅkyaputta, delighted, applauded his words.

Introduction to the Upāli Sutta

(Majjhima Nikāya No. 56)

During the Buddha's lifetime, the world was particularly fortunate in great teachers. Contemporaneous with him were the great philosophic movements of China, Persia and Greece. There is no doubt that the giant intellects of that period, roughly about 500 B.C., have left an ineradicable stamp on the culture of humanity.

In India, at that time, there appears to have been a general religious awakening. Many were the devout enthusiasts and teachers who, renouncing the world, sought paths of deliverance from suffering. Among these the name of Nātaputta, the founder of the Nigaṇṭhas, is frequently mentioned in our books. This discourse gives some indication of the Nigaṇṭha doctrines and the marked difference of view with regard to the importance and effect of "mental action," between Nātaputta and the Blessed One.

We would invite the non-Buddhist reader to note particularly the Buddha's admonition to one ardently eager to be his disciple to make a thorough investigation before he decides to adopt the new faith. What modern religionist would thus repress a possible convert, especially a highly educated millionaire convert, and a poet of no mean order as his verses (whose beauty is difficult to reproduce in translation) disclose!

This has ever been the triumphant achievement of Buddhism. It sets out to help others to deliver themselves from pain, but its wide tolerance has never permitted it to have and to hold converts merely for the sake of its own prestige. It welcomes criticism and investigation from within and without. It discredits blind faith. It does not forbid the reading of alien religious literature. Indeed, we make bold to claim that Buddhism is the only religion that positively demands the exercise of cold reason and investigation from its converts. No man's freedom of thought is interfered with by the Master, who would guide, but never coerce, into channels of spiritual betterment and uplift. The reason for all this is the Buddhist belief in kamma.

A good action, mental, verbal or physical, remains a "good" action whatever the external religious label of the agent. As the word "agent" may mislead the reader, it is well to insist here that *Buddhism recognises no "performer."*

There is only a performance; and every "individual," man, god or animal, is only a "being," a becoming, consisting of present fresh performance added to the sum-total of that particular being's past action—the whole constituting a coherent flux that is conventionally called "an individual."

This absence of a "thing-in-itself"—soul, or *attā*, in the Buddha's teaching—at once raises it above the ruck of ordinary religious levels. There is always the possibility that any particular flux, or being, may now or hereafter, in this "life" or in a future one, purge itself of its errors and work out its salvation. There is every need for him of the tender heart to extend a helping hand. But he of the tender heart must first make sure of his own correctness and stability; for a tender heart without supporting wisdom, may, all unconsciously, mislead and betray where it would only lead and save. In any case there is no need to worry and fret about a possible "eternal damnation" for those we love. Such a doctrine has no place in Buddhism. Whatever is gained is never lost, though, temporarily, passing clouds of ill may obscure and perplex.

So it has never been the habit of the Buddhist to force, or desire to force, his convictions on those of alien faiths. He is not over-anxious to make converts. Wherever any moral good is contemplated, he bestows his hearty approval, even as his Master did, when advising Upāli to continue bestowing alms on the Nigaṇṭhas, an alien sect. The Buddhist is glad to welcome, as brothers, any truly devout and earnest men, whatever the religion they outwardly profess. What grieves the sincere Buddhist, today is to observe so few of truly religious bent in the fold of any religion. The West is slave to Mammon and materialism, and the East bids fair to follow suit.

Upāli Sutta

Upāli, the Householder

Thus have I heard:

On one occasion the Blessed One was dwelling at Nālandā[36] in the mango grove of Pāvārika.[37] Now, Nigaṇṭha[38] Nātaputta was also staying at Nālandā at that time in a large company of naked ascetics. And Dīgha Tapassī,[39] the naked ascetic, having been for alms in Nālandā and returned from his begging round,[40] proceeded,

---

36. Nālandā, a town near Rājagaha, afterwards renowned by reason of its famous Buddhist university.

37. That is, in the monastery erected by the millionaire Pāvārika in his mango grove.

38. Nigaṇṭha, the name of a sect of naked ascetics who vainly opposed the Buddha and his disciples—Translators. Prof. Hermann Jacobi writes in Hastings, *Encyclopaedia of Religion and Ethics:*

"The canonical books of the Buddhists frequently mention the Jains as a rival sect, under their old name Nigaṇṭha (Sanskrit - *Nigaṇṭha*; Prakrit—*Niggantha*) and their leader in Buddha's time, Nātaputta (Nāta or Nātiputta, being an epithet of the last prophet of the Jains, Vardhamāna Mahāvira), and they name the place of the latter's death, Pāvā, in agreement with Jain tradition. On the other hand, the canonical books of the Jains mention as contemporaries of Mahāvīra the same kings as reigned during Buddha's career. Thus it is established that Mahāvīra was a contemporary of the Buddha, and probably somewhat older than the latter, who outlived his rival's decease at Pāvā."

39. Lit. "Long Tapassī" probably owing to long limbs or height.

40. *"Begging-round."* The Pāli term *piṇḍapāta* means "dropping by morsels." The bhikkhus go begging to each Buddhist house and stand near the door, bowl in hand, without any other intimation of their presence. Then the residents come and serve them with rice, etc., according to their means. The bhikkhus say in acknowledgment "*Sukhī hotu*" (May you be happy) and pass on. They live on such morsels dropped into their bowls, and on alms given by generous supporters. Though the identical term is here used with reference to Dīgha Tapassi, the Commentator says that this term is not usually applied to the process of begging as practised by alien orders.

after the meal was over, to the mango grove of Pāvārika, where the Blessed One was.[41] Coming into his presence, he exchanged friendly greetings with the Blessed One, and after the customary words of courtesy remained standing nearby. Standing thus at a little distance, the Blessed One addressed him as follows:

"There are seats, Tapassī. Be seated, if you wish."

Thereupon Dīgha Tapassī, the naked ascetic, took one of the low seats and sat on one side. Then the Blessed One spoke to him thus:

"Well, Tapassī, how many modes of action[42] does Nigaṇṭha Nātaputta declare there are, in doing and perpetrating evil deeds?"

"No, Venerable Gotama, 'action' is not the word used by Nigaṇṭha Nātaputta in his teaching. 'Offence.'[43] 'Offence' is the word he uses."

"Well, Tapassī, how many modes of 'offence' does he declare there are, in doing and perpetrating evil deeds?"

"Verily, Venerable Gotama, there are three (modes of) 'offence,' declares Nigaṇṭha Nātaputta, in doing and perpetrating evil deeds, namely: 'Offence' of body, of word, and of mind."

"Then, Tapassī, is bodily offence one, verbal offence another, and mental offence still another?"

"Bodily offence, Venerable Gotama, is one, verbal another and mental still another."

"Then, Tapassī, these three offences, thus analysed and differentiated, which offence does Nigaṇṭha Nātaputta declare to be the most heinous in doing and perpetrating evil deeds? Is it bodily, verbal or mental offence?"

"Of these three offences, Venerable Gotama, thus analysed and differentiated, bodily offence, declares Nigaṇṭha Nātaputta, is the most heinous in doing and perpetrating evil deeds; verbal offence and mental offence are not so (heinous)."[44]

---

41. The followers of other sects frequently visited the Buddhist monasteries and the bhikkhus also visited their monasteries. Often, points of religious controversy were debated at such meetings.

42. *Kammāni*—"actions."

43. *Daṇḍāni*—Note the distinction between the terms employed. The former merely implies "action," the latter "punishment" or "offence."

44. According to the doctrine of the Nigaṇṭhas bodily offence is considered

"Bodily offence! you say, Tapassī?"
"Bodily offence! I say, Venerable Gotama."
"Bodily offence! you say, Tapassī?"
"Bodily offence! I say, Venerable Gotama."
"Bodily offence! you say, Tapassī?"
"Bodily offence! I say, Venerable Gotama."

Thus did the Blessed One make Dīgha Tapassī confirm this statement even unto the third time.[45]

Thereupon Dīgha Tapassī, the naked ascetic, addressed the Blessed One as follows:

"Well, Venerable Gotama, how many modes of offence do you declare there are, in doing and perpetrating evil deeds?"

"No, Tapassī, the Accomplished One does not use the word 'offence' in His Teaching. 'Action.' 'Action' is what he recognises."

"Well, Venerable Gotama, how many modes of 'action' do you declare there are, in doing and perpetrating evil deeds?"

"Verily, Tapassī, there are three modes of 'action' I declare, in doing and perpetrating evil deeds, namely: 'Action' of body, of word, and of mind."[46]

---

to be the most heinous. The Commentator states that the Nigaṇṭhas declare the first two to be non-volitional. For instance, when the wind blows, branches are stirred and waters are ruffled. Again the blowing of the wind causes leaves to rustle and waters to give forth sound. In these cases no mind is involved, but there is visible action and audible sound. Therefore they posit that bodily and verbal "offences" are non-volitional, mental offences alone being volitional.

45. Why did the Buddha make Tapassī confirm his statement thus? The Commentator says that it was because he anticipated the conversion of Upāli who, hearing of this conversation, would be enticed to come personally to hear the Truth from the Buddha.

46. *Kāya kamma, vacī kamma* and *mano kamma* are the terms employed by the Buddha to signify bodily, verbal and mental actions. Here it should be noted that according to Buddhism all "actions" are volitional. Bodily actions are those done by the mind through the instrument of the body. Similarly verbal actions are those done by the mind by means of speech. Purely mental actions have no other instrument but the mind. The Commentator says that bodily and verbal actions, therefore, constitute the twelve types of immoral consciousness and the eight types of moral consciousness that arise through the agency of body and speech. Mental actions constitute all the twenty-

"Then, Venerable Gotama, is bodily action one, verbal action another and mental action still another?"

"Bodily action, Tapassī, is one, verbal another and mental still another."

"Then, Venerable Gotama, of these three actions, thus analysed and differentiated, which action do you declare to be the most heinous in doing and perpetrating evil deeds? Is it bodily, or verbal or mental action?"

"Of these three actions, Tapassī, thus analysed and differentiated, mental action,[47] I declare, is the most heinous in doing and perpetrating evil deeds. Bodily action and verbal action are not so (heinous)."

"Mental action! you say, Venerable Gotama?"

"Mental action! say I, Tapassī."

"Mental action! you say, Venerable Gotama?"

"Mental action! say I, Tapassī."

"Mental action! you say, Venerable Gotama?"

"Mental action! say I, Tapassī."

Thus did Dīgha Tapassī, the naked ascetic, make the Blessed One confirm this statement for the third time; and rising from his seat he went to Nigaṇṭha Nātaputta.

Now Nigaṇṭha Nātaputta was seated at that time with many large companies of laymen, including the villagers of Bālaka[48] headed by Upāli. Nigaṇṭha Nātaputta, perceiving Dīgha Tapassī, the naked ascetic, coming in the distance addressed him as follows:

"Well, Tapassī, from where do you come in the middle of the day?"

"I come, Venerable Sir, direct from the presence of the Samaṇa Gotama."[49]

---

nine types of *kammic* consciousness (i.e., five moral states of consciousness pertaining to the form sphere, four pertaining to the formless sphere, and the above twenty).

47. Actions are moral, immoral or amoral. With respect to immoral actions, bodily deeds and verbal deeds such as matricide, causing schism in the Order, etc., are the most heinous. Mental actions, such as ecstasies (*jhānas*) are the most powerful with reference to moral actions.

48. Bālaka was a salt-makers' village. Upāli, the owner of the village, had requested his men to pay a visit to their teacher, Nātaputta—Commentary.

49. *Samaṇa Gotama.* We prefer to retain the word *samaṇa* for which,

"Had you any conversation, then, with the Samaṇa Gotama?"

"Indeed, Venerable Sir, I had some conversation with the Samaṇa Gotama."

"Well, Tapassī, what was the trend of the conversation you had with the Samaṇa Gotama?"

Thereupon Dīgha Tapassī, the naked ascetic, told Nigaṇṭha Nātaputta everything, the exact conversation he had with the Blessed One.

When he had finished, Nātaputta said to him:

"Excellent, excellent, Tapassī! As by a learned disciple who knows the doctrine of his teacher perfectly, even so by Dīgha Tapassī, the naked ascetic, was it explained to the Samaṇa Gotama. Of what avail is the insignificant[50] mental offence when compared with the gross bodily offence? Hence, bodily offence is the most heinous in doing and perpetrating evil deeds; verbal offence and mental offence are not so (heinous)."

Thereupon Upāli, the householder, addressed Nigaṇṭha Nātaputta as follows:

"Excellent, excellent, Venerable Sir, [on the part of] Dīgha Tapassī! As by a learned disciple has it been expounded to the Samaṇa Gotama, by the Venerable Sir Tapassī, that bodily offence is the most heinous, whereas verbal offence and mental offence are not so (heinous).

"Well, Venerable Sir, I shall go and refute the Samaṇa Gotama on this matter. If the Samaṇa Gotama should affirm likewise to me as he was made to affirm by the Venerable Tapassī, then, just as a strong man would seize a long-haired ram by its fleece and pull it along, draw it towards him and drag it hither and thither, even so will I pull up, draw towards me and drag the Samaṇa Gotama hither and thither in the debate. Or, just as a sturdy distillery-man would fling a huge distillery strainer into a deep vat and holding

---

unless we create such a word as 'calmist,' there is no English equivalent (the restricted meaning allowed to "pacifist" renders it unsuitable). *Samaṇa* is usually rendered "ascetic" or "recluse". Neither fits the case of the Buddha and members of his order. "Ascetic" implies severe abstinence and austerity and "recluse" involves isolated seclusion. Neither word can be applied to the Buddha, who taught and trod the Middle Path, rejecting asceticism just as much as self-indulgence, and was always accessible to all men.

50. *Chavo* = *lāmaka*—low, mean.—Commentary. Also: dead, non-effective.

the rim pull it up, draw it towards him and drag it hither and thither ... or, just as a strong distillery labourer would grip the sieve by the rim and turn it over, turn it back and shake it to and fro ... or, just as an elephant of sixty years plunges into a deep lake and plays a kind of game called 'the washing of hemp,'[51] even so will I sport, as it were, with the Samaṇa Gotama. Well, Venerable Sir, I shall go and refute the Samaṇa Gotama on this matter."

"Go, householder, and refute the Samaṇa Gotama on this matter; for either I or Dīgha Tapassī, the naked ascetic, or you should refute the Samaṇa Gotama."

When he had spoken thus, Dīgha Tapassī, the naked ascetic, addressed Nigaṇṭha Nātaputta as follows:

"Really, Venerable Sir, it does not please me that Upāli, the householder, should engage the Samaṇa Gotama in debate; for the Samaṇa Gotama, Venerable Sir, is a magician; he knows an enticing spell by which he lures the disciples of other religions."

"It is absolutely impossible,[52] Tapassī; it can never happen that Upāli, the householder, should become a disciple of the Samaṇa Gotama; but there is certainly a possibility of this—that the Samaṇa Gotama might become a disciple of Upāli, the householder! Go, householder, and refute the Samaṇa Gotama on this matter; for Dīgha Tapassī, the naked ascetic, or you or I should refute the Samaṇa Gotama."

For a second and a third time did Dīgha Tapassī, the naked ascetic, address Nigaṇṭha Nātaputta thus:

"Really, Venerable Sir, it does not please me that Upāli should engage the Samaṇa Gotama in debate. The Samaṇa Gotama lures the disciples of the other religions."

"It is absolutely impossible, Tapassī, (that Upāli should be

51. That is the elephant playfully splashes the water right and left with his trunk, reminding one of the beating and combing of hemp.

52. Nigaṇṭha Nātaputta had not yet met the Buddha, and was consequently in ignorance of the Buddha's personality and the sublimity of his Teachings. Dīgha Tapassi on the other hand, used to frequent the Buddha's monastery and discuss the Dhamma. He was fully aware that Upāli would be impressed by the personality of the Buddha and would most probably become a convert to his Teaching. The Nigaṇṭhas would thereby lose one of their staunchest supporters—Commentary.

converted). One of us should refute the Samaṇa Gotama."

"Certainly, Venerable Sir," said Upāli, the householder, in response; and rising from his seat he respectfully saluted Nigaṇṭha Nātaputta, passed round him to the right[53] and proceeded to the mango grove of Pāvārika, where the Blessed One was. Approaching the Blessed One, he respectfully saluted[54] him and sat on one side. Thus seated, Upāli, the householder, addressed the Blessed One as follows:

"Venerable Sir, did Dīgha Tapassī, the naked ascetic, come this way?"

"He came this way, householder."

"Had you, Venerable Sir, any conversation with him?"

"Certainly, householder, I had some conversation with him."

"What then, Venerable Sir, was the trend of the conversation you had with him?"

Thereupon the Blessed One told him everything, the exact conversation he had with Dīgha Tapassī, the naked ascetic.

When he had finished, Upāli, the householder, said to the Blessed One:

"Excellent, excellent, Venerable Sir, [on the part of] Dīgha Tapassī! As by a learned disciple who knows the doctrine of his teacher perfectly, even so by Dīgha Tapassī, the naked ascetic, was it explained to the Blessed One. Of what avail is the insignificant mental offence when compared with the gross bodily offence? Hence, bodily offence is the most heinous in doing and perpetrating evil deeds; verbal offence and mental offence are not so (heinous)."

"If you, O householder, holding fast to the truth, would debate, then, we may have a conversation on this matter."

"I, holding fast to the truth, Venerable Sir, will debate. Let us have a talk on this matter."

"What then do you think, householder? Suppose there was a naked ascetic here, afflicted with disease, suffering, seriously ill,

---

53. To present the left shoulder to a superior was considered disrespectful.

54. Some salute the Buddha impressed by the dignity of his appearance, others thinking that he is worthy of salutation as he comes of a noble family. On this occasion Upāli, the staunch follower of an alien teacher, was so impressed by the Buddha's noble bearing that he respectfully saluted him, despite his former intention of deriding him.

who refused cold water[55] and lived on hot water. He, not taking cold water, would die. Now, householder, where does Nigaṇṭha Nātaputta hold that he would be reborn?"

"There are, Venerable Sir, deities known as 'mind-attached'; there is he reborn—and for what reason? Because, Venerable Sir, he dies with mental attachment."

"Householder, householder, think carefully before you reply. The latter does not agree with your former (statement), nor the former with the latter;[56] and these, householder, were the words spoken by you: 'I, holding fast to the truth, Venerable Sir, will debate. Let us have a talk on this matter.'"

"Although, Venerable Sir, the Blessed One speaks thus, nevertheless, Venerable Sir, bodily offence is certainly the most heinous in doing and perpetrating evil deeds; verbal offence and mental offence not being so (heinous)."

"What then do you think, householder? Suppose there was a naked ascetic here restrained with the four kinds of restraint: He is restrained as regards all evil; is devoted to restraint as regards all evil;[57] has shaken off all evil; is pervaded with restraint[58] as regards all evil; he, whilst walking up and down, inflicts destruction upon many tiny creatures. Now, householder, what does Nigaṇṭha

55. As the Nigaṇṭhas believe there is life in water.—Commentary. The Buddhist standpoint is eminently practical. Water itself has no life; but if it contains living beings, it should be filtered before drinking. Bhikkhus always filter their drinking water.

56. The Buddha made Upāli admit that mental offence is the most heinous. The Nigaṇṭha, in the imaginary proposition, is ill with a bilious derangement which requires the use of cold water. Mentally he craves for water, cold water; but fearing to commit either a bodily or a verbal offence he refrains from it, thereby guarding these two doors. But he commits a mental offence and is therefore reborn among the deities known as "mind-attached"—Commentary.

57. The four forms of Nigaṇṭha "restraint" are referred to, by Rhys Davids in *Sacred Books of the Buddhists*, Vol. II, p. 74, but the rendering is inaccurate.

58. The Commentary gives the following four "forms of restraint":

He neither kills, causes to kill, nor consents to killing;

He neither steals, causes to steal, nor consents to stealing;

He neither lies, causes to lie, nor consents to lying;

He neither craves sensual pleasure, nor causes others to crave, nor approves of others craving for such pleasure.

Nātaputta declare is the result of this?"

"Nigaṇṭha Nātaputta, Venerable Sir, declares that what is unintentional is not heinous."

"But, householder, if it is intentional?"

"Then, Venerable Sir, it is heinous."

"In which (offence), O householder, does Nātaputta recognise intention?"[59]

"In mental offence, Venerable Sir."

"Householder, householder, think carefully before you reply. This latter does not agree with your former statement ..."

"Although, Venerable Sir, the Blessed One speaks thus, nevertheless bodily offence is certainly the most heinous."

"What then do you think of this, householder? This (town of) Nālandā has flourished and prospered, has a vast population, and is crowded with men?"

"Yes, Venerable Sir, this (town of) Nālandā, it is true, has flourished and prospered, has a vast population, and is crowded with men."

"And what then do you think, householder? Suppose someone were to come here with uplifted sword and say: 'In one moment—no, in an instant, I will make a shambles—one single mass of flesh, of every living creature in this (town of) Nālandā.'

"Do you think, householder, that it is really possible for that individual in one moment—no, in an instant, to make a shambles—one single mass of flesh, of every living creature in this (town of) Nālandā?"

"Even ten persons, Venerable Sir—no, twenty, thirty, forty, or even fifty persons, will not suffice! Then of what avail is one insignificant person."

"What then do you think, householder? Suppose a Samaṇa or Brahmin, possessed of supernormal psychic powers and mastery of mind, were to come here and say: 'This (town of) Nālandā will I reduce to ashes by one thought of intense hatred.'

"Do you think, householder, that it is really possible for such

---

59. *Cetanā.* Usually rendered "volition," which is better than 'will.' Buddhism recognises no such entity *per se* as "will"; but the exercise of willing, an all-important activity, is considered to be the basis of the perpetuation of sorrow.

a one to reduce this Nālandā to ashes by one thought of intense hatred?"

"Even ten Nālandās—Venerable Sir—no, twenty, thirty, forty, or even fifty Nālandās, is that Samaṇa or Brahmin, possessed of supernormal psychic powers and mastery of mind, able to reduce to ashes by one thought of intense hatred! What, then, does one insignificant Nālandā avail?"

"Householder, householder, think carefully before you reply. This does not agree with your earlier views."

"Nevertheless, Venerable Sir, bodily offence is the most heinous; verbal and mental offence not being so (heinous)."

"What then do you think of this, householder? You have heard of the forests—Daṇḍaka, Kālinga, Mejjha and Mātaṅga—and how they became forests?"

"Yes, Venerable Sir, I have heard of them, and of how they became forests."

"And what do you think (of them), householder? What have you heard? By what means did they become forests?"

"This is what I have heard, Venerable Sir: It was by a mental act of intense hatred of the ascetics[60] that they became forests!"

"Householder, householder, think carefully before you reply. ... The latter does not agree with your former (statement), nor the former with the latter; and verily these, householder, were the words spoken by you: 'I, holding fast to the truth, Venerable Sir, will debate. Let us have a talk on this matter.'"

"With the very first illustration, Venerable Sir, I was satisfied and delighted with the Blessed One. Nevertheless, as I wished to hear the Blessed One's beautiful expositions of these problems, I thought of contradicting the Blessed One.

"Excellent, Venerable Sir, excellent! It is, Venerable Sir, as if a man were to set upright that which was overturned, or were to reveal that which was hidden, or were to point the way to one who had gone astray, or were to hold a lamp amidst the darkness, so that those who have eyes may see.

---

60. *Isinaṃ manopadosena.* The Commentary says that the gods, annoyed at maltreatment of the sages who dwelt in these once populous sites, destroyed the cities there so utterly that only a waste remained which, later, became forests. But popular belief was that they were destroyed by the ascetics themselves.

"Even so has the doctrine been expounded in various ways by the Blessed One.

"I, too, Venerable Sir, take refuge in the Buddha, the Doctrine and the Order. May the Blessed One receive me as a follower, as one who has taken refuge from this very day to life's end."

"Householder, make a thorough investigation! It is good for a distinguished man like you to (first) make a thorough investigation."

"Venerable Sir, I am still more satisfied and delighted with the Blessed One because he cautions me thus: 'Householder, make a thorough investigation! It is well for a distinguished man like you to (first) make a thorough investigation.' For, Venerable Sir, other religious bodies having acquired me as a disciple, would carry banners round the whole of Nālandā, saying, 'Upāli, the householder, has become a disciple of ours!' The Blessed One, on the contrary, admonishes me to (first) make a thorough investigation. For the second time, Venerable Sir, I take refuge in the Buddha, the Doctrine and the Order."

"For a long time now, householder, your family has been like a fountain to the naked ascetics. Hence, you must bear in mind that alms should be given to those who come."

"Such words, Venerable Sir, make me still more satisfied and delighted with the Blessed One.

"I have heard, Venerable Sir, that the Samaṇa Gotama speaks thus: 'To me alone should alms be given, not to others; to my disciples alone should alms be given, not to the disciples of others. Alms given to me alone is productive of much fruit, not so the alms given to others; alms given to my disciples alone is productive of much fruit, not so the alms given to the disciples of others.'

"But, on the contrary, the Blessed One advises me to bestow alms on the naked ascetics also! Well, Venerable Sir, we shall know when that is suitable.

"For the third time, Venerable Sir, I take refuge in the Buddha, the Doctrine, and the Order.

"May the Blessed One receive me as a follower, as one who has taken refuge from this very day to life's end."

Then the Blessed One discoursed to him a graduated sermon,[61] that is to say, he spoke on the subjects of liberality, virtue, the heavens; on the evil consequences, the vanity and the depravity of sensual pleasures; and on the advantages of renunciation.[62]

When the Blessed One perceived that the mind of Upāli, the householder, was prepared, pliant, free from obstacles, elevated and lucid,[63] then he revealed to him that exalted doctrine[64] of the

---

61. *Ānupubbikathaṃ*—"a graduated discourse." All Buddhas teach in this methodical manner. Although their special message is the Four Noble Truths, they do not propound this advanced teaching until the pupil is clearly ready to appreciate its sublimity. In order to prepare the seeker, the Buddhas commence with exposition and extolling of elementary virtues. Liberality is the foremost virtue to be practised, for it strikes at the root of that deep-seated vice, "Greed," which holds sway over all. Then they explain the importance of morality or regulated clean behaviour, which is the second step on the path of spiritual progress. But no ordinary man is content to do good merely for its own sake. He expects rewards. Therefore the Buddhas next tell him of happier planes, heavenly bliss, only to be obtained as the result of good action performed here and now. This is the only stimulus to virtue that the masses perceive. When the Buddhas know that a seeker is above the average, one wise and brave enough to look deeper, then the trend of the discourse undergoes a profound change. To such a fortunate one, the Buddhas explain the utter vanity of all cosmic pleasure, human and divine. From its unstable complexity come only pain and woe. "All that is, when clung to, fails." Understanding this, at last, the seeker is ripe enough to hear the doctrine of complete renunciation.

62. *Nekkhamma*:—renunciation is five-fold, viz.

1. Ordination (pabbajjā) being the renunciation of household life.
2. The first ecstasy (paṭhama jhāna) being inhibition of the five hindrances.
3. Nibbāna, the renunciation of everything cosmic.
4. Insight (vipassanā), the getting rid of the conceptions of permanence, happiness and soul.
5. The adoption of all moral conditions and opposition to all immoral states.

In this instance the Buddha is referring to the renunciationof sensual pleasures—a variation of the last division.

63. An oft-recurring sequence of technical words used to describe the mind of one who is ready to comprehend the Truth.

64. *Buddhānaṃ sāmukkaṃsikā dhammadesanā*, the teaching particular to Buddhas, i.e., the Four Noble Truths, which a Buddha discovers by himself and

Buddhas, viz. Suffering, its Cause, its Ceasing and the Path.

Just as a clean cloth, free from stain, would take the dye perfectly, even so, to Upāli, the householder, whilst seated in that place, there arose (in him) the spotless, stainless vision of Truth.[65] He knew "Whatsoever has causally arisen must inevitably pass utterly away."[66]

Then Upāli, the householder, having thus, in the Dispensation[67] of the Exalted One seen[68] the Truth;[69] attained to the Truth; comprehended the Truth; penetrated the Truth; overcome doubt;[70] cast off uncertainty;[71] and gained full confidence[72] without dependence on another,[73] said to the Blessed One:

---

understands by self-won knowledge, which he has not in common with others.

65. *Dhamma-cakkhu.* The Vision of Truth. Sometimes this phrase is applied to the First Three Paths, at others times to the Arahant Path only. Here it is applied to the *sotāpatti* Path (first stage of Sainthood)—Commentary.

66. That is, he realised the Truth of Transience (*anicca*).

67. *Satthusāsane.* The word *sāsana* has no closer English equivalent than "dispensation." The Buddha's Sāsana is his system of the highest Truth. Beginning with the cosmic, it soon transcends this and reaches the hypercosmic. Any Buddha's Sāsana includes:

his message,
the guiding rules he promulgates,
the relationship he reveals between bondage and
deliverance,
the Holy Order of Saints and even the wordlings who follow His Path.

68. What follows is another formula describing the first stage of sainthood.

69. That is, the Four Noble Truths.

70. It is only when one attains to the first stage of sainthood that all doubts with respect to the Buddha, Dhamma and Sangha are absolutely discarded. Prior to this attainment one does not possess the "steadfast confidence" (*acala saddhā*) of the saint. Then only is one fully entitled to be" called *sammā diṭṭhika*, a right believer.

71. *Vigatakathaṅkatho,* lit. "He who has cast off saying how, how?" I.e., having shed all indecision and uncertainty with regard to his past, present and future.

72. *Vesārajjapatto,* i.e., free from timidity; having gained personal realisation; wise; skilled.

73. *Aparappaccayo,* i.e., his attainment was absolutely a personal experience, and not the gift of another. Even a Buddha cannot make a thoroughly bad

"Well, Venerable Sir, we must be going now. We have much to do."

"You, householder, are aware of the hour."

Thereupon Upāli, the householder, delighted with the words of the Blessed One, having expressed his gratitude, rose from his seat, saluted the Blessed One respectfully, passed round him to the right, and proceeded to his residence.

Reaching home, he summoned his gatekeeper: "From today, my good gatekeeper, to naked ascetics, male and female, my gates are shut; but wide open are they to bhikkhus and bhikkhunis, male and female lay disciples of the Blessed One. If any naked ascetic comes, you should say to him: 'Halt, Venerable Sir, do not enter. Henceforth Upāli, the householder, having become a disciple of the Samaṇa Gotama, shuts the gate against the naked ascetics, male and female, but open are they to the bhikkhus, the bhikkhunis, and to the male and female lay disciples of the Blessed One. If, Venerable Sir, you are in need of alms, stand just here; they will bring it here to you.'"

"Very good, Venerable Sir," said the gatekeeper, in response to Upāli, the householder.

Now Dīgha Tapassī, the naked ascetic, heard that Upāli, the householder, had become a disciple of the Samaṇa Gotama. So he went to Nigaṇṭha Nātaputta and said:

"I am given to understand Venerable Sir, that Upāli has become a disciple of the Samaṇa Gotama."

"It is absolutely impossible, Tapassī; it can never happen that Upāli, the householder, should become a disciple of the Samaṇa Gotama; but there is certainly a possibility of this—that the Samaṇa Gotama might become a disciple of Upāli, the householder!"

A second and third time did Dīgha Tapassī, the naked ascetic, address Nātaputta thus:

"I am given to understand, Venerable Sir, that Upāli has become a disciple of the Samaṇa Gotama."

"It is absolutely impossible, Tapassī, but the Samaṇa Gotama may have become a disciple of Upāli, the householder!"

"Yet, Venerable Sir, I am going to find out whether Upāli has

---

man good, leaving alone making the gift of sainthood. The Buddhas only "point out the way."

become a disciple of the Samaṇa Gotama or not."

"Go, Tapassī, and find out whether Upāli has become a disciple of the Samaṇa Gotama or not."

Then Dīgha Tapassī proceeded to the residence of Upāli, and the gatekeeper, seeing him coming in the distance, said, "Halt, Venerable Sir, do not enter. Henceforth, Upāli, the householder, having become a disciple of the Samaṇa Gotama, shuts the gate against the naked ascetics, male and female, but open are they to the bhikkhus, the bhikkhunīs and to the male and female lay disciples of the Blessed One. If, Venerable Sir, you are in need of alms, stand just here; they will bring it here to you."

"I am not in need of alms, friend," said he.

Thereupon turning back, he went to Nigaṇṭha Nātaputta and said, "It is only too true, Venerable Sir, that Upāli has become a disciple of the Samaṇa Gotama. I was not heeded by you, Venerable Sir, with regard to my disapproval of his going to refute the Samaṇa Gotama. Undoubtedly, he is enticed from you, Venerable Sir, by the alluring magic of the Samaṇa Gotama."

"It is absolutely impossible, Tapassī, but the Samaṇa Gotama may have become a disciple of Upāli, the householder!"

For a second and a third time did Dīgha Tapassī, the naked ascetic, address Nātaputta thus:

"It is only too true, Venerable Sir, that Upāli has become a disciple of the Samaṇa Gotama. I was not heeded by you, Venerable Sir, with regard to my disapproval of his going to refute the Samaṇa Gotama. Undoubtedly he is enticed from you, Venerable Sir, by the alluring magic of the Samaṇa Gotama."

"It is absolutely impossible, Tapassī, but the Samaṇa Gotama may have become a disciple of Upāli, the householder! Nevertheless, Tapassī, I shall go and find out whether Upāli has become a disciple of the Samaṇa Gotama or not."

So Nigaṇṭha Nātaputta with a large company of naked ascetics proceeded to the residence of Upāli. Seeing him coming in the distance, the door-keeper said:

"Halt, Venerable Sir, do not enter. If you are in need of alms, stand just here; they will bring it here to you."

"Well then, my good gatekeeper, go and inform Upāli that Venerable Sir Nigaṇṭha, the son of Nāta, with a large company of naked ascetics, is standing (in the porch) outside the gates and wishes to see him."

"Very good," replied the gatekeeper, and going to Upāli, the householder, he informed him to that effect.

"In that case, my good gatekeeper, prepare seats in the central vestibule."[74]

"Very good, Venerable Sir," he replied.

Having prepared seats in the central vestibule, he went and informed Upāli, "The seats are arranged, Venerable Sir, in the central vestibule. Now (we can proceed), if you consider it is time for it."

Thereupon Upāli, the householder, went to the central vestibule, and sitting on the highest, finest, greatest and most valuable[75] seat, he said to the gatekeeper:

"Now then, my good gatekeeper, go to Nigaṇṭha Nātaputta and say: 'Venerable Sir, Upāli, the householder, says 'You may enter, Venerable Sir, if you wish.'"

"Very good, Venerable Sir," replied the gatekeeper.

Going to Nātaputta he said: "Venerable Sir, Upāli, the householder, says 'Enter then, Venerable Sir, if you wish'"

So Nigaṇṭha Nātaputta, with the large company of naked ascetics, proceeded to the central vestibule.

Now, on previous occasions, immediately Upāli sees Nigaṇṭha Nātaputta coming in the distance, instantly he goes forward to meet him; and having dusted with his upper garment the highest, finest, greatest, and most valuable seat there, holding (the Nigaṇṭha) lightly (by means of the garment), makes him sit down. But on this occasion, Upāli himself occupied the highest, finest, greatest, and most valuable seat there and spoke thus to Nigaṇṭha:

"There are seats, Venerable Sir, be seated if you wish."

When he spoke thus, Nigaṇṭha said to Upāli, "Are you mad,

---

74. *Majjhimāya dvārasālāya.* Upāli's residence is said to have had seven enclosing walls, each with its gate. This "halt at the mid-gate" would therefore be at the fourth gate, Upāli evidently wishing to meet his late preceptor Nātaputta halfway and no more.

75. Ordinarily, the follower, however great, would take the meanest seat, or remain standing before his spiritual preceptor. Upāli, by taking the best available seat, signifies, in an unmistakable manner, that he has, under the Buddha, attained a higher spiritual level than his former teacher.

or are you stupid, householder! 'I go, Venerable Sir' (you said) 'and I shall refute the Samaṇa Gotama,' but you have returned bound by the great *entanglement* of controversy. It is as if, householder, a gelder were to go and return emasculated himself,[76] or else, as if a person who throws a casting net (for fish) were to go and return with the mesh destroyed. Just so, householder, you went saying that you would refute the Samaṇa Gotama, but you have returned bound by the great entanglement of controversy. Verily, you are caught in the alluring juggling of the Samaṇa Gotama."

"Excellent, Venerable Sir, is the enticing juggling! Beautiful, Venerable Sir, is the enticing magic! If, Venerable Sir, my beloved kinsmen and blood relatives were caught in this alluring magic, long would it conduce to their well-being and happiness. If, Venerable Sir, all the warriors, Brahmins, merchants, menials[77] were caught in this alluring magic long would it conduce to the well-being and happiness of all. If, Venerable Sir, the world, together with the worlds of the Gods, of Māras, and Brahmas, including the communities of Samaṇas and Brahmins, gods and men, were caught in this alluring magic, long would it conduce to their well-being and happiness. Well, then, Venerable Sir, I will give you an illustration, for, in this world, certain intelligent people perceive the meaning of what is said by means of an illustration.

"It happened long ago, Venerable Sir, that a certain decrepit hoary old Brahmin had a very young wife who was about to be confined. Then, Venerable Sir, that young woman said to the Brahmin:

'Go, Brahmin; purchase and bring from the market a young monkey. It will be a plaything for my child.'

"When she spoke thus, Venerable Sir, he said to her, 'Wait, dear, until the advent of your confinement. If, dear, a boy is born to you, I will purchase and bring you from the market a young male monkey, which will be a plaything for him. But, dear, should a girl be born to you, I will purchase and bring you from the market a

76. Nātaputta, says the Commentator, was so overcome by grief over the loss of a prominent supporter that he was unmindful of the coarse language he used.

77. These were the four great castes of those times: the Khattiyas, Brāhmaṇas, Vessas and Suddas.

young female monkey, which will be a plaything for her.'

"For a second time she repeated her request, and he again advised her to wait.

"For a third time she repeated her request.

"Then, Venerable Sir, that Brahmin, moved by the powerful bond of love for that young woman, purchased and brought from the market a young male monkey and said to her, 'I have purchased and brought you, dear, this young male monkey from the market. It will be a plaything for your boy.'

"When he had spoken thus, that young woman said to the Brahmin, 'Take this young monkey, Brahmin, and go to Rattapāṇi, the son of the laundryman, and tell him, "My good Rattapāṇi, I want this young monkey to be dyed the kind of colour known as Golden Perfume[78] to be pounded and beaten repeatedly (in the dye), and smoothed[79] back and front."'

"Then, Venerable Sir, that Brahmin, moved by the mental bond towards the young woman, took that young monkey to Rattapāṇi, the son of the laundryman, and gave him the necessary instructions.

"Whereupon Rattapāṇi said to the Brahmin, 'This young monkey of yours, Venerable Sir, can certainly be dyed but it cannot be pounded or smoothed'[80]

"In the same way, Venerable Sir, the doctrine of the Nigaṇṭhas can certainly delight foolish people, but not the wise. It cannot be applied or investigated.[81]

"Then, Venerable Sir, that Brahmin, on a subsequent occasion, taking a couple of new cloths, went to Rattapāṇi, the son of the laundryman, and said, 'My good Rattapāni, I want this couple of new cloths dyed the kind of colour known as Golden Pride, to be pounded and turned repeatedly (in the dye) and smoothed back and front.'

78. *Pītāvalepana,* "Golden Perfume," apparently a fashionable dye at that time.

79. That is, ironed.

80. This was intended to show Nātaputta that his teaching does not lead to salvation, whereas the Teaching Upāli has now embraced does, as he has personally experienced—Commentary.

81. "Like searching in the chaff for one grain of rice after threshing," as the Commentator puts it; or, as Shakespeare says, "searching for a grain of wheat in a bushel of chaff."

"Whereupon Rattapāṇi said to the Brahmin, 'Certainly, Venerable Sir, this couple of new cloths of yours can be dyed, and can also be pounded and smoothed.'

"In the same way, Venerable Sir, the doctrine of that exalted, fully enlightened Blessed One can delight the wise only, but not the foolish. It can be applied and investigated."[82]

"The people, householder, together with the king, know that you, Upāli, the householder, are a disciple of Nigaṇṭha Nātaputta. But, as whose disciple shall we (now) regard you, householder?"

Thereupon Upāli rose from his seat, covered one shoulder with his upper garment and raising joined hands in reverence in the direction of the Blessed One, said to Nigaṇṭha Nātaputta, "Well, then, Venerable Sir, hear whose disciple I am—

Of him who is wise, free from ignorance,
who has destroyed obstinacy, victor over conquerors,[83]
who is free from suffering, possesses a perfectly impartial mind,
has developed conduct, possesses excellent wisdom,
has passed beyond insecurity, is without stain,
of that Blessed One am I a disciple.

Of him who has no perplexities, is content,
has rejected worldly pleasures, is sympathetic,
has completed the duties of one who renounces the world,
is born as man, bears his last body,
the Man incomparable and without blemish,
of that Blessed One am I a disciple.

Of him who has no doubts, is skilful,
disciplines others, is an excellent guide,
unrivalled, whose nature is pure,
who is free from uncertainty, an Enlightener,
who has cut off pride and is heroic,

---

82. Wherever one plunges into the Buddha Word, it is deep like the great ocean—Commentary.

83. *Vijitavijayo*, "Conqueror of conquerors." Who are the conquerors (*vijaya*)? They are: Māra whose name is Death; Māra the Passions; and Māra the Deva Tempter. These are called "conquerors" because they have conquered, are conquering and shall ever conquer the worldling. The Buddha is "Victor over conquerors" because these conquerors were vanquished by him.—Commentary.

of that Blessed One am I a disciple.

Of him who is supreme, immeasurable,
profound, has attained to wisdom,
establishes security, learned, righteous, restrained,
has overcome passion and is delivered,
of that Blessed One am I a disciple.

Of him who is faultless, abides in seclusion,
has cast off the fetters, is emancipated,
possesses the power of wise discussion, sage,
has done away with his banner (i.e., the fight being over),
subdued and free from obsessions,
of that Blessed One am I a disciple.

Of him who is the Seventh of the Sages,[84]
is not a hypocrite, is possessed of the threefold knowledge,[85]
has attained to supremacy, has washed off impurity,
skilful in the composition of verses, is tranquillised,
has comprehended knowledge, gave alms in the past[86]
and is capable,
of that Blessed One am I a disciple.

Of him who is noble, is developed,
has attained to advantage, mindful, intuitive,
free from like and dislike,
is devoid of craving and has attained mastery,
of that Blessed One am I a disciple.

Of him who has fared well, is absorbed in meditation,
is independent, is pure, is unattached, is to be abandoned,
is secluded, has attained to pre-eminence,
has crossed (the Ocean of Sorrow) and causes others to cross,
of that Blessed One am I a disciple.

Of him who is calm, greatly wise, profoundly wise,
who is devoid of greed, accomplished, exalted,

---

84. *Isi-sattama.* The seven sages are the seven Buddhas reckoned from Vipassī: Vipassī, Sikhī, Vessabhū, Kakusandha, Konāgama, Kassapa and Gotama.

85. Reminiscence of previous births, divine eye, and knowledge as to the extinction of passions.

86. *Purindadassa.* According to Commentary, this term means that the Buddha was the very first who gave the gift of the Dhamma.

unequalled, peerless, is confident and skilful,
of that Blessed One am I a disciple.

Of him who has cut off craving, enlightened,
devoid of fumes (of desire), free from taint,
worthy of personal offerings, powerful,
the Highest of Individuals, incomparable,
worshipful and attained to supreme glory,
of that Blessed One am I a disciple."[87]

"And when, householder, were these accomplishments of the Samaṇa Gotama gathered thus by you?"

"It is as if, Venerable Sir, there were a huge heap of flowers of many kinds and a skilful garland-maker, or garland-maker's apprentice, were to make a beautiful garland of it. In the same way, Venerable Sir, many hundreds are the virtues of the Blessed One. Then, Venerable Sir, who will not extol one who is so worthy of praise?"

Then and there hot blood gushed from the mouth of Nigaṇṭha Nātaputta, who could not endure the homage paid to the Blessed One.

87. For a metrical rendering see *Early Buddhist Poetry*, by I. B. Horner (published by Ānanda Semage, Colombo 11) p. 14.

Buddhism in Sri Lanka

A Short History

By

H. R. Perera

WHEEL PUBLICATION NO. 100

Preface

The present treatise, *Buddhism in Sri Lanka: A Short History,* deals with the history of Buddhism in this island from the time of its introduction in 250 BCE in the reign of King Devānampiyatissa, up to the present time (1966). The work is the outcome of an attempt to revise Dr. W. A. de Silva's monograph entitled "History of Buddhism in Ceylon," appearing in *Buddhistic Studies* of Dr. B. C. Law (Calcutta, 1931). It should be mentioned, with due respect to the great scholar and national leader, that several of the chapters of his monograph have been reproduced here while many have been revised and enlarged. A few new chapters too have been added where it was deemed necessary.

The author's and the publisher's thanks are due to Messrs. Thacker, Spink & Co., Calcutta, the publishers of *Buddhistic Studies*, for their kind permission to make use of Dr. W. A. de Silva's article.

The writer of the present work has made use of a large number of other works, both ancient and modern, in its compilation. The chronicles of Sri Lanka, mainly the *Mahāvaṃsa* and the *Dīpavaṃsa, The History of Ceylon* (University Press), Vol. I, Parts I & II, and the article on "Mahayanism in Ceylon" by Dr. S. Paranavitana, *Early History of Buddhism in Ceylon* by Dr. E. W. Adikaram, *History of Buddhism in Ceylon* by the Ven. W. Rāhula, *The Pali Literature of Ceylon* by Dr. G. P. Malalasekera, *Bauddha Toraturu Prakāsaka Sabhāve Vārtāva* (Sinhalese), the *Buddhist Commission Report* (Sinhalese) and the *Diamond Jubilee Souvenir* of the Maha Bodhi Society of India, should be especially mentioned among them, with gratitude to their authors and editors.

The relevant material from these numerous works has been synthesised to give the reader a basic knowledge of the history of Buddhism in Sri Lanka from the earliest time up to the present. It is hoped that this book will serve this purpose, especially to those who wish to gain this knowledge by reading a single short treatise.

H. R. Perera

Publisher's Note

In accordance with the official change of the island's name in 1972, throughout the text the word "Ceylon" has been changed to "Sri Lanka" or "Lanka," except in a few cases where it was thought necessary or desirable to retain "Ceylon."

Buddhism in Sri Lanka

A Short History

1. State of Sri Lanka before the Introduction of Buddhism

Buddhism was introduced to Sri Lanka in 236 BE (cir. 250 BCE)[1] and became the national religion of the Sinhalese from that date. It is, however, necessary for a proper study of the history of Buddhism in the island to consider the state of the island and its social and political developments and the culture and character of the people immediately preceding this period. This will enable us to get a clear understanding of the manner in which such a far-reaching revolution in the beliefs, manners, customs and character of a people was affected by the introduction of this new religion and the progress in literature, art and culture that has been manifested through its influence.

2. Early Traditions

According to the early chronicles relating the historical traditions of Sri Lanka, a prince named Vijaya and his followers who came from India and landed in Lanka on the day of the Parinibbāna of the Buddha were the first human inhabitants of this island. When they came the island was occupied by "yakkhas" (sprites, demons). "Yakkhas" and "nāgas" are also said to have inhabited Lanka in the time of the Buddha. A legend relating the existence of a great civilization before this time, under a king named Rāvana, is also current, though the early chronicles make no mention of it.

The Vijaya legend of these chronicles is taken by modern historians as a poetic expression of the actual Aryanisation of Sri Lanka in about the sixth century BCE. The term "yakkhas" and "nāgas" may refer to the aborigines who occupied the island before

1. According to the tradition current in Sri Lanka, the date of the Buddha's Parinibbāna is 543 BCE, but most modern historians tend to place it at 486 BCE, which has here been adopted.

their arrival. No traces of an advanced civilization, however, have yet been discovered to support the Rāvana legend. Archaeologists have discovered chert and quartz implements and tools at various sites, believed to have been used by aborigines of Sri Lanka, and they indicate that these people were a primitive tribe who lived by hunting. These aborigines have not left traces of a strong political organisation or an advanced culture. The present Veddas are believed to be their descendants.

3. Colonisation by Prince Vijaya and his Followers

Vijaya and his 700 followers are described in the Lankan chronicles as a set of adventurous young men who, when they were banished from their Indian homeland Lāla (or Lāta), came in search of new land for settlement. Other legends, some of which are even older, relating how the first Aryan inhabitants came to settle down in Lanka, are found in several Pali and Sanskrit works. Most of them show that the settlement of early Aryan settlers is due to the enterprise of the pioneering merchant mariners who came to this island for pearls and precious stones. Historians thus do not lay much reliance on the details of the Vijayan legend but they accept Vijaya as the first traditional ruler of the newcomers—the Sinhalese.

Vijaya, who was a Kshatriya,[2] landed in Lanka, according to the chronicles, on the day of the Parinibbāna of the Buddha. He allied himself with an aboriginal princess named Kuveni and married her and with her influence soon became the master of the country. Later he drove Kuveni away and obtained a princess from Madurā whom he made his queen. Maidens of high birth came from the Pandyan kingdom as wives of his followers.

Vijaya ruled from his settlement Tambappaṇṇi and his ministers founded other settlements like Anurādhagāma, Upatissagāma, Ujjeni, Uruvelā and Vijitapura. Thus the earliest settlements that were founded in the time of King Vijaya were located along the river banks in the northwestern region of Lanka like the Malvatu-oya and the Kalā-oya.

2. A member of the ruling caste in the Indian caste system.

4. Political Development and Social Organisation after Vijaya

Vijaya died after a rule of 38 years. Since he had no son to succeed him, before his death he sent messengers to his brother Sumitta in Sīhapura to come and rule here. Sumitta sent his youngest son Panduvāsudeva, since he himself was king of Sīhapura and was also too old. Panduvāsudeva, Vijaya's nephew, arrived one year after Vijaya's death, during which period the ministers of Vijaya ruled the country. When Panduvāsudeva came he brought with him 32 sons of ministers.

The early chronicles preserve an episode which connects the Sakka family of the Buddha with the sovereignty of Lanka from the time of King Panduvāsudeva. According to this account, Bhaddakaccānā, who also arrived in Lanka with 32 other maidens shortly after Panduvāsudeva arrived, was the daughter of Pandu Sakka, who himself was the son of Amitodana, an uncle of the Buddha.

Panduvāsudeva ruled for 30 years and was succeeded by his eldest son, Abhaya, who ruled for 20 years. Abhaya's successor was Pandukābhaya, the son of his sister Ummādacitta. Pandukābhaya was a great ruler in whose reign Anurādhapura developed into a great city with well-marked boundaries. After a long reign of 70 years, Pandukābhaya was succeeded by his son Mutasiva, who ruled for 60 years. Mutasiva's second son, Devānampiyatissa, succeeded him in 250 BCE, that is, 236 years after the accession of Vijaya.

These 236 years could be reckoned as a separate period in the history of Sri Lanka, for it formed the background for the official introduction of Buddhism, which occurred during the opening years of the next ruler, King Devānampiyatissa. During this period the Aryan colonists founded settlements along the fertile river banks almost throughout the island. They chose the river banks because they were mainly agriculturists. Thus the regions watered by the Malvatu-oya, Kalā-oya, Valave-ganga, Kirindi-oya, Menik-ganga and Kumbukkan-oya, the Kelani-ganga and some regions around the Mahaveli-ganga soon became populated. Anurādhapura became a well-organised city with boundaries marked, lakes dug and hospitals and other buildings constructed.[3]

---

3. See the article on Anurādhapura by D. T. Devendra, in the *Encyclopaedia of Buddhism*, pp. 754–765.

In the south, Mahāgāma (Māgama) became the centre of activity. The majority of the aboriginal inhabitants were absorbed into the new community through intermarriage while a few withdrew to the Malayadesa, the highlands.

5. Pre-Buddhist Religion in Sri Lanka

It is evident from the chronicles relating the early history of Sri Lanka that before the introduction of Buddhism in the reign of King Devānampiyatissa (250–210 BCE) there was no single religion which was widely accepted as the national religion of the country. Nevertheless, there was a wide range of religious beliefs and practises, different from one another, and each individual seems to have freely observed his religion according to his belief.

A noteworthy feature of the pre-Buddhist religion of Sri Lanka is that it was a mixture of the aboriginal cults and the beliefs of the Aryan newcomers.

The worship of yaksas and yaksinis was a widely prevalent aboriginal custom of pre-Buddhist Lanka. King Pandukābhaya, the grandfather of Devānampiyatissa, provided shrines for many of these spirits and also gave them sacrificial offerings annually. Some of these yaksas and yaksinis mentioned by name are Kālavela, Cittarāja, Vessavana, Valavāmukhi and Cittā. Vyādhadeva, Kammāradeva and Pacchimarājini, though not known as yaksas and yaksinis, also belong to the same category of aboriginal spirits. Trees like the banyan and palmyrah were also connected with the cults of these spirits, showing that tree-worship was also prevalent.

Many scholars agree that these yaksas and other non-human beings are none but the spirits of the dead relatives and tribal chiefs who, the people believed, were capable of helping friends and harming enemies. This belief, as is widely known, formed one of the main features of the primitive religion and is extant even today.

Accounts relating the pre-Buddhist history of Sri Lanka also show a considerable influence of the religious trends of India on the society of Lanka. Several Nigaṇṭhas (Jainas) such as Giri, Jotiya and Kumbhaṇḍa lived in the reign of Pandukābhaya and hermitages were constructed for them and other ascetics like ājivakas, brahmins and the wandering mendicant monks. Five hundred families of heretical beliefs also lived near the city of Anurādhapura. The brahmins occupied a high place in society and their religious beliefs were also respected. The worship of Siva too may have been prevalent.

The account in the *Mahāvaṃsa*[4] of the settling of the adherents of various sects by King Pandukābhaya does not specifically mention the presence of any adherents of Buddhism among them. But the work refers to three visits of the Buddha to Sri Lanka, a statement which, though not corroborated by other evidence, has not been disproved. Legendary accounts also claim that two stupas—the Mahiyaṅgana and the Girihandu—were constructed before the introduction of Buddhism. Among the newcomers too there could have been some members who were acquainted with Buddhism, especially as Bhaddakaccānā, who arrived with 32 other maidens in the guise of nuns, was a close relative of the Buddha.

6. Emperor Asoka and Buddhism in India

Buddhism as a form of religious expression gained ascendency in India during this period. Emperor Asoka was crowned, according to the chronicles, in the year 218 of the Buddhist era (i.e., 268 BCE). Like his father, Bindusāra, and grandfather, Candragupta, Asoka was a follower of the brahminical faith at the beginning of his reign. In the early years of his reign he followed an expansionist policy and in the eighth year of his coronation he conquered Kāliṅga, in the course of which 100,000 were slain and 150,000 taken prisoners. But the carnage of the Kāliṅga war caused him much grief and the king was attracted towards the humanistic teachings of Buddhism. According to the Sri Lanka chronicles, it was a young novice named Nigrodha who converted Asoka.

After the conversion of this great emperor Buddhism flourished under his patronage. He inculcated the teachings of the Buddha and set up edicts of morality at numerous places of his vast empire so that his subjects would adhere to them and his successors might follow him. He himself followed those morals and set an example to the others. The king is reputed to have

4. "The Great Chronicle" of Sri Lanka; see Ch. 24.

built 84,000 stupas. The monks were lavishly provided with their requisites.

The king even permitted his son Mahinda and daughter Saṅghamittā to join the Order when they were twenty and eighteen years of age respectively. These two illustrious disciples became noted for their piety, attainments, learning and profound knowledge of the Dhamma.

Vast numbers joined the Order in the reign of Asoka solely to share the benefits showered on it by the king, and such people were not only lax in their conduct, but also held doctrines counter to the teachings of the Buddha.

It was this dissenting element that led to the holding of the Third Buddhist Council under the patronage of King Asoka in order to purify the Buddhist religion (Sāsana). It was at this Council, held by a thousand theras (elders) under the leadership of Moggaliputta Tissa, at Pāṭaliputta, that the Pali Canon of the Theravāda, as it exists today, was finally redacted.

At this Council was also taken the important decision of sending missionaries to different regions to preach Buddhism and establish the Sāsana there. Thus the Thera Moggaliputta Tissa deputed Majjhantika Thera to Kasmīra-Gandhāra, Mahādeva Thera to Mahisamaṇḍala, Rakkhita Thera to Vanavāsi, Yona-Dhammarakkhita Thera to Aparāntaka, Dhammarakkhita Thera to Mahāraṭṭha, Mahārakkhita Thera to Yonaloka, Majjhima Thera to Himavanta, theras Soṇa and Uttara to Suvaṇṇabhūmi, and Mahinda Thera with theras Itthiya, Uttiya, Sambala and Bhaddasāla to Lanka, saying unto the five theras: "Establish ye in the delightful land of Lanka the delightful religion of the Vanquisher."

7. The Mission to Sri Lanka

Mahinda was thirty-two years old when he undertook the mission to Sri Lanka. He had adopted the religious life at the age of twenty, mastered the doctrines and attained the highest spiritual life, i.e., Arahatship. Pondering on the fitting time to come to Lanka, he perceived that Mutasiva, the ruler at that time, was in his old age, and hence it was advisable to tarry until his son became ruler.

In the meantime Mahinda visited his relatives at Dakkhināgiri and his mother at Vedisagiri along with his companions. His mother, Devi, whom Asoka had married while he was yet a prince, was living at Vedisagiri at that time. Having stayed for six months at Dakkhināgiri and a month at Vedisagiri, Mahinda perceived that the right time had come, for the old ruler was dead and his son Devānampiyatissa had become king.

Devānampiyatissa was the second son of Mutasiva. He was a friend of Asoka even before he became king but the two had not seen each other. The first thing that Devānampiyatissa did when he became king was to send envoys to Asoka, bearing costly presents. The envoys, when they returned, brought among other things the following message from Asoka:

> *"Ahaṃ Buddhañca Dhammañca Saṅghañca*
> *saraṇaṃgato upāsakattaṃ vedesiṃ Sākyaputtassa sāsane*
> *tvamp'imāni ratanāni uttamāni naruttama cittaṃ pasādayit-*
> *vāna saddhāya saraṇaṃ bhaja."*

> *"I have taken refuge in the Buddha, his*
> *Doctrine and his Order, I have declared myself*
> *a lay-disciple in the religion of the Sākya son; seek then, O best of men, refuge in these best of gems, converting your mind with believing heart."*

This message of Asoka was conveyed to King Devānampiyatissa in the month of Vesākha and it was the full-moon day of the following month Jeṭṭha (Sinh. Poson) that Mahinda fixed for his arrival in Sri Lanka. Among the companions of Mahinda were the theras Itthiya, Uttiya, Sambala and Bhaddasāla, the sāmaṇera Sumana, who was the son of Saṅghamitta, and the lay-disciple Bhanduka, who was the son of a daughter of Devi's sister and had become an *anāgāmi* (once-returner) on hearing a sermon of Mahinda preached to Devī.

8. Arrival of Mahinda

Thus on the full-moon day of the month of Jeṭṭha in the year 236 BE (i.e., 250 BCE) Mahinda and his companions, departing from Vedisagiri, rose up in the air and alighted on the Silakūta of the pleasant Missaka hill, presently Mihintale, eight miles east of Anurādhapura. The thera alighted here for he had perceived that he would meet the king there on that day.

The first meeting of the king of Lanka and the Thera Mahinda is graphically described in the chronicles of Sri Lanka. The full-moon day of Jeṭṭha was a day of national festival in Lanka. Men and women were engaged in amusing themselves. The king with a large party of followers went to Mihintale hills on a hunting expedition. There he saw the theras with shaven heads dressed in yellow robes, of dignified mien and distinguished appearance, who faced him and addressed him not as ordinary men addressing a king but as those to whom a king was their inferior. The conversation impressed the king and his immediate surrender to the wisdom and piety displayed by the thera was complete. Mahinda Thera, in reply to the king's inquiry as to who, they were and whence they had come, said:

"Samaṇā mayaṃ Mahārāja Dhammarājassa sāvakā
tav'eva anukampāya Jambudīpā idhāgatā."

"We are the disciples of the Lord of the Dhamma.
In compassion towards you, Mahārāja,
We have come here from India."

When he heard these words of the thera, the king laid aside his bow and arrow, and approaching the thera, exchanged greetings with him and sat down near him. Mahinda then had a conversation with the king, and realising that the king was intelligent enough to comprehend the Dhamma, preached the *Cūlahatthipadopama Sutta.*[5] At the end of the discourse the king and his retinue of forty thousand people embraced the new faith. Having invited the missionaries to the city the king left for his palace. Mahinda spent his first day in Sri Lanka at Mihintale, where he solemnised the first ecclesiastical act by admitting to the Order the lay-follower Bhanduka, who had accompanied him from India.

9. Entry into the Capital

On the invitation of the king, Mahinda and the other theras arrived at Anurādhapura the following day. Going forward to meet the theras, the king respectfully led them into the palace

5. "The Lesser Discourse on the Elephant's Footprint Simile" (MN 27. See Bodhi Leaves B 5).

where he himself served them with dainty food. After the meal Mahinda preached the *Petavatthu*, the *Vimānavatthu* and the *Sacca-saṃyutta* to the royal household.

The people of the city who heard of the theras flocked near the palacegate to see them and the king prepared a hall outside the palace so that the townspeople could see the theras. On this occasion Mahinda preached the *Devadūta Sutta* (Majjhima Nikāya, No. 130).

This hall too was not spacious enough for the vast gathering and seats were prepared for the theras in the Nandana-garden in the royal park, where Mahinda preached the *Bālapaṇḍita Sutta* (Majjhima Nikāya, No. 129).

In the evening the theras expressed their desire to go back to Mihintale. The king, who wished them to stay in his capital, granted to the Sangha the royal park Mahāmegha for their residence. The king himself marked the boundaries by ploughing a furrow. Thus was established the Mahāvihāra, which became the earliest celebrated centre of the Buddhist religion. Having spent twenty-six days in the Mahāmegha Park, the theras returned to Mihintale for the rain-retreat (*vassa*). This was the beginning of the Cetiyagiri-vihāra, another great monastic institution of early Buddhist Sri Lanka.

10. Saṅghamittā and Women Disciples

Many women of Sri Lanka, headed by Queen Anulā, desired to enter the Order of disciples and thus it came about that emissaries led by the king's nephew Ariṭṭha were sent to Emperor Asoka to obtain the help of female disciples to enable the women of Lanka to obtain ordination.

Saṅghamittā, the sister of Mahinda Thera, who had entered the Order and had received ordination, was sent out to Lanka at the request of the king and the people and on the recommendation of Mahinda Thera.

The message sent by Thera Mahinda to Emperor Asoka pleased him very much, for in it he realised that the mission to Lanka had been eminently successful and the king and the people of Lanka had accepted the new doctrine with enthusiasm.

11. Arrival of the Sacred Bo-Tree

Emperor Asoka decided on sending a token of the Great and Enlightened One to the land of Lanka and prepared a branch of the Sacred Bodhi Tree under which the Lord attained enlightenment. He planted the branch in a golden vessel and, when it had taken root, conveyed it to the ship, depositing it in the ship. He also sent a large number of attendants to accompany the tree. The chronicles mention that these were selected from the brahmins, nobles and householders and consisted of 64 families. Saṅghamittā Therī and her attendants embarked on the same ship as well as the ambassadors and messengers who came from Lanka.

The ship sailed from Tāmralipti (Tamluk) and arrived at the port in Lanka in seven days. The port was known as Jambukola and was situated in the north of the island. The king of Lanka on hearing of the arrival of the ship had the road from Jambukola to the capital city of Anurādhapura gaily decorated. He arrived in state and himself took charge of the Sacred Bodhi Tree. This tree was planted in the Mahāmegha garden of Anurādhapura with great festivities and tended with honour and care. Up to this date it flourishes as one of the most sacred objects of veneration and worship for millions of Buddhists.

12. The Firm Establishment of the Sāsana

Ariṭṭha, the king's nephew who had obtained the king's permission to enter the Order of monks on his return from India, did so with five hundred other men and all became Arahants. With the ordination of Anulā and the other women both the bhikkhu-sāsana and the bhikkhunī-sāsana were established in the island. Separate residences for monks and nuns were built by the king. The Thūpārāma-cetiya enshrining the right collarbone and other bodily relics of the Buddha was built, and the Sacred Bodhi Tree was planted for the devotion of the laity. When these acts of religious devotion were accomplished, the king asked Mahinda Thera whether the Sāsana had been firmly established in the island, to which the latter replied that it had only been planted but would take firm root when a person born in Sri Lanka, of Sinhalese parents, studied the Vinaya in Sri Lanka and expounded it in Sri Lanka.

Ariṭṭha Thera had by this time become noted for his piety and his learning and on an appointed day, at a specially constructed preaching hall, in the presence of numerous theras, the king, and the chiefs, Ariṭṭha Thera was invited to give a discourse on the Vinaya in the presence of the Thera Mahā Mahinda. And his exposition was so correct and pleasing that there was great rejoicing as the condition required for the firm establishment of the Sāsana was fulfilled by him.

13. Progress of Buddhism in Lanka

Devānampiyatissa ruled in Sri Lanka for forty years. It was in the first year of his reign that Buddhism was introduced and from that time the king worked for the progress of the new faith with great zeal. Apart from the Mahāvihāra, the Cetiyapabbatavihāra, the Thūparāma and the Sacred Bodhi Tree, he established numerous other monasteries and several Buddhist monuments. The chronicles mention that he built monasteries a yojana from one another. Among these monuments the Isurumuni-vihāra and the Vessagiri-vihāra are important centres of worship to this day. He is also credited with the construction of the Paṭhamaka-cetiya, the Jambukola-vihāra and the Hatthālhaka-vihāra, and the refectory.

Thousands of men and women joined the Order during his reign. The king not only built vihāras for their residence but also provided them with their requisites. It was not only in the capital city that Buddhism spread in his reign but even in distant regions like Jambukola in the north and Kājaragāma and Candanagāma in the south.

The remarkable success of Mahinda's mission and the rapid spread of the religion in a very short time were mainly due to the efforts of Mahinda and the unbounded patronage of King Devānampiyatissa. Apart from them, the people of Lanka too were eminently ripe at this period for receiving and adopting the teachings of the Buddha. The people in the land were prosperous, their wants were few, and these were supplied by the fertile soil. There was prosperous trade, for merchants came from all lands to barter goods; their art was well developed, for in the leisure people enjoyed they were able to build cities and tanks, great and small, and to perform works both of utility and artistic value. Contentment reigned supreme. Where such conditions existed the people were ready to embrace new ideals that had the prospect of helping their culture and elating their thoughts and activities, and as such the new doctrine preached by Mahinda Thera fell on a fertile soil, where it soon rose to its full height. Hundreds of thousands of men and women rose to high spiritual attainments on hearing the new message and thus the Law of the Blessed One was firmly established.

14. The Passing Away of Mahinda and Saṅghamittā

Both Mahinda and Saṅghamittā survived Devānampiyatissa. Mahinda lived to the age of 80 years and Saṅghamittā to the age of 79 years. They spent nearly 48 years in the island. The former died in the eighth year and the latter in the ninth of the reign of King Uttiya, brother and successor of Devānampiyatissa. Uttiya performed their funerals with great honour and built stupas over their relics. The king himself died in the following year, 286 BE, after a reign of ten years.

The hierarchy of the disciples was continued in pupilary succession. Ariṭṭha Thera succeeded Mahinda Thera; he was in turn succeeded by Isidatta, Kālasumana, Dīghanāma and Dīghasumana.

15. Invasion of Tamils and Restoration of the Sāsana by King Duṭṭhagāmaṇi

Twenty years after the death of Uttiya foreign usurpers from South India seized Anurādhapura. Two of them, Sena and Guttika, reigned together for twenty-two years and another Tamil usurper, Elāra, reigned for forty-four years. The lack of interest of these Tamil rulers in the Buddhist faith and the vandalism of their supporters evidently retarded the progress of the religion. Furthermore, the Sinhalese rulers were not free to work for the religion during these periods of political unrest. Nevertheless, the people held strongly to their new religion and showed no signs of laxity.

It was a young prince from Māgama of the southeastern principality of Ruhuna who restored the lost glory of the Sinhalese and their religion. He was Abhaya, known to posterity by a nickname which means "disobedient," Duṭṭhagāmaṇi. He was a descendant of

Mahānāga, who had established himself at Māgama when his older brother Devānampiyatissa was ruling at Anurādhapura. Kākavaṇṇa Tissa and Vihāramahādevī were his parents.

After a thorough preparation for war Duṭṭhagāmaṇi defeated and killed Elāra in battle and became the ruler of Anurādhapura. Thus the sovereignty of the Sinhalese rulers of Anurādhapura was once more established.

Duṭṭhagāmaṇi reigned for twenty-four years. The advancement of the Buddhist religion was his main concern. The Ruvanveli-sāya, the most celebrated stupa in Sri Lanka, was his greatest work. The magnificent edifice of nine storeys and nine hundred chambers, called the Lohapāsāda, "the Brazen Palace," was constructed by him for the use of the monks. Mirisaveti-dāgaba was another of his works.

Duṭṭhagāmaṇi was not only a supporter of Buddhism but was also a zealous follower himself. Many episodes in the Pali commentaries depict him as a pious monarch. Under his patronage there flourished several learned monks during his reign.

16. Social and Cultural Development due to Buddhism

It is well to find out the social and cultural development of the Sinhalese during the two centuries following their acceptance of the Buddhist religion. We have many incidents and stories in the Sri Lanka chronicles from which a definite idea regarding these conditions can be inferred. For instance, the *Rasavāhinī*, a Pali work composed in the thirteenth century of the Christian era, contains over a hundred stories of the life of the people during this early period. According to these stories, among the Sinhalese there do not appear to have been any caste divisions. Brahmins are mentioned as living apart in their own villages, and they were more or less counted as foreign to the Sinhalese. The members of the royal families were held in a class by themselves, and those of such families who aspired to the kingdom had to marry a member of a royal family or at least from a Brahmin family. The rest of the people were *grihapatis* (householders with settled abodes).

The Caṇḍālas (despised) were those without a fixed abode; they were despised on account of being tramps and vagrants with no fixed residence. In some cases the word Caṇḍāla was used in a self-deprecatory manner in order to indicate unworthiness. There is the instance of Prince Sāli, son of King Duṭṭhagāmaṇi, who fell in love with a village artisan's daughter, Devī (Asokamālā). In addressing the prince she said that she was a Caṇḍāli as she did not belong to a family into which a member of the royal family was allowed to marry. The two divisions of people merely appear to be those who had a fixed abode and those who had no fixed abode. There were at this time no special caste divisions for trades or occupations, for a householder or members of a family were, in general, expected to engage themselves in one of the three occupations, as traders, as artisans or as cultivators.

Prince Dīghābhaya, when appointed as governor of Kasātota, required attendants and asked each chief family of a village to send one of its sons for service and sent a messenger to Sangha, the chief of the village. The chief called together his seven sons. The elder six asked him to send the youngest to the king's service as he was idling his time at home without engaging in any work. "We six are engaged in such occupations as trade, industries and cultivation and work hard at our occupations." Again, in another story, the father, a chief of a village, addressing his daughter regarding her husband, tells her that her husband is living in idleness, and like her brothers should engage himself in an occupation such as cultivation, industry and commerce. Thus it appears all trades were common, and the same family engaged in work as artisans, tradesmen and cultivators without distinction.

The religion of the Sinhalese during this period was purely and entirely Buddhist and the stories indicate much practical activity in religious affairs, both in endowment and maintenance of religious institutions and the practice of religious principles. The Orders of bhikkhus and bhikkhunīs flourished during this period; a very large number of men and women entered the religious Orders. Some of the vihāras (monasteries) had thousands residing in them. There were also large numbers who were practising meditation in forests and rock caves. They were well supported by the laity. There were four classes of disciples: the novices (*sāmaṇera*), bhikkhus (fully ordained), theras (elders) and mahātheras (chief elders.) There are no Saṅgharājas (heads of the entire Sangha) mentioned in any of the stories and no interference by kings or ministers in appointment or in giving ranks to the members of the Order. The affairs of the Sangha were managed by the monks themselves under well-established rules of the Vinaya.

There appear to have been large numbers of disciples who had attained to the state of Arahant, i.e., saints who had gained emancipation. In addition practically every man or woman was an *upāsaka* or *upāsikā*, a devotee who regularly performed religious duties. The bhikkhus lived in their vihāras during the rainy season and at other seasons travelled far and wide in the country, visiting villages, other vihāras, and as pilgrims worshipping at shrines. Both laymen and bhikkhus are frequently mentioned as going on pilgrimages to Gayā in India to worship at the sacred Bodhi Tree there. These parties of pilgrims sometimes crossed over to Southern India and walked all the way to Gayā, taking about six months on the journey; sometimes they went by sea and landed at Tāmralipti at the mouth of the Ganges and reached Gayā in half the time.

The canonical scriptures had not been committed to writing at this time though writing was known. The bhikkhus learned the Dhamma and many committed to memory the scriptures or parts of them, thus preserving the tradition by frequent rehearsal. That the art of writing was probably introduced to Sri Lanka only after the introduction of Buddhism seems deducible from the circumstance that, so far, no pre-Buddhist writing, lithic or other, has been identified. The earliest lithic records date back to the time of King Uttiya, successor of Devānampiyatissa.

The bhikkhus were the instructors of the people. This was practically a duty. The Dhamma was expounded individually on every occasion and sermons to congregations were also held from time to time. There is mention of the periodical expounding of the Dhamma at a temple. Each temple in a district sometimes took its turn once a year to preach the *Ariyavaṃsa Sutta*,[6] which was continued each time for seven days; the gatherings on these occasions appear to be very large as in instances mentioned it is said that the crowds were so great that large numbers usually had to stand outside the hall for the whole night and listen to the Dhamma, the audience including bhikkhus and the laity. There is also mention of discourses by lay preachers well versed in the

6. Translated in *With Robes and Bowl* by Bhikkhu Khantipālo (Wheel No. 83/84).

Dhamma employed by the king at halls of preaching.

It is not clearly stated whether brahmins who lived in brahmin villages practised their own religion. Mention is made of sannyāsis or yogis who practised asceticism and sometimes lived in cemeteries scantily clad, with bodies covered with ashes, and as the story says, pretending to be saints while at the same time they led sinful lives. There is no mention of brahmin temples or places of worship.

Women had a very high status in society during this period. Practically in every strata of society the position of women showed no distinction from that of men. They freely took part in every activity of life and their influence is well marked. Their character is depicted in most favourable terms; they were gentle, courteous and good natured, hospitable, tender and intelligent, ever ready to help others, to preserve the honour of their families, devoted to religion and country with untrammelled freedom of action. The position of women is further seen from the fact that monogamy was a definite institution. There is no mention of any other form of marriage. Women had freedom to choose their husbands.

17. Vaṭṭagāmaṇi Abhaya

After the death of King Duṭṭhagāmaṇi his younger brother Saddhātissa ruled for eight years and did a great deal for Buddhism. He was succeeded by his sons Thūlatthana, Lanjatissa, Khallāta Nāga and Vaṭṭagāmaṇi Abhaya, in succession.

The period of Vaṭṭagāmaṇi Abhaya, also known as Valagambahu, is noteworthy in the history of early Buddhism in Sri Lanka. Five months after his accession to the throne, in 103 BCE a brahmin named Tiya (or Tissa) from Ruhuna, South Lanka, revolted against him. At the same time a Tamil army led by seven Tamil chiefs landed at Mahātittha and waged war against the king. The Tamil army vanquished Tiya and defeated Vaṭṭagāmaṇi in battle after which the latter fled and lived in exile for fourteen years.

These fourteen years of Tamil domination were disastrous to the cause of Buddhism, especially because the country was also ravaged by an unprecedented famine during that period. Food was so scarce during that time that even cases of cannibalism are said to have occurred. Many thousands of monks and laymen died of starvation. The monasteries were deserted. The Mahāvihāra of Anurādhapura was completely abandoned and the Mahāthūpa was neglected. Trees grew in the courtyards of vihāras. Twelve thousand Arahants from the Tissamahārāma and another Twelve thousand from the Cittalapabbata-vihāra passed away in the forest due to lack of food. While thousands of monks died in the country, many left the country and went to India.

As a result of the death of most of the learned monks there was even the fear that some parts of the scriptures would be lost. The *Mahāniddesa* of the Sutta Piṭaka, for instance, was on the verge of being lost, for this text was known by only one monk at that time. The monks, in their earnestness to preserve the teachings of the Buddha, subsisted on roots and leaves of trees and recited the scriptures, lest they should forget them. When they had the strength they sat down and recited and when they could no longer keep their bodies erect they lay down and continued their recitation. Thus they preserved the texts and the commentaries until the misery was over.

18. The First Schism

After Vaṭṭagāmaṇi Abhaya regained the throne he demolished the monastery of a Nigantha (Jain ascetic) named Giri for having mocked him when he was fleeing. He built a Buddhist monastery called the Abhayagiri-vihāra over it, which he presented to a monk named Kupikkala Mahā Tissa, who had helped the king in his exile. Later, the monks of the Mahāvihāra imposed the punishment of expulsion on Tissa on the charge of improper contact with lay families. Tissa's pupil Bahalamassu Tissa, who resented the punishment imposed upon his teacher, was likewise expelled from the Mahāvihāra. He then went away with a following of five hundred monks and lived at Abhayagiri-vihāra, refusing to return to the Mahāvihāra. There was thus a group of monks who broke away from the Mahāvihāra and lived separately in the Abhayagiri-vihāra, but they did not yet disagree with each other either in the theory or the practice of the Dhamma.

The actual schism occurred only when monks of the Vajjiputta sect in India came to Sri Lanka and were received at the Abhayagiri, not long after Tissa and his followers occupied that monastery. Tissa and his followers liked the new monks and adopted their doctrines. Thenceforth they came to be known as the Dhammaruci sect, after the name of the great Indian monk who was the teacher of the newcomers to Abhayagiri. There was no official suppression of the new sect, presumably because the king was in their favour, but the Mahāvihāra monks opposed them as unorthodox and heretical. From this time the Abhayagiri existed as a separate sect opposed to the Mahāvihāra.[7]

19. Writing of the Sacred Books

It is stated in the early chronicles that after the acceptance of Buddhism by the people in Lanka and after the formation of a hierarchy of disciples who were Sinhalese, a council was held under Mahinda Thera, where all the leading theras were present and the teachings were recited and authoritatively laid down, as was done in the third convocation held in India under the direction of Emperor Asoka. Theravāda was thus established in Sri Lanka and according to tradition and custom the various parts of the Tipiṭaka were learned by the members of the Order, committed to memory, and preserved as oral traditions. It was seen how, during the famine that broke out in the time of King Vaṭṭagāmaṇi Abhaya, a great strain was put on the continuance of this form of preserving the teachings of the Tipiṭaka. When conditions became normal, the members of the Order considered that they could lose the teachings if any similar calamity or calamities were to occur in the future, and they decided that the time had arrived for committing these teachings to writing so that they might be preserved for future generations. The advent of schisms about this time might also have weighed strongly in favour of this decision.

Thus the members of the Order assembled at the Mahāvihāra at Anurādhapura, took counsel together and with the permission and encouragement of the king a convocation was held. The teachings were recited and scribes were engaged to commit to writing, on palm leaves, the Pali canonical texts (the Tipiṭaka), consisting of Vinaya, Sutta and Abhidhamma, and the Sinhalese commentaries. According to the *Nikāya Sangraha,* a Sinhalese

7. See the articles on Abhayagiri in *Encyclopaedia of Buddhism*, Vol. 1, pp. 21–28.

work of the fourteenth century dealing with the history of the Buddhist order, after the convocation at the Mahāvihāra at Anurādhapura, the selected number of reciters and scribes, 500 in all, went to Alulena (Aluvihāra) cave temple close to Matale, in the central province. There in retirement they completed the work assigned to them and thus for the first time brought out in book form the teachings of the Buddha.

20. The Growth of Dissentient Schools

About two centuries after the formation of the Dhammaruci sect at the Abhayagiri-vihāra, in the days of King Vohārika Tissa (214–236 CE), the monks of the Abhayagiri-vihāra adopted the *Vaitulyavāda*. Thereupon the monks of the Mahāvihāra, having compared it with their own texts, rejected the Vaitulya doctrines as being opposed to traditional doctrine. The king, who had them examined by a learned minister named Kapila, burnt them and suppressed the Vaitulyavādins.

Despite the suppression by Vohārika Tissa, the Vaitulyavādins began to assert themselves again and a few years later, in the time of King Gothābhaya (Meghavaṇṇa Abhaya, 253–266 CE), the Dhammaruci monks of Abhayagiri again accepted Vaitulyavāda. When this happened, about three hundred monks left the Abhayagiri-vihāra to reside at the Dakkhinavihāra, founding a new sect known as Sāgaliya. The king, having assembled the bhikkhus of the five great monasteries of the Theriya Nikāya (Mahāvihāra Nikāya), had the Vaitulya books examined, ordered the books to be destroyed, and expelled the Vaitulya monks. Sixty of them left for the Chola country in South India.

The struggle did not end here, for the adherents of the new doctrine were firmly established in South India and they planned to undermine the Mahāvihāra Nikāya in Sri Lanka. With this object a very learned monk by the name of Saṅghamitra came to Sri Lanka and obtained the post of tutor to the king's two sons. Saṅghamitra gained considerable influence over the young pupil, Mahāsena, and was able to instil into him the new doctrine and make him a follower of his views. When Mahāsena ascended the throne, the opportunity looked forward to by the Vaitulyans came. The new king became a great supporter of his tutor and as such persecuted the Mahāvihāra monks. The king, at the instigation of Saṅghamitra Thera, ordered that no one should give food to the monks of the Mahāvihāra. The Mahāvihāra, as a result, had to be abandoned for nine years. The supporters of Saṅghamitra destroyed the buildings of the Mahāvihāra and carried away their material to construct new buildings for the Abhayagiri-vihāra.

Two persons, a minister and a queen, came forward this time to suppress Vaitulyavāda and save the Mahāvihāra. The minister, Meghavaṇṇābhaya by name, managed to persuade the king to rebuild the Mahāvihāra. The queen caused Saṅghamitra to be put to death and burned the Vaitulya books.

But the king, who was yet favourable towards the followers of Saṅghamitra, built and gave the Jetavana-vihāra to a monk named Tissa. Tissa, who was later charged by the Mahāvihāra monks of a grave offence, was expelled from the Order. The monks of the Sagaliya sect at Dakkhina-vihāra then came to reside in the Jetavana-vihāra. In the reign of Silākāla (522–535) a Vaitulyan book called the *Dharmadhātu,* which was brought to Sri Lanka from India, was kept at the Jetavana-vihāra and venerated. Thus from this time the monks of Jetavana-vihāra too became adherents of Vaitulyavāda.

In the reign of King Aggabodhi I (575–608) a great monk and teacher named Jotipāla, coming from India, so exposed the fallacies of the Vaitulya doctrines that in his day they fell into disrepute and disappeared from Sri Lanka. Since that time the monks of the Abhayagiri and Jetavana vihāras who adhered to Vaitulyan doctrines abandoned their pride and lived in submission to the monks of the Mahāvihāra.

Intercourse with India was so frequent that from time to time other unorthodox doctrines occasionally found favour with certain monks, but these had no marked effect on the general progress or the stability of the Mahāvihāra Nikāya.

For nearly three centuries after the time of Aggabodhi I the chronicles make no mention of the Vaitulyavāda or any other heretical teaching, until in the reign of King Sena I (833–853) a monk of the Vājraparvata Nikāya came to Sri Lanka from India and introduced Vājiriyavāda, converting the king to his doctrines. It was at this time that teachings like the *Ratnakūta-sūtra* were also introduced to Sri Lanka and another heresy called *Nīlapata-darsana* appeared. Sena II (853–887), who succeeded Sena I, managed to suppress these new doctrines. From his time until the Chola conquest in the early eleventh century there is no mention of any heretical sect in Sri Lanka. However, a survey of the religious monuments of that period clearly shows that their teachings survived side by side with the teachings of the Theravāda.

21. The Nature of the New Doctrines

It is opportune here to enquire about the nature of the new doctrines that were mentioned in the previous section as having been introduced into Sri Lanka from time to time since the first century CE. It was the monks of the Vajjiputra sect in India who were the first to introduce a new teaching. The Vajjiputra sect is mentioned in the Sri Lanka chronicles as one of the groups that parted from the Theriya Nikāya after the Second Buddhist Council to form a new sect. They thus evidently held some views different from those of the orthodox teachings. Buddhaghosa mentions in the Pali commentaries that the Vajjiputrakas held the view that there is a persistent personal entity, which is opposed to the accepted theory of *anattā* of the Theravāda teachings. They also believed that Arahants may fall away from their attainment.

These followers of the Vajjiputraka doctrines, residing at the Abhayagiri-vihāra, became adherents of the Vaitulya doctrines about two centuries afterwards, and until the beginning of the seventh century Vaitulyavāda became closely associated with Abhayagiri-vihāra and Jetavana-vihāra.

Like the Vajjiputra sect the Vaitulyavāda is mentioned in the *Nikāya Saṅgraha* as one of the sects that arose in India after the Second Buddhist Council. The *Nikāya Saṅgraha* also states that the Vaitulya Piṭaka was composed by heretic brahmins called Vaitulyas who entered the Order in the time of King Asoka to destroy Buddhism. It has been noticed that the terms Vaitulya, Vaipulya and Vaidalya are commonly used as a designation for Mahāyāna sūtras and hence the term Vaitulyavāda is used in the Sri Lanka chronicles to denote Mahāyānism in general without having a particular Buddhist school in view.

The Vaitulyavādins were considered even more heretical than the Vajjiputrakas. The Pali commentaries mention some of their heretical views. They held the view that the Buddha, having been born in the Tusita heaven, lived there and never came down to earth and it was only a created form that appeared among men. This created form and Ānanda, who learned from it, preached the doctrine. They also held that nothing whatever given to the Order bears fruit, for the Sangha, which in the ultimate sense of the term meant only the path and fruitions, does not accept anything. According to them any human pair may enter upon sexual intercourse by mutual consent. The *Dīpavaṃsa* used the term Vitaṇḍavāda in place of Vaitulyavāda and the Pali commentaries mention them as holding unorthodox views regarding the subtle points in the Dhamma, particularly the Abhidhamma.

Buddhaghosa also refers to the Vaitulyavādins as Mahāsuññavādins. The philosophy of the Mahāyāna as expounded by the great Mahāyāna teacher Nāgārjuna was Sūnyavāda. Thus the fact that the first appearance of Vaitulyavāda in Sri Lanka took place shortly after Nāgārjuna's teachings spread in South India, and that "Vaitulyavāda" is also identified with Sūnyavāda of Nāgārjuna, suggests that it was the teaching of Nāgārjuna that was received by the monks of Abhayagiri-vihāra in the days of Vohārika Tissa.

The book called *Dharmadhātu,* which was brought to Lanka in the reign of Silākāla, is described in the chronicles as a Vaitulyan book. The monks of the Abhayagiri-vihāra and the Jetavana-vihāra are connected with the honours paid to it. It has become evident that a book named *Dharmadhātu* was known and held in high esteem in the tenth century in Lanka and it is quite probable that this book was a Mahāyānistic treatise dealing with the doctrine of the three bodies of the Buddha found among the teachings of the Mahāyāna.

Vājiriyavāda was introduced in the reign of King Sena I by a monk of the Vajraparvata Nikāya. Scholars have pointed out that the Vājiriyavādins are identical with the Vajrayānists, a school of Buddhism which flourished in eastern India about this time and which was an exponent of the worst phases of Tantrism. The *Nikāya Saṅgraha* describes their writings as "secret teachings" and the Gūdhavinaya, i.e., the "secret Vinaya," is one of the compositions of the Vajrayānists.

The *Nikāya Saṅgraha* mentions that about this time the *Ratnakūta-sūtra* was introduced to Sri Lanka. In the Chinese Canon the second of the seven classes of the Mahāyāna-sūtras is called the Ratnakūta. The *Nīlapata-darsana*, which was also introduced about this time, was also an extreme form of Tantrism. Blue has been a colour often favoured by Tantrists.

22. The Sacred Tooth Relic

An important event in the early history of Buddhism in Sri Lanka is the arrival of Buddha's Tooth Relic, the left eye-tooth, from India about 805 BE (311 CE), during the time of King Sirimeghavaṇṇa, son and successor of King Mahāsena. Ever since this Sacred Tooth Relic was received in Sri Lanka it has been a national treasure of great value and a tangible token of the attachment of the Sinhalese to the doctrine of the Blessed Tathāgata. King Sirimeghavaṇṇa held a great festival for the Tooth Relic and decreed that it should be brought every year to the Abhayagiri-vihāra and the same ceremonial should be observed. Today it is enshrined in golden caskets in the Temple of the Tooth Relic (Daladā Māligāwa) in Kandy, which has become the centre of devout pilgrims from all over the island and from Buddhist lands elsewhere.

Ancient customs and ceremonies are scrupulously kept up, offerings are made daily, and in honour of the Sacred Relic an annual festival lasting fourteen days is held in Kandy every year during August. The Perahera, or procession, on these occasions is conducted by the temple authorities with elephants, lights, music and dancers, and is witnessed by thousands of devotees. Chiefs in full ancient attire accompany the procession. Large tracts of land have been set apart as fees for services at this temple and the tenants of these lands have various services apportioned to them. The exhibition of the Sacred Relic itself takes place at rare intervals when tens of thousands of pilgrims find their way to the temple to worship and view the Relic. A medieval chronicle, chiefly of the eastern part of the island, mentions the existence of the right eye-tooth and its enshrinement in Somavati Cetiya in pre-Christian times.

The Sacred Tooth Relic was in the possession of King Guhasiva of Kālinga before it was brought to Sri Lanka. When he was about to be defeated in battle he entrusted it to his daughter Hemamālā. Hemamālā with her husband Dantakumāra brought the Sacred Tooth to Lanka and handed it over to King Sirimeghavaṇṇa at Anurādhapura. From this date the Sacred Tooth Relic became the care of the kings of Lanka, who built special temples for it. During the many vicissitudes of the fortunes of the kings of Lanka, the Sacred Relic was conveyed from place to place, where the fortunes of the king happened to take him. Replicas of the Sacred Tooth were made at various times and were owned by princes claiming the throne. About the year 1071 King Anawrahta (Anuruddha) of Burma sent various presents to King Vijayabāhu I of Sri Lanka and in return received a duplicate of the Sacred Tooth Relic, which he received with great veneration, and a shrine was built for it in Burma.

The Portuguese, in one of their expeditions to Sri Lanka, claim to have captured the Sacred Tooth Relic at Jaffna in the year 1560. Jaffna was an outlying port away from the strongholds of Sinhalese kings and the relic said to have been found by the Portuguese in a temple at Jaffna appeared to be one of the several duplicates which had been made at various times. On this question Prof. Rhys Davids wrote in the *Academy* of September 1874: "Jaffna is an outlying and unimportant part of the Ceylon kingdom, not often under the power of the Sinhalese monarchs, and for some time before this it had been ruled by a petty chieftain; there is no mention of the Tooth brought by Dantakumāra having been taken there—an event so unlikely and of such importance that it would certainly have been mentioned had it really occurred. We have every reason to believe therefore that the very Tooth referred to in the *Dāṭhāvaṃsa* is preserved to this day in Kandy."

In 1815 the British occupied Kandy. As usual the Sacred Tooth Relic had been taken to the mountains for security and one of the earliest tasks of the Agent of the British Government in the Kandyan Province was to arrange for the bringing back of the Relic with due ceremony. The houses and streets of Kandy were decorated, the surface of the streets whitened, and the Relic was brought in a magnificent procession. In 1818 there was a rebellion in the Kandyan provinces and the Sacred Tooth Relic was taken away from Kandy and hidden in a forest. After the suppression of the rebellion the British were able to find the Sacred Tooth Relic and bring it back to Kandy. The Sacred Tooth Relic continued to be in the custody of the British Government till 1853, when by order of the Secretary of State for the Colonies, the charge was given over to the Diyawadana Nilame (lay custodian) and the chief monks of Malwatte and Asgiriya monasteries in Kandy.

23. Buddhaghosa Thera and the Compilation of the Pali Commentaries

The compilation of the Pali Aṭṭhakathā (commentaries) by Buddhaghosa Thera is another important event in the annals of Sri Lanka, which marks the progress of Buddhism. As has already been stated, the Piṭakas or the teachings of the Buddha which were being handed down orally were committed to writing in 397 BE (89 BCE) and the commentaries on these, composed in Sinhalese, were also committed to writing at this time. Since this period much by way of exegetical works in Sinhalese was added from time to time and during the next five hundred years literary activity progressed considerably. By about 896 BE (410 CE), when King Mahānāma reigned at Anurādhapura, the fame of Buddhist literature in Sri Lanka was well recognized throughout India and tradition mentions Sinhalese Buddhist monks visiting India, China and other countries and introducing the literature produced in Sri Lanka. Monks from India and China also visited Anurādhapura during this time to procure Buddhist books.

It was about this time that Buddhaghosa Thera came to Sri Lanka in the reign of King Mahānāma (410–432). Mahānāma succeeded to the throne 79 years after the death of King Sirimeghavaṇṇa, during whose reign the Sacred Tooth Relic was brought to Sri Lanka, and three rulers, namely, Jeṭṭhatissa II, Buddhadāsa and Upatissa I, reigned in between. The story of Buddhaghosa is given in detail both in the *Mahāvaṃsa* and the Sinhalese works composed in later times. According to these sources Buddhaghosa was a brahmin youth who was born in the vicinity of Buddha Gayā and became well known as an exponent of Veda and philosophy. He was such a proficient scholar that in his youth he was able to assert his knowledge among the great scholars of the time. He travelled from place to place, from one seat of learning to another, from one set of teachers to another, triumphantly asserting his knowledge and scholarship.

At a well-known Buddhist monastery at Tamluk, he met Revata Mahāthera, one well versed in the doctrines and philosophy of Buddhism. There he entered into discussions and found not a peer but one superior to him in knowledge and understanding.

This made him join the Order of Buddhist monks as a pupil of Revata Mahāthera. At this vihāra he studied Buddhist philosophy diligently and produced a treatise on Buddhism, he also planned to compose commentaries on the Abhidhamma and the suttas. His teacher at this stage advised him to go to Anurādhapura before undertaking this work, as he said that in Lanka were preserved not only the Tipiṭaka, the teachings of the Buddha himself, but also the Sinhalese commentaries and various expositions of the teachings which were very valuable and of high repute.

Buddhaghosa Thera proceeded to Sri Lanka and stayed at the Mahāpadhānaghara of the Mahāvihāra. He then asked the monks at Anurādhapura for access to books for the compilation of commentaries. The learned theras at Anurādhapura tested his knowledge and ability by setting him a thesis on which he compiled the well-known *Visuddhimagga.* They were so pleased with this work that he was given facilities for his projected work and books were placed at his disposal for the preparation of Pali commentaries.

The old Sinhalese commentaries from which Buddhaghosa drew material for the compilation of his Pali commentaries are occasionally named in his works. The *Mahā* (or *Mūla*) *Aṭṭhakathā* occupied the foremost position among them while the *Mahāpaccāri Aṭṭhakathā* and the *Kurundi Aṭṭhakathā* were also important. These three major works probably contained exegetical material on all the three Piṭakas. Apart from these there were other works like the *Saṅkhepa Aṭṭhakathā*, *Vinaya Aṭṭhakathā*, *Abhidhamma Aṭṭhakathā* and separate commentaries on the four Āgamas or Nikāyas, namely, the *Dīgha Nikāya Aṭṭhakathā*, *Majjhima Nikāya Aṭṭhakathā*, *Saṃyutta Nikāya Aṭṭhakathā* and the *Aṅguttara Nikāya Aṭṭhakathā*. References to numerous other sources like the *Andhaka Aṭṭhakathā*, the Ācariya (or Teachers), and the *Porāṇā* (or Ancient Masters) are also found in Buddhaghosa's works.

Utilising the copious material of these commentaries and other sources, which sometimes contained conflicting views and contradictory assertions, Buddhaghosa compiled his Pali commentaries, including all authoritative decisions, sometimes giving his own views but leaving out unnecessary details and repetitions as well as irrelevant matter. The first of such commentaries was the *Samantapāsādikā* on the Vinaya Piṭaka. The *Kaṅkhāvitaraṇī* on the Pātimokkha of the Vinaya Piṭaka was compiled later. These books were followed by the commentaries on the four Nikāyas, the *Sumaṅgalavilāsinī* on the Dīgha Nikāya, the *Papañcasūdanī* on the Majjhima Nikāya, the *Sāratthappakāsinī* on the Saṃyutta Nikāya and the *Manorathapurāṇī* on the Aṅguttara Nikāya. The *Dhammapadaṭṭhakathā* on the Dhammapada, the *Jātakaṭṭhakathā* on the Jātaka, and the *Paramatthajotikā* on the Khuddaka Nikāya, are also ascribed to him. On the books of the Abhidhamma Piṭaka, Buddhaghosa compiled the *Atthasālinī* on the Dhammasaṅgaṇī, the *Sammohavinodanī* on the Vibhaṅga, and the *Pañcappakaraṇa-ṭṭhakathā* on the other five books.

The voluminous literature which Buddhaghosa produced exists to this day and is the basis for the explanation of many crucial points of Buddhist philosophy which without them would have been unintelligible. His commentaries become all the more important since the old Sinhalese commentaries gradually went out of vogue and were completely lost after the tenth century. Buddhaghosa's activities gave an impetus to the learning of Pali in Sri Lanka, which resulted in the production of many other Pali commentaries and other literary works, and also established the pre-eminence of Sri Lanka as the home of Theravāda Buddhism.

24. The Pali Chronicles

Some time before and after the compilation of the Pali commentaries by Buddhaghosa two important literary works of a different type were produced in Sri Lanka. They are the *Dīpavaṃsa* and the *Mahāvaṃsa*, described in the foregoing pages either as the Sri Lanka chronicles or the Pali chronicles. These two works are the earliest extant literary records giving a continuous history of the activities of the kings of Sri Lanka from pre-Buddhistic times up to the end of the reign of King Mahāsena. Both works are composed in Pali metrical verses.

The *Dīpavaṃsa* is the earlier of these two chronicles. It is not a compilation of one individual author but is the outcome of several previous works to which additions have been made from time to time, taking its present form about the fourth century CE. The chronicle does not name any author but it has been held by some scholars, from the abundant material it contains about nuns, that the *Dīpavaṃsa* is a work compiled and continued by nuns from time to time.

The *Dīpavaṃsa* consists of twenty-two chapters. They contain accounts of the three visits of the Buddha to Sri Lanka, the ancestry of the Buddha, the three Buddhist councils and the different Buddhist schools which arose after the Second Council, the activities of King Asoka, the colonisation of Sri Lanka by Vijaya, his successors, the introduction of Buddhism in the reign of King Devānampiyatissa and the activities of his successors, especially Duṭṭhagāmaṇi, Vaṭṭagāmaṇi and Mahāsena. The narrative ends with the reign of Mahāsena (276–303).

The *Dīpavaṃsa* has obtained its material from different sources of which the *Sīhala Mahāvaṃsa Aṭṭhakathā* (also called the *Sīhala Aṭṭhakathā* or *Porāṇa Aṭṭhakathā* or merely *Aṭṭhakathā*) was pre-eminent. Besides this there were several other sources like the *Uttaravihāra Mahāvaṃsa*, *Vinaya Aṭṭhakathā* and the *Dipavaṃsa Aṭṭhakathā*. By these names were known the records collected and preserved in the Mahāvihāra and the other monasteries.

The *Mahāvaṃsa*, which is the better work in its comprehensiveness, arrangement of facts and high literary standard, was compiled by a thera named Mahānāma either in the late fifth century or the early sixth century CE. It also covers the same period of history and its material is drawn from the same sources as the *Dīpavaṃsa*, but it contains much more additional material presented in a better form.

The *Mahāvaṃsa* contains 37 chapters in all. They deal mainly with the same events as those of the *Dīpavaṃsa*, but there are much longer accounts and greater details of the activities of several kings such as Paṇḍukābhaya and Duṭṭhagāmaṇi and events like the establishment of Buddhism and the rise of new schools.

These two chronicles contain many myths and legends. Yet they are among the primary sources for the reconstruction of the early history of Sri Lanka for they contain a great deal of historical facts, especially in the narratives dealing with the period after the 2nd century BCE, corroborated by epigraphical, archaeological and other evidence.

The *Mahāvaṃsa* has been continued in later times, at three stages, giving a connected history of the island up to modern times. This continuation of the chronicle, which is in three parts, is called the *Cūḷavaṃsa*. The first part brings the history down to the twelfth century, the second part to the fourteenth century and the third part to modern times.

25. Political Unrest and the Decline of Buddhism

The political situation in Sri Lanka from about the middle of the fifth century BCE until the third quarter of the eleventh century CE was not favourable towards the progress of Buddhism. This period of Sri Lankan history is marked with continuous warfare between the reigning king and his rival claimants or the foreign invaders. Often when the reigning king was defeated in battle he fled to India and came back with a Tamil troop to regain his lost throne, and as a result the Tamils who thus settled down in Sri Lanka from time to time also became an important element, even powerful enough to seize political power for themselves.

Such a political situation evidently did not give the rulers an opportunity to work for the religion and as a result the community and the monasteries were neglected. Some rulers like Aggabodhi III and Dāthopatissa I even resorted to the evil practice of robbing monasteries of their gold images, precious gems and other valuables which had accumulated there for centuries, for the purpose of financing their military operations when the royal treasury had become empty. Dāṭhopatissa I also removed the gold finial of the Thūpārāma and the gem-studded umbrella of the cetiya. Relic chambers of stūpas were opened and valuable offerings were removed. Their Tamil soldiers were allowed to burn down monastic buildings like the Sacred Tooth Relic Temple and take away the valuables. The Pāṇḍya and the Chola invaders from South India who also attacked Sri Lanka several times during this period ransacked the monasteries and carried away vast treasures. These conditions necessarily worsened when Sri Lanka passed into the hands of the South Indian Cholas in 1017 and remained a part of the Chola empire until 1070.

Amidst this political unrest and the resultant religious decline several events important in the history of Buddhism in Sri Lanka occurred. In the reign of Moggallāna I (495–512) the Sacred Hair Relic of the Buddha was brought to Sri Lanka from India and the king placed it in a crystal casket in an image house and held a great festival. The writing of the *Mahāvaṃsa* by a Mahāvihāra monk is ascribed to the reign of his successor Kumāra Dhātusena (512–520). In the reign of Silākāla (522–535) the Mahāyāna book, the *Dharmadhātu*, was brought to Sri Lanka and in the reign of Aggabodhi I (575–608) the monk Jotipāla defeated the Vaitulyavādins in a public controversy. Apart from these special events several rulers purified the Sāsana and repaired the old and neglected monasteries. They also encouraged the recital of Dhamma.

26. Vijayabāhu I and the Revival of Buddhism

In the year 1070 Vijayabāhu I succeeded in defeating the Cholas and becoming the king of Sri Lanka. Residing at Polonnaruwa, which he made the capital of his kingdom, he turned his mind to the noble task of repairing the damage that had been inflicted upon the national religion by the invaders. The great religious edifices, the pirivenas and the monasteries which were in utter destruction were restored and new ones were built. But the greatest of his tasks was the restoration of ordination of monks. When he found that the five ordained monks required to carry out an ordination ceremony could not be found in the whole island, he sent an embassy to his friend and ally, King Anuruddha (i.e., Anawrahta) of Burma, soliciting his help in restoring the Sāsana in Sri Lanka. King Anuruddha sent a number of eminent theras who re-established the Sāsana in Sri Lanka and instructed a large number of monks in the three Piṭakas and the commentaries. The king also brought about a reconciliation of the three Nikāyas of the Mahāvihāra, Abhayagiri and Jetavana, and restored their ancient monasteries to them. Thousands of laymen joined the Order.

The religious revival inaugurated by King Vijayabāhu led to a great intellectual reawakening and a large number of religious literary works in Pali and Sanskrit were written. King Vijayabāhu also encouraged learned men to come and settle down in Sri Lanka and also induced his courtiers to engage in literary pursuits. These activities suffered temporarily with his death in 1110, but were revived after the accession of Parākramabāhu the Great in 1153.

27. Revival of Buddhism under Parākramabāhu the Great

King Parākramabāhu the Great (1153–1186) ascended the throne after a great struggle with rival claimants and even after his accession he had to suppress many rebellions. Being a great leader of men he was able to restore order and even carry his prowess as a conqueror to foreign lands including South India and Burma. He rebuilt the city of Polonnaruwa. King Parākramabāhu also undertook the restoration of the ancient capital city of Anurādhapura which had been neglected and abandoned after the Cholas had captured and devastated it about a century and a half earlier. The four great stupas were overgrown with trees, and bears and panthers dwelt there. The king restored all the important monuments at Anurādhapura and the entire Mihintale monastery.

But the most important task which the king performed for the establishment of the Sāsana was its purification and the unification of the Sangha. In spite of the activities of King Vijayabāhu I, there were by this time members of Sangha who were unfit to lead the monastic life. Some of the monks are said to have even supported wives and children. With a learned thera named Mahā Kassapa of Udumbaragiri Vihāra (Dimbulāgala near Polonnaruwa) at its head, the king convened a Council of the leading monks of the dissentient schools and was convinced that the teachings of the Mahāvihāra were correct and their claims were in keeping with the Dhamma. Consequently with great care and patience, the king made investigations into the members of the schismatic schools. Many of the unworthy monks were persuaded to leave the Order and those who were not open to persuasion were expelled. Some monks were made to return to the status of novices. After that the three fraternities of the Mahāvihāra, the Abhayagiri-vihāra and the Jetavana-vihāra remained united.

Subsequent to this purification of the Sangha the king, with the assistance of the leading monks, proclaimed a code of regulations for the guidance of the bhikkhus. After the proclamation of that code the internal discipline of the Sangha was in the hands of the monks themselves and the king acted only when a necessity arose. The code of regulations enforced by King Parākramabāhu became a royal proclamation. It gave directions for the proper observance of the Vinaya rules and dealt with the procedure that should be followed by his subjects who had become or who wished to become lay pupils, novices and subsequently ordained monks. The king also caused this proclamation to be engraved on the rock surface of the Uttarārāma, presently known as Gal-vihāra, which exists to this day. It is now known as *Polonnaru-katikāvata* or the *Parākramabāhu-katikāvata*.

The great interest taken by the king in the affairs of the religion coupled with internal peace and prosperity brought about a revival of Buddhist learning, which created a rich literature during this period.

28. Compilation of Religious Treatises

It has been mentioned earlier that Buddhaghosa Thera compiled the Pali commentaries to many of the texts of the Tipiṭaka in the early part of the fifth century. Buddhaghosa was, however, not able to compile commentaries to all the books of the Tipiṭaka due perhaps to the fact that the illness of his teacher, Revata, in India caused him to leave Sri Lanka before he finished the entire work. Fortunately, there were several other scholars who took up the work left undone by Buddhaghosa, and in the succeeding years they compiled commentaries to the rest of the texts of the Pali Canon.

Thus the commentator Dhammapāla Thera compiled the commentaries to the Udāna, Itivuttaka, Vimānavatthu, Petavatthu, Theragāthā, Therīgāthā and Cariyāpiṭaka of the Khuddaka Nikāya; all these commentaries are known by the name *Paramatthadīpanī.* Upasena Thera compiled the *Saddhammappajjotikā* on the Niddesa. Mahānāma Thera compiled the *Saddhammappakāsinī* on the Paṭisambhidāmagga, and Buddhadatta Thera compiled the *Madhuratthavilāsinī* on the Buddhavaṃsa. The author of the *Visuddhajanavilāsinī*, which is the commentary on the Apadāna, is not known. Of these commentators Buddhadatta was a contemporary of Buddhaghosa; Upasena and Mahānāma flourished about the latter part of the sixth century, and Dhammapāla about the latter part of the tenth century.

The political disturbances from the time of King Dhātusena until the reign of Vijayabāhu I greatly hampered literary activities and as a result only a few religious works were composed during this period. About the end of the tenth century, a thera named

Khema wrote an expository work on the Abhidhamma, called the *Paramatthadīpanī.* To the same period belongs also the Pali *Mahābodhivaṃsa,* which gives primarily the history of the Sacred Bodhi Tree at Anurādhapura and the ceremonies connected with it. A poem entitled *Anāgatavaṃsa* on the future Buddha Metteyya is also ascribed to this period. To the tenth or the early part of the eleventh century belongs a Pali poem of 98 stanzas, called the *Telakaṭāhagāthā,* in the form of religious exhortations of a great elder named Kalyāniya Thera, who was condemned to be cast into a cauldron of boiling oil.

King Vijayabāhu I, in whose reign occurred a great intellectual reawakening, was himself a great patron of literature and a scholar of high repute. Many Sinhalese works including a Sinhalese translation of the Dhammasaṅgaṇī are attributed to him but not one of them exists today. About this time a monk named Anuruddha composed the *Anuruddhaśataka,* the *Abhidhammatthasaṅgaha,* the *Nāmarūpaparicheda* and the *Paramattha-vinicchaya.* The first is a Buddhist devotional poem of 101 stanzas, in elegant Sanskrit. The second work is a compendium on the teachings of the Abhidhamma and is held in high esteem by all Buddhists of the southern school. The third and fourth are two short works in verse on the Abhidhamma, giving the reader a general idea of the subjects dealt with in the Abhidhamma Piṭaka.

The reign of King Parākramabāhu the Great ushered in another great epoch of literary activity. Three great scholarly monks flourished in his reign, namely, Mahā Kassapa of Dimbulāgala Vihāra, Moggallāna Thera and Sāriputta Thera. Mahā Kassapa was the author of a Sinhalese paraphrase (*sannē*) to the *Samantapāsādikā,* which is now lost. He is also reputed to have written a sub-commentary to the *Abhidhammatthasaṅgaha.* It is probable that he was also the author of several other works such as the *Mohavicchedanī,* which is a treatise on the Abhidhamma, and *Vimativinodanī,* which is a commentary on the Vinaya. Moggallāna, a contemporary of Mahā Kassapa, was the author of the Pali grammar, *Moggallāna-vyākaraṇa.* He is also credited with the authorship of the *Abhidhānappadīpikā,* which is the only ancient Pali dictionary in Sri Lanka.

Sāriputta was the most prominent scholar of the reign of Parākramabāhu the Great. A clever Sanskrit scholar as he was,

Sāriputta compiled two works on Sanskrit grammar. Another work by him, the *Vinayasaṅgaha*, was a summary of the Vinaya Piṭaka. This work was known by several titles and was widely known in Burma. On this work Sāriputta himself wrote a sub-commentary (*ṭīkā*) and a Sinhalese paraphrase. The most comprehensive and therefore important work of Sāriputta is the masterly sub-commentary called the *Sāratthadīpanī*, which he composed on Buddhaghosa's commentary on the Vinaya, the *Samantapāsādikā*. The immense and valuable information it contains shows that his knowledge was extensive and profound even as that of the great commentator Buddhaghosa.

He further wrote a Sinhalese paraphrase to the *Abhidhammatthasaṅgaha* of Anuruddha Thera and this paraphrase is still held in high esteem by modern scholars. Sāriputta is also credited with the authorship of two other *ṭīkās*, the *Sāratthamañjūsā* on the *Manorathapuraṇī* and the *Līnatthappakāsinī* on the *Papañcasūdanī*, which are commentaries on the Aṅguttara and Majjhima Nikāyas, respectively, by Buddhaghosa. To this period also belong the *ṭīkās* on the other three Nikāyas of the Sutta Piṭaka, collectively known as the *Sāratthamañjūsā-ṭīkā*.

It should be mentioned here that the *ṭīkās* named above formed one of the major groups of Pali literature compiled during this period. As described in the *Saddhammasaṅgaha*, a Pali work of the 14th century, Mahā Kassapa and a large congregation of monks who assembled at the Jetavana Vihāra at Polonnaruwa decided to compose exegetical commentaries since the existing sub-commentaries on the old *Aṭṭhakathas* were unintelligible. Acting on this decision they compiled *ṭīkās*, namely, the *Sāratthadīpanī* on the Vinaya Piṭaka, the *Saratthamañjūsā* in four parts on the first four Nikāyas of the Sutta Piṭaka, and the *Paramatthadīpanī* in three parts on the Abhidhamma Piṭaka.

These *ṭīkās* or sub-commentaries were works containing expositions of points in the *Aṭṭhakathas* compiled by Buddhaghosa and other commentators, which needed further elucidation for their correct interpretation. There were *ṭīkās* compiled from time to time subsequent to the compilation of the commentaries, and what the council headed by Mahā Kassapa performed was the bringing of these various *ṭīkās* together and making a synthetic summary of them. Though the *Saddhammasaṅgaha* does not give any prominence to the part played by Sāriputta at this council, it is well known that several *ṭīkās* were compiled either by him or under his supervision.

Several religious works written in Sinhalese also belong to this period. The Sinhalese exegetical works on which the Pali commentaries were based were preserved in the Mahāvihāra as late as the tenth century. Likewise there were the collections of Jātaka stories and the stories connected with the verses of the Dhammapada, in the Sinhalese language. A collection of stories from which the Pali *Rasavāhinī* drew material and a work called the *Sīhalaṭṭhakathā Mahāvaṃsa,* on which the Pali chronicles were based, also existed in Sinhalese. None of these works is now extant. Several Sinhalese religio-literary works which were composed in or about the twelfth century are popular even today. Among them are the *Sasadāvata,* which is a poem on the Sasa Jātaka; the *Muvadevdāvata,* which is a poem on the Makhādeva Jātaka; and the *Kavsilumina,* which is a poem on Kusa Jātaka. Gurulugomi's *Amāvatura* and *Dharmapradīpikāva* and Vidyācakravarti's *Butsaraṇa* are also generally ascribed to the twelfth century.

29. Decline of Buddhism after Parākramabāhu I and Restoration by Parākramabāhu II

After the death of Parākramabāhu the Great there was much internal disturbance in the country caused by rival claimants to the throne and invasions by foreigners. As a result Buddhism was on the decline again. Parākramabāhu's immediate successor, Vijayabāhu II, promoted trade and religious relations between Burma and Sri Lanka but was slain after a year's rule by a usurper. The usurper was, however, slain five days later by Nissaṅkamalla, who thereafter reigned for nine years (1187– 1196). Nissaṅkamalla was a great benefactor of Buddhism. He built several notable religious edifices in Polonnaruwa, his capital. Some of these, like the Ruvanveli-dāgaba (now called Rankot-vehera), the beautiful Vaṭadā-gē, the Sacred Tooth Relic Temple (Haeṭadāge), and the Nissankalatā-maṇḍapa exist to this day. He made occasional tours in his kingdom, visiting places of religious significance like the Sumanakūta (Sri Pāda, or as called by the English, Adam's Peak) and the Dambulu-vihāra. He built alms-houses at several important places and purified the Sāsana by expelling corrupt bhikkhus from the Order.

The period of two decades that followed the death of King Nissaṅkamalla was one of the most disturbed periods in Sri Lanka, during which time occurred several assassinations of rulers and invasions by foreigners. In 1214 a foreigner named Māgha invaded, defeated the Sinhalese ruler and reigned for thirty-six years (1215–1251). His reign was one of the most disastrous for Buddhism, for he plundered the monasteries and made them over to his soldiers to dwell in. The people were persecuted by torture and were forced to adopt a different faith. He also destroyed libraries containing many valuable books. The situation was temporarily saved by Parākramabāhu II, who ruled from Dambadeniya from 1236 while Māgha was still dominating north Lanka. Parākramabāhu II, who was a ruler of great learning, earned for himself the title Kalikāla Sahitya Sarvajña Pandita. He made efforts to restore the Sāsana by bringing over monks from the Chola country in South India and holding a festival to admit monks to the higher ordination. He established several monasteries and pirivenas and encouraged learning. The king also held a great council of monks under the leadership of the great thera Araññaka Medhaṅkara and purified the Sāsana. Subsequently, like Parākramabāhu I, he formulated rules for the proper conduct of the monks, the code of these rules being known by the name Dambadeni Katikāvata. At Palābatgala he constructed a great monastery for the hermit-monks who were full of virtue and were able to undergo strict austerities. Two succeeding kings, Vijayabāhu IV (1270–1272) and Parākramabāhu III (1287–1293), took much interest in maintaining Buddhism and consolidating the efforts of their predecessor.

30. The Literary Revival

The religious revival brought about by Parākramabāhu II continued until about the fifteenth century, though there was not much political stability in the country during that period. The outstanding feature of the period is the compilation of a large number of religio-literary works. Parākramabāhu II himself obtained teachers from India to teach Lankan monks. He persuaded his younger brother Bhuvanekabāhu to become a scholar and be a teacher to many thousands of elders. The king's minister

Devapatirāja was a great patron of learning. To Parākramabāhu II is ascribed the authorship of the Sinhalese translations to the *Visuddhimagga* and the *Vinayavinicchaya,* the Sinhalese poem *Kavsilumiṇa,* the masterpiece of Sinhalese poetry, based on the Kusa Jātaka, and the Sinhalese prose work *Daladāsirita.* In the reign of Parākramabāhu II lived the Thera Dharmakirti, who was the author of the Pali poem *Dāṭhāvaṃsa* and the first part of the *Cūḷavaṃsa.*

The *Thūpavaṃsa* on the erection of stūpas in Lanka, the *Hatthavanagallavihāravaṃsa* on the history of the ancient vihāra at Attanagalla, the *Rasavāhinī* which is a collection of stories about ancient India and Sri Lanka, the *Samantakūta-vaṇṇanā* on the Buddha's visit to Sumanakūṭa (Adam's Peak), the *Kesadhātuvamsa* on the history of the hair-relics of the Buddha, the *Pāramīmahāśataka* on the ten perfections (*parāmitā*), and the *Saddhammasaṅgaha* which gives an account of the history and development of Buddhism in Lanka, are several of the religious works of merit composed in Pali from the time of Parākramabāhu II until the fifteenth century.

A large number of Sinhalese works on religious subjects too belongs to this period. The *Saddharmaratnāvalī,* which narrates the stories of the Pali *Dhammapadaṭṭhakathā* in Sinhalese, the *Pūjavalī* which relates the honour and offerings received by the Buddha, the *Pansiyapanas-jātaka* based on the Pali Jātaka commentary, the Sinhala *Bodhivaṃsa* on the history of the Bodhi Tree, the *Elu-Attanagaluvaṃsa* which is a translation of the Pali work, the *Saddharmālankāra,* based on the Pali *Rasavāhinī,* the *Guttilakāvyaya* based on the Guttila Jātaka, the *Kāvyasekharaya* based on the Sattubhatta Jātaka, the *Buduguṇālankāraya,* which narrates the dispelling of the calamity in Vesāli by the Buddha, and the *Lovaeda-sangarāva,* containing religious instructions for the laity, are the standard works among them.

31. Embassy from Burma to Obtain Ordination

As a result of this religious revival, the reputation of the Sangha in Sri Lanka became so well established that in the year 1476 King Dhammaceti of Burma decided to send twenty-two selected bhikkhus to Lanka to obtain ordination and bring back to Burma the traditions of Lanka. He sent these bhikkhus with numerous presents in charge of two ministers, Citradūta and Rāmadūta. They came in two ships. The first ship with eleven bhikkhus and their attendants, in charge of the minister Citradūta, arrived in Colombo and the other ship in charge of Rāmadūta with eleven bhikkhus and attendants arrived at Weligama on the southern coast of Lanka. These deputations were received with due ceremony and given a cordial reception by King Buvanekabāhu VI (1470–1478), who reigned at Kotte (Jayawardhanapura), six miles from Colombo.

The king of Burma sent the following message to the chief theras of Lanka: "My Lords, I am sending many articles to be offered to the Sacred Tooth Relic, etc., and I request you to make an endeavour to offer these to the Sacred Tooth Relic. May the noble ones obtain facilities for the twenty-two bhikkhus and their pupils and the two ministers, Citradūta and Rāmadūta, who are attending on these bhikkhus to assist them in worshiping, honouring and viewing the Sacred Tooth Relic if they are so fortunate as to get an opportunity to do so; after which may the Noble Ones be pleased with their endeavour to enable the twenty-two bhikkhus and their pupils to be ordained in the community of succession from Mahāvihāra fraternity founded by the great thera Mahinda by selecting such bhikkhus who hold an established high reputation and giving the ordination of Upasampadā in the Sīmā (ordination hall) in the river Kalyāṇi, which has been made sacred by its association with our Great Lord."

The request made by the king of Burma was duly granted, the bhikkhus were ordained in the Sīmā in the Kalyāṇi River. The minister Rāmadūta with twenty bhikkhus and thirty-three pupils, duly ordained, returned to Burma. The other minister, Citradūta, and his party of bhikkhus were shipwrecked and six of these bhikkhus met with their death. The remaining ones reached their country.

32. Establishment of Mahāvihāravaṃsa in Burma

In Burma King Dhammaceti built an ordination hall, known as Kalyāṇi Sīmā, and the bhikkhus ordained there went by the name of Kalyāṇivaṃsa. At a later period ordination of this Nikāya was carried to Siam from Burma. The connection with Burma at this period has an important bearing on the fortunes of Buddhism in Sri Lanka, for through these embassies the books that existed in Lanka were taken to Burma, Siam and Cambodia and the Mahāvihāra Nikāya was established in these countries. This helped Lanka to reobtain the books and the ordination at a subsequent period, when ordination had disappeared in the island and the books were lost.

33. The Arrival of the Portuguese and the Persecution of Buddhism

The political stability that was maintained by Parākramabāhu II and his successors until about the fifteenth century began to weaken by the end of that century. At this time the Sinhalese king who ruled at Kotte was the head of a very small territory. The interior regions of the country were in the hands of several petty chiefs who did not care about the religion or the welfare of the people. The Moors on the other hand controlled the trade of the coastal regions. Economically too the country had sunk to such a very low level that by this time Sri Lanka had become dependent on India even for food.

Such was the condition when the Portuguese, who were engaged in discoveries and conquests in the East and were in pursuit of Eastern trade, landed in Lanka in 1505, when Vīra Parākramabāhu VIII (1484–1508) was ruling at Kotte. The Portuguese promised him military aid against his rivals and great riches from the trade which they proposed to establish. They then gained a foothold in Lanka by erecting a fortress on the rocky beach in Colombo and establishing many trading settlements. Before long the entire coastal region passed into the hands of the Portuguese and the kings of Kotte were entirely at the mercy of their allies. They even made several assaults on the interior of the country in order to become masters of the whole island.

The Portuguese arrived in Colombo in 1505 and, gradually occupying all maritime provinces, Lanka remained in their possession up to 1658. The Lanka chronicles as well as the records of their friendly historians describe them as cruel, inhuman, rapacious, bigoted and savage persecutors of Buddhism in their endeavour to impose their own faith—Roman Catholicism—on the people of Sri Lanka.

A few decades after the arrival of the Portuguese, King Bhuvanekabāhu VI (1534–1551), who ruled at Kotte, sought the assistance of his allies, the Portuguese, to ensure the succession of his grandson Dharmapāla to the throne. For this purpose an ivory image of Dharmapāla was sent to Portugal, where a coronation of the effigy was held by the Portuguese emperor. When the Sinhalese ambassadors returned they were accompanied by a party of Franciscans who, under the direction of the Portuguese emperor and with the permission of the king of Kotte, preached the Christian Gospel in Lanka. Thus for the first time Christian communities were organised in the maritime provinces of Lanka. Dharmapāla, who had become a baptised Christian under the name of Don Juan Dharmapāla, as an expression of thankfulness to the Portuguese gave them a deed of gift (*sannas*) after his accession, transferring to them the Daladā Māligāwa (i.e., the Temple of the Tooth), the temple at Kelaniya and all the temple revenues in the island for the maintenance of the missionary establishments.

Thus there was the necessary assistance given to the Portuguese by the rulers of Kotte to suppress the national religion of the Sinhalese and propagate their own religion—Catholicism. With this support they set about their task. In their conversions they adopted two distinct methods, namely, inducement by offices and other temporal favours, and brutal punishment where inducement failed. People who wished to obtain high offices under them and who wished to earn the goodwill of those in power readily adopted the new faith and took up new Biblical names. Others who hesitated to give up their national faith and showed resistance were brutally punished.

There are lurid accounts of men thrown into rivers to be eaten by crocodiles, babies spitted on the soldiers' pikes and held up before the parents, or crushed between millstones before the eyes of their mothers who later were to be tortured to death. Those who dared to worship in public or wear the yellow robe were put to death. Buddhist monasteries and institutions were destroyed and their treasures looted. Libraries were set on fire. Thus did the period of Portuguese rule become one of the darkest periods of Buddhism in Sri Lanka.

34. Persecution of Buddhism by Rājasiṃha I

The Portuguese were not the only enemies of Buddhism at this period. King Rājasiṃha I (1581–1592), who was the son of Mayādunne, a brother of Bhuvenekabāhu VI, ruled from Sitawaka when the Portuguese were holding power at Kotte. A gallant leader as he was, Rājasiṃha succeeded in gaining the confidence of the Sinhalese who opposed the Portuguese rule and winning several battles against the Portuguese, the battle at Mulleriyāwa being the most famous. But, as the chronicles mention, his popularity was short-lived. The foolish king, in his thirst for power, slew his old father with his own hands. Later, being seized with the fear of his crime, Rājasiṃha sought the advice of the monks for setting himself free from the sin. When the monks explained to him that it was too great a crime to be absolved, the king was provoked to anger.

He then became a follower of the Saivites, in whose advice he took refuge, and became an enemy of Buddhism. The chief Buddhist elder was stoned to death, and many other monks were buried neck-deep in the earth and their heads ploughed off. Some others were put to the sword. The sacred edifices and the monasteries were pulled down, and the sacred books were reduced to ashes. The lands which had been endowed in earlier times to the monastic establishments were taken away and Sri Pāda, the Sacred Footprint of the Buddha on Adam's Peak, was handed over to the Saivites. Those monks who managed to escape from the king's wrath disrobed themselves and fled.

35. Vimala Dharmasuriya's Attempt at Restoring Buddhism

In 1592, the year in which Rājasiṃha died, a Sinhalese ruler, Vimala Dharmasuriya I, ascended the throne of the hill capital, Kandy, and ruled for twelve years. Though he had been educated by the Portuguese and was originally favoured by them, the king soon after his accession turned against them out of his love for the country and the religion.

Vimala Dharmasuriya I was a great patron of Buddhism of that time. After his wars with the Portuguese he set his heart on repairing the damage done by Rājasiṃha. Several Buddhist monuments were restored. Finding that there was hardly a single monk left in the country who was properly ordained, Vimala

Dharmasuriya sent an embassy to the country of Arakan (now part of Burma) to obtain monks to restore ordination in Sri Lanka. The mission was successful; several monks led by the elders Nandicakka and Candavisāla came to Kandy and in the year 1597 an ordination ceremony was held in the Udakukkhepa Sīmā at Getambe, near Kandy, many men of noble families entering the Order on this occasion. The king also built a storeyed pavilion and, bringing back the Sacred Tooth Relic from the Delgamuvihāra where it was hidden, deposited it in the pavilion. The control of Sri Pāda was taken from the Saivites and handed over to the Buddhist monks.

36. Successors of Vimala Dharmasuriya I and the Arrival of the Dutch in Sri Lanka

Vimala Dharmasuriya was succeeded on the throne of Kandy by Senarat, a man zealous in religious works. In his reign the Portuguese invaded Kandy and the king carried away the Sacred Tooth Relic to Mahiyangana for safety. Senarat's son and successor Rājasiṃha II (1634–1687) was a great warrior but was not zealous. In his reign ended the Portuguese rule in the maritime provinces of Lanka, a feat which the king accomplished with the aid of the Dutch in June 1658.

It was as early as 1602 that the Dutch visited the court of Kandy, in the reign of Vimala Dharmasuriya I, seeking an alliance. In 1612 a treaty was agreed upon between the Dutch and King Senarat, the then king of Kandy, and in accordance with this agreement, in 1638 Rājasiṃha II sought Dutch assistance against the Portuguese. From that time the two European nations fought each other until in 1658 the Portuguese were expelled from the country and the Dutch came to occupy those regions which formerly were occupied by the Portuguese. They remained in possession until 1796, in which year they were ousted by the British.

The Dutch, whose religion was Protestant Christianity, followed a policy which was in marked contrast to that of the Portuguese. Extension of commerce was their main concern and since peace was essential to achieve this end, they even endured with subdued humbleness and patience whatever insult and provocation came from the Sinhalese. They even assisted the

Sinhalese in two embassies to Siam which were sent to obtain monks to re-establish higher ordination in Sri Lanka.

The Dutch, however, had an established system of education throughout their territories. The school building was both church and school, the schoolmaster was both teacher and representative of the religion. Services were held regularly at these places; births and marriages were registered according to Christian rites. When the agent of the Church was so disposed, he was able to get those who did not attend church punished for the alleged offence. All civil rights and inheritance depended on a person's church affiliation. No person who was not a Christian could hold even a minor office under government, no person who was not a Christian could get married legally or register the birth of a child.

There was, however, one redeeming feature of this system. The organisation was so extensive that they had to employ Sinhalese as their teachers and agents of religion. The vast majority of these Protestant agents were at heart Buddhists; they were Christians only in the sense of their office. The people themselves followed this plan: they were Buddhists inwardly but were officially Christians, for the purpose of registering their marriages, the births of their children, for holding office, etc. Thus the efforts of the Dutch in the propagation of their religion did not affect Buddhism much. On the other hand the Portuguese, where they had priests and where they had established churches under the direct control of these priests, were able to look after the congregations and gradually established their religion in such centres. Most of them were zealous and earnest in their duties and took a genuine interest in the welfare of their flocks.

37. Vimala Dharmasuriya II and His Successors

When the Dutch were occupying the maritime provinces, several Sinhalese rulers of the Kandyan kingdom made attempts to restore Buddhism. One of them was Vimala Dharmasuriya II (1687–1706), son and successor of Rājasiṃha II. He constructed a three-storied pavilion for the Sacred Tooth Relic. The king also made a pilgrimage to Sumanakūta (Adam's Peak) on foot. Seeing that the state of the Order of monks was unsatisfactory again to such an extent that not more than five ordained monks were found in the whole country, the king sent an embassy to Arakan and obtained monks for an ordination ceremony. With the help of these monks an ordination ceremony was held at Getambe, at the place where a similar ceremony had been held formerly in the reign of Vimala Dharmasuriya I. At this ceremony thirty-three novices were given higher ordination and another one hundred and twenty persons were admitted to the Order.

Vimala Dharmasuriya II was succeeded by his son Sri Viraparākrama Narendrasinha (1706–1739), a just ruler, mindful of the welfare of the religion. He constructed a two-storied building for the Sacred Tooth Relic, provided the monks with their requisites, and induced several members of the laity to enter the Order. However, during his reign many a monk had resorted to scandalous practises.

His successor Sri Vijaya Rājasiṃha (1739–1747), also a pious ruler, induced many a young person to join the Order and also held several religious festivals. He spent money on getting religious books written, caused preaching halls to be constructed at several places, and took measures to educate the people in the doctrine. Discovering that the Order of the Sangha was almost extinct in the island, he sent two missions to Siam, with the help of the Dutch, who lent a ship for the voyage. The first expedition proved disastrous due to shipwreck, and before the second mission returned the king died. Thus his attempt to restore higher ordination failed.

38. The Reign of Kirti Sri Rājasiṃha

Sri Vijaya Rājasiṃha was succeeded by King Kirti Sri Rājasiṃha, whose reign proved to be one of the most inspiring periods for Buddhism in that century. At the time of his accession the Order of monks had sunk to very low levels of degeneracy. There was not a single monk in the whole island who had received the higher ordination. There were plenty of novices (i.e., sāmaṇeras), but apart from a few skilful and pious ones among them the majority were leading a life unbecoming to monks. They set aside the study of Dhamma and Vinaya and resorted to the study of astrology, medicine and devil worship, led scandalous lives and engaged in cultivation of land and in trade. The older sāmaṇeras ordained only the sons of their relatives so that they could obtain the immense wealth which the generations of kings and ministers had dedicated to the service of the Order.

Kirti Sri Rājasiṃha was determined to set right this state of affairs. With the aid of the Dutch, who gave a vessel for the voyage, the king sent an embassy to King Dhammika of Siam and re-established the higher ordination in Sri Lanka. Several hundreds were ordained and education was fostered. The king also proclaimed a code of conduct (*katikāvata*) for the guidance of the monks.

39. Velivita Sri Saranaṅkara

In all these religious activities of King Kirti Sri Rājasiṃha he was inspired and guided by a great personality, a sāmaṇera who was distinguished for his piety, enthusiasm, learning and determination. He was Velivita Pindapātika Sri Saranaṅkara. Born in 1698 at Velivita, a village near Kandy, he became a novice at the age of sixteen as a pupil of an elder sāmaṇera called Sūriyagoda. With great effort and devotion he studied the Pali language and the doctrine, for which purpose he traveled from place to place in search of books and tutors. Later he went about preaching the Dhamma, thus encouraging others to rise up for the welfare of the religion. These activities of Saranaṅkara Sāmaṇera soon made him popular as a teacher of great renown who devoted his life to his own welfare and that of others, a poet, preacher and controversialist.

Apart from his skill as a scholar he was also known for his austere practises. When he went round the country learning or preaching, he depended for his sustenance on the ancient practice of a bhikkhu, called *piṇḍapāta,* gathering his food from house to house in his almsbowl. For this he became known as Piṇḍapātika Saranaṅkara. When King Vimala Dharmasuriya II reigned he was a sāmaṇera, but his sincere devotion had pleased the king so much that he made a gilt casket set with seven hundred gems and presented it to Saranaṅkara Sāmaṇera, with many books. This king also provided the monk with the requisites and induced him to write several literary works.

When King Sri Vijaya Rājasiṃha came to the throne it was at the request of Saranaṅkara Sāmaṇera that the king sent two embassies to Siam. In the reign of King Kirti Sri Rājasiṃha, Saranaṅkara Sāmaṇera offered his fullest cooperation in his activities in the revival of Buddhism and the king depended upon the sāmaṇera for guidance, advice and inspiration. He urged the king to send the embassy to Siam and himself wrote the messages that were taken to the Siamese king and the Saṅgharāja of that country. The king's ministers who constituted the embassy were chosen on his advice and this mission was successful mainly due to his exertions. After the return of the embassy Saranaṅkara Sāmaṇera was given higher ordination and was appointed Saṅgharāja of Sri Lanka, the highest office conferred on a monk.

The activities of Saranaṅkara Thera not only restored the higher ordination and the purity of the Sangha but also brought about a literary revival as a result of the impetus given by him to the study of the Pali language and the Buddha's teachings.

Saranaṅkara Thera himself compiled several important religious works such as the *Muniguṇālankāra,* a Sinhalese poem in praise of the Buddha, the *Sārārtha Saṅgraha,* a treatise on various doctrinal teachings in Buddhism. *Abhisambodhi-alaṅkāra,* a Pali poem in a hundred stanzas on the life of the Buddha from the time of Dipankara up to his enlightenment, the *Madhurārtha Prakāsanī,* which is a Sinhalese commentarial paraphrase to the Pali *Mahābodhivaṃsa,* and the *Rūpamālā,* a work on Pali grammar. Several others who were pupils of Saranaṅkara Thera also composed many literary works. The great monk died in 1778 CE at the age of 81.

The successors of Sri Saranaṅkara Thera are known as belonging to the Syāmopāli Nikāya, now popularly called the Siyam (Syāma) Nikāya. Only those who belonged to what was regarded as the highest caste could obtain higher ordination in that Nikāya. In the year 1799 a sāmaṇera named Ambagahapitiya Kalyāṇavimalatissa, who did not belong to that caste, went to Amarapura in Burma to obtain higher ordination and on his return he established the Amarapura Nikāya in 1803. Subsequently, in 1863 Ambagahawatte Sri Saranaṅkara Thera established the Rāmañña Nikāya. These three Nikāyas exist up to this day, with no doctrinal differences between them.

40. The Arrival of the British and the End of Sinhalese Rule in Sri Lanka

King Kirti Sri Rājasiṃha, whose reign, as was seen above, was one of the most fruitful for the cause of Buddhism, was succeeded by his brother Rājādhi Rājasiṃha. A scholar of Pali, Sanskrit and Sinhalese as he was, the king himself composed the beautiful Sinhalese poem *Asadisa-dā-kava* and worked for the religion by taking necessary steps to preserve the purity of the Sāsana. His nephew, Sri Vikrama Rājasiṃha, was the next and last king of Lanka. This ruler, who was in constant fear of the intrigues of his Adigar Pilima Talawe and his allies, had recourse to intoxicating drinks, hoping thus to forget his sorrows, and tortured all his enemies with appalling cruelty. There was general unrest in the kingdom and these conditions were evidently not conducive to the progress of Buddhism.

It was in 1796, during the reign of Rājādhi Rājasiṃha, that the Dutch, who were defeated in battle, surrendered their territories to the British colony and Sir Frederick North was sent as the first British governor.

Before long North realised that the opportunity would come soon for them to possess the whole island, for Pilima Talawe, the Adigar of King Sri Vikrama Rājasiṃha of Kandy, disclosed his plans to ruin the king to the British governor himself. However, this plan of Pilima Talawe was revealed to the king, and the Adigar was beheaded in 1812. Ehelepola, who became the next Adigar, was detected in an attempt to organise a general rebellion against the king, and as punishment, the king tortured his wife and children cruelly. Subsequently the king punished all whom he suspected and as a result, unrest and disorder became the order of the day.

In these circumstances, Ehelepola appealed to the British for help. In January 1815 a British army marched to the capital city of Kandy and took the Sinhalese king captive. On the 2nd of March 1815, at a solemn assembly of the Kandyan chiefs and the monks, the king was deposed and his dominions were vested in the British Crown. Thus ended the glamour of the Kingdom of Kandy which had withstood the invasions and attacks of the Portuguese and the Dutch and for some time the English. Thus ended too the line of the Buddhist kings of Lanka, who for 2301 years, from the accession of Vijaya in 486 BC, brought glory and fame to their country and religion.

41. The British Attitude towards Buddhism

It was seen in the previous section how the British occupied the low-country of Lanka in 1796 and the Kandyan territories in 1815. These territories remained in their hands until 1948, in which year Sri Lanka regained her independence.

Mention has already been made of the solemn assembly of the 2nd of March 1815 held in Kandy. At this assembly a treaty was signed between the British rulers and the Kandyan chiefs, by which the chiefs handed over the country to the British and the British promised to safeguard Buddhism, declaring its rites and ceremonies sacred and inviolate.

The inclusion of this clause referring to Buddhism in the very treaty by which the chiefs handed over the country to the British is very significant. On the one hand, it indicates how concerned the Sinhalese leaders were about the future of Buddhism even in the hour of their misfortune. On the other hand, the British had obviously considered that its omission would bring disastrous results.

However, the British attitude towards Buddhism soon caused dissatisfaction among the Sinhalese chiefs. The chiefs and the Buddhist monks realised that the British had no desire to respect the clause of the treaty relating to Buddhism, and that they were keen to convert the people to their own faith.

During the early years after the signing of the treaty the British governor took part in the annual ceremonies connected with the Sacred Tooth Relic and appointed the chief theras, as had been done by the Sinhalese kings in former times. This created resentment on the part of the Christian missionaries in Sri Lanka and the Christian authorities in England, and soon both practices were dropped, severing whatever connection they had with Buddhism. From 1847 the bhikkhus were required to elect and appoint their own chiefs and in 1853 the British government handed over the Tooth Relic from their custody to the Diyawadana Nilame and the chief monks of the Malwatte and the Asgiriya monasteries.

While thus violating the treaty of 1815 the British rulers even prohibited the Buddhists from enjoying some of the privileges that were granted to the followers of the Christian faith. Thus, for instance, even as late as 1905 no child could be legally registered without previous baptism by a Christian minister, and the clergy did not solemnise the marriage of unbaptised individuals. Further, only those who adopted the Christian faith were favoured with government employment. This attitude of the British made vast numbers of Buddhists adopt the new faith without any understanding of its teachings. These people saw in Christianity "not only happiness in the world which is to come, but, what was more important to them, the promise of this life as well!"

Some of the British governors in their attempt to disrupt the Buddhist organisation even tried to bring about disunity between the monks and the laity and also to win over some of the leading Buddhist monks to their side. For they realised that the monks were the main obstacle to their conversions and that as long as the monks and the laity remained united their attempts would not meet with great success.

Lastly, the British rulers gave all possible support to the Christian missionaries to carry out their educational and missionary activities. How these missionary bodies attempted the Christianisation of Lanka will be discussed in the next section.

42. The Christian Missionary Activities

From the beginning of the period of British rule several Christian missionary bodies engaged themselves actively in missionary activities in Sri Lanka. The Baptists had already started their activities in 1792. They were followed by the Wesleyan Methodists in 1814, the Americans in 1816, and the Church of England in 1818. These missionary bodies received every encouragement and assistance from the government.

The establishment of missionary schools in various parts of the island was one of the principal undertakings of these missionary bodies. These schools were manned and managed by the missionary societies with the assistance of the British government and were partly financed by public funds. The schools attracted large numbers of Buddhist children because they were the centres where young men were trained for high government offices. Hitherto the temple had been the village school and the monks were the instructors of the village children in secular learning as well as in spiritual wisdom. But under the British government temple education could not provide the learning necessary for government employment. Thus the Buddhist parents who wished to see their children in high government offices willingly sent them to the new missionary schools.

In these schools the children were moulded according to the requirements of the missionary bodies. The authorities did not insist that one should become a Christian before admission, but each student was required to learn the Christian religion and to participate in the morning and evening religious services in the school. They had no opportunity of participating in their own religious observances. Almost every school had its own church. The lessons imparted to these children were arranged with a view to undermining their Buddhist religion. The teaching of the Buddha was criticised and condemned and the Buddhist practises were ridiculed. Buddhism was held up as a religion of the vulgar masses as opposed to the Christianity of civilised people.

This disparagement in course of time naturally had its expected result. People gradually began to give up their national faith for the new faith which they were trained to think of as more refined and cultured. It now became the fashion to adopt the Christian faith and Christian names and customs. Even those who did not embrace Christianity became indifferent to their own religion. When they grew up they did not even mind their conversion to any religion.

The missionaries also did not neglect the education of the girls. Convents were opened up with boarding facilities and in them the girls were brought up and educated with the utmost care until they were married in due time, with the sanction of the Christian guardians.

The following table enumerating the assisted schools in Sri Lanka in 1886 belonging to the different denominations shows the extent of missionary activities in Lanka in the sphere of education:

Number of Assisted Schools in 1886

	English	Bi-lingual	Vernacular	Total
Wesley Miss	18	18	170	206
Rom. Cath.	25	5	175	205
C.M.S.	28	18	178	224
Amer. Miss	8	9	116	133
Baptist	1	5	32	38
Private	7	5	13	25
Hindu	0	0	5	5
Buddhist	0	1	11	12

Apart from the Christianisation carried out through schools these missionary bodies sought conversion by distributing books and pamphlets which criticised and ridiculed the Buddhist religion and sang the praises of Christianity. For this purpose the missionaries themselves studied the doctrines of Buddhism and the Buddhist literature and also the Sinhalese language, thus enabling them to write tracts in Sinhalese attacking the Buddhist religion and extolling the virtues of Christianity. Christian preachers went about from village to village distributing these books and pamphlets and denouncing Buddhism and exhibiting the supremacy and the divine origin of Christianity.

43. Mohottiwatte Guṇānanda Thera and the Buddhist Reawakening

When the Christian missionaries were thus active in towns and villages propagating their gospel and converting the Buddhists to their faith, the Buddhist monks were not able enough to offer much resistance. When the villagers assembled in the temple on Poya (*uposatha*) days, they attempted to refute the arguments of the Christian preachers in the course of their sermons, but this method was not very effective.

It was at this time, about 1860, that a young Buddhist sāmaṇera named Mohottiwatte Guṇānanda appeared on the scene and challenged the Christian missionaries to meet him in open debate. This young novice had obtained his early education in Christian schools and had thus studied the Christian scriptures and was also well versed in the Buddha's teachings. He went from village to village making public speeches and held meetings in several Christian strongholds, often challenging the Christian clergy to face him in open debate. Soon he earned a great reputation for his eloquence and people flocked in thousands to hear him.

The Christian clergy at first took no notice of the challenge of this monk, but later, quite confident of their success, they accepted the challenge. This resulted in three public controversies, one at Udanvita in 1866, another at Gampola in 1871 and the last at Pānadura in 1873.

The Pānadura controversy, which lasted for a week, was the most important of them all. It was the culmination of his efforts and it led to a Buddhist reawakening. The controversy was to take place in the presence of leading Sinhalese Christians and Buddhists. Rules were laid down so that the meeting could be held in a fair manner. The leading English newspaper of the time, *The Ceylon Times,* sent a special representative to report the proceedings. A complete report of all the speeches corrected by the speakers themselves was published in English day by day.

The controversy ended with victory for the Buddhists. The Buddhist orator not only replied effectively to the fallacies of the Christian speakers, but also enlightened them on the principles and tenets of the Buddhist doctrine. When the Christians retired from the debate defeated, the Buddhists were overjoyed. Festivities were held in every temple to mark their triumph and the effigy of Guṇānanda Thera was carried in procession in every village.

The triumph of the Buddhists over their Christian adversaries at the Pānadura controversy flushed into their veins vigour and enthusiasm to work for the recovery of their lost glory.

44. Colonel Olcott and Buddhist Activities

An American scholar named Dr. Peebles, who happened to be in Sri Lanka on a visit about the time of this Pānadura controversy, was so impressed with it that he published its proceedings in book form on his return to America. The attention of Colonel Henry Steele Olcott was first drawn towards Buddhism by this report of the controversy, which he happened to read in a public library in America. Olcott was an American by birth who had spent his early life as a very successful farmer and a colonel of both the army and the navy. At an early age of 43 years in 1875 he gave up all worldly fortunes and together with Madame Blavatsky formed the Theosophical Society for the quest of truth in all religions. Having read the reports of the Pānadura controversy, he realised the importance of the teachings of the Buddha and in 1880 he came over to Lanka along with Madame Blavatsky to gain a first-hand knowledge of Buddhism. When his studies soon convinced him of the teachings of the Buddha, he embraced Buddhism and worked for the uplift of the Buddhists in Lanka.

Olcott showed the Buddhist leaders of Sri Lanka that if Buddhism was to raise its head against the Christian missionary activities, they should open up Buddhist schools to educate their children. Under his guidance and leadership, and with the support of all the leading Buddhist monks, the lay Buddhist leaders in Sri Lanka at that time founded the Buddhist Theosophical Society on 17th June 1880. The primary objects of the society were the establishment of Buddhist schools, and the bringing together of Buddhist workers in a cooperative body without distinction of caste or position for the purpose of promoting the welfare of the Buddhists of Lanka.

At the time of Olcott's arrival there were only three Buddhist schools in Sri Lanka which obtained government grants, one at Dodanduwa, another at Pānadura, and the third at Bandaragama. In 1897, twelve years after the establishment of the society, there were 25 boys' schools, 11 girls' schools, and 10 mixed schools founded by the society. In 1903 there were 174 schools under the management of the society with an attendance of about 30,000 children. In 1940 the number of schools had risen to 429.

Olcott and his supporters went from village to village appealing to the people to donate subscriptions for the maintenance of these schools, and funds were readily forthcoming. Several leading educationists of his day made his educational plans a great success. Mention should be made among them of C. W. Leadbeater, Bowles Daly, F. L. Woodward, A. E. Bultjens and Mrs. M. Museus Higgins. Mrs. Higgins was particularly responsible for the successful education of the Buddhist girls. The leading Buddhist schools of the present day such as Ānanda and Nalanda Colleges in Colombo, Dharmarāja in Kandy, Mahinda in Galle, Dharmasoka in Ambalangoda, Visakha in Bambalapitiya, and Museus in Colombo are outstanding examples of the success of his efforts.

Olcott pointed out to the Sinhalese Buddhist leaders of his time that they should have their own publications to give publicity to Buddhist and national opinion. For this purpose the Buddhist Theosophical Society started the Sinhalese newspaper, *Sarasavisandarasa*, in December 1880, and later its English supplement, *The Buddhist*, now a monthly of the YMBA, Colombo. Colonel Olcott worked hard to win back for the Sinhalese their lost rights. It was as a result of his efforts that the Buddhists of Lanka gained freedom to hold their Buddhist processions and that the full-moon day of Vesak was declared a public holiday. The present Buddhist flag is also a creation of Olcott, which he appealed to the Buddhists to hoist on all important Buddhist occasions. His efforts also resulted in the appointment of Buddhist registrars of marriages.

Of the Pānadura controversy and the consequent arrival of Colonel Olcott, it could justly be said that these two events jointly closed down a dark period in Lankan Buddhism and ushered in a new bright era.

This noble personality who awakened the Sinhalese Buddhists and showed them the path on which they should proceed passed away in 1907 while he was in India.

45. Other Activities of the Buddhist Renaissance Movement

Apart from meeting the Christian opponents in open debate, Mohottivatte Guṇānanda Thera and his companions had planned other devices to counteract the anti-Buddhist propaganda of the Christian missionaries and revive the Buddhist faith in the country. One of these devices was the establishment of a printing press whereby they could reply to the criticisms of the Christians and also publish books for the study of Buddhism.

Thus the first press, controlled by Sinhalese Buddhists, was established in 1862 under the name of Lankopakāra Press. It was a donation by the king of Siam. In the same year Mohottivatte Guṇānanda Thera established the Sarvajña-sāsanābhivurddhi-dāyaka Press at Kotahena, near Colombo. Consequently the Lakrivikirana Press was established in 1863 and the Lankabhinavavisruta Press in 1864.

In the meantime learned monks of the period, with the assistance of lay followers, brought about a revival of Buddhist learning. Pioneers among them were the venerable Hikkaduve Sri Sumaṅgala, who founded the Vidyodaya Pirivena of Maligakanda in Colombo in 1874 and the venerable Ratmalāne Sri Dhammāloka, who founded the Vidyālankara Pirivena of Peliyagoda in Colombo in 1875. In these two great centres of learning a vast number of monks and lay people received education and in a short time the fame of these two pirivenas spread even in foreign countries.

The scholars whom these two centres produced opened up other pirivenas in different parts of the country and also contributed to Buddhist studies by compiling and editing numerous books. It was also about this time that devoted scholars from foreign countries who happened to be in Sri Lanka evinced a great interest in Buddhism, its culture and literature, and created an interest in their kinsmen in the West through their valuable treatises. Turner, Tennant, Childers, Rhys Davids and Geiger were but a few among them.

46. Anāgārika Dharmapāla and the Buddhist Cultural Revival

A different type of revivalist activity was carried out by a group of lay Buddhist leaders just at this time, the foremost of this group being Anāgārika Dharmapāla. The fame of this great personality lies in his successful effort of reforming the Buddhist society in Sri Lanka, which had fallen into a very low moral state, and also in his activities in India for the purpose of reviving Buddhism in that country and for winning back the Buddhist sacred places there for their rightful owners, the Buddhists. We are presently concerned only with his social reformation in Sri Lanka.

Anāgārika Dharmapāla, formerly known as David Hewavitarana, was born in 1864 as the eldest son of a leading businessman in Colombo who had migrated to the capital city from Mātara in south Lanka. The father, mother and the grandfather of the child were devoted Buddhists who were close associates of the venerable Hikkaduve Sri Sumaṅgala Thera. At home the child was thus brought up in a Buddhist environment though he received his education in Christian schools. Those were the days when Mohottiwatte Guṇānanda Thera was engaged in verbal battles against the Christian missionary activities, and young Dharmapāla had not only listened to the orations of the great speaker with much inspiration, but also had become a favourite of the monks by his constant visits to the temple at Kotahena. When Colonel Olcott and Madame Blavatsky arrived in Lanka in 1880, Dharmapāla, then a youth of sixteen years, naturally became a great favourite of the two foreigners through his association with Guṇānanda Thera.

The speeches and activities of Colonel Olcott greatly inspired the young enthusiast. In 1883, consequent upon a brutal assault on a Buddhist procession by a Catholic mob at Kotahena, Dharmapāla left his Catholic school and in the following year became a member of the Buddhist Theosophical Society in Colombo, of which his grandfather was the president. At the age of twenty, Dharmapāla obtained permission from his father to leave home and lead a celibate life as he wished to devote all his time to the welfare of the Sāsana. From that time he stayed at the headquarters of the Buddhist Theosophical Society.

In 1886, when Colonel Olcott returned to Sri Lanka after a short stay abroad and planned to go round the country addressing public gatherings and collecting money for the Buddhist Educational Fund, Anāgārika Dharmapāla joined him as his interpreter. For this purpose he obtained leave from the Education Department where he was working as a junior clerk and subsequently vacated his post in order to dedicate all his life to the good of the religion.

As the interpreter of Colonel Olcott, Dharmapāla gained immense experience as a speaker. He now travelled throughout the country with or without his companion, Olcott.

Those were the days when the Buddhists of Lanka were reluctant to declare themselves Buddhists, for Buddhism was considered to be the faith of the rural masses. It was the fashion at that time to become a Christian, to study English and other allied subjects, to adopt a foreign name and to imitate the dress of the foreigners and their customs and manners. Buddhism and Buddhist culture were subjected to ridicule and were the heritage of villagers in the interior.

Anāgārika Dharmapāla was the foremost among those who rose against this mentality of the Buddhists. Through his public speeches and numerous articles in newspapers and journals he vehemently opposed the habit of imitating foreigners in religion, names and customs. He emphatically pointed out that this tendency to imitate was a clear manifestation of a lack of the primary element of self-esteem. In keeping with his preaching he himself changed his name from David to Dharmapāla. The people listened to his sermons and attentively read his articles in journals and newspapers and were convinced of the truth of his philosophy. Gradually there came about a cultural revival. The people began to take pride in their religion, their language and their customs.

Above all, several younger men of his time joined the Buddhist forward movement to guide the destinies of future generations of Buddhists in Sri Lanka.

This great personality, who indefatigably gave his services for the revival of Buddhism in Lanka, India and other parts of the world, in his last days entered the Order as the Venerable Devamitta Dhammapāla Thera. He passed away in the year 1933, while he was in India. To perpetuate his memory Sri Lanka and India celebrated his birth centenary in 1964–1965.

47. Buddhism in Sri Lanka in the First Half of the Twentieth Century

The leading men in the Buddhist community at the beginning of the twentieth century were inspired by the activities of Anagārika Dharmapāla and they formed into organised bodies for the promotion of the Buddhist revivalist movement. Among them were great personalities such as Sir D. B. Jayatilleke, F. R. Somnayake, Valisinha Harishchandra and W. A. de Silva. To them the Buddhist revival was the national revival. These prominent men, whose names have gone into history, became active members of leading Buddhist associations like the Buddhist Theosophical Society (founded 1880), the Colombo Young Men's Buddhist Association (1898), the Maha Bodhi Society (1891), and the Ceylon Buddhist Congress (1918), and worked with remarkable success to achieve the aims and objects of those organisations. Through such organisations these Buddhist leaders were able to unite and bring together all Buddhists in Sri Lanka, to inspire them to be active, to collect funds for educational and other religious purposes, to give the Buddhist children a sound religious and secular education, to do a great deal of social work and to raise the spiritual and moral standard of the people.

A great deal of literary work was produced during this period. The Vidyodaya and the Vidyālankāra Pirivenas and their affiliated institutions, which numbered about two hundred, had produced many scholars who edited several canonical and commentarial works in the early twentieth century. Simon Hewavitarana, the youngest brother of Anāgārika Dharmapāla, had left a large legacy which was to be used for the printing and publishing of Pali books, and this greatly facilitated the production of books at this time. From about 1930 many modern scholars, both monks and laymen, have edited and published many more texts of Pali Buddhism and have also compiled several secondary works on the different aspects of Buddhism. To name these scholars and their publications is not necessary since they and their works are very well known.

A great enthusiasm was also created for the rebuilding of ancient Buddhist shrines in the old capitals of Sri Lanka. The Ruwanveli Dāgaba was the first to receive attention. The other shrines too were renovated one by one and today the old city of Anurādhapura has once more become a sacred city with the Catholic Church and the commercial sites which were in the city being moved to other places.

Sri Lanka has not only reorganised her Buddhist activities within the country but has also taken a leading part in sending *Dhammadūtas*, "messengers of the Dhamma," abroad. In 1950 the World Fellowship of Buddhists was set up in order to bring all Buddhist countries together, and several conferences were held in the subsequent years.

It is a very significant fact that this revival of Buddhism in the twentieth century was accelerated towards the middle of that century as a result of the Sinhalese Buddhist leaders of the time gaining control of the reins of government. Ultimately in 1948 Sri Lanka regained its independence after a period of British rule of 133 years. The Buddhist leaders who worked indefatigably for the cause of Buddhism were also the Sinhalese national leaders who led the struggle for liberation from foreign rule. It was therefore to be expected that when these leaders gained national freedom and took over the reins of government from the British rulers, they were mindful of their national faith and its culture and therefore took the necessary steps to set things right so that Buddhism would once more receive its rightful place.

48. The Buddha Jayanti and After

In the year 1956, on the 23rd of May, which was the Vesak full-moon day of that year, the Buddhists in Sri Lanka and other parts of the world celebrated the Buddha Jayanti. That was the 2500th anniversary of the Buddha's Parinibbāna, a day especially significant to the Buddhists the world over on account of the tradition that it constitutes half the life-span of the Sāsana and that from that year the Dhamma would flourish and spread far and wide.

The history of Buddhism in Sri Lanka from the closing years of the nineteenth century has clear indications that the prophecy, as far as Lanka is concerned, is coming true. In other parts of the world too it is seen that more and more people who were not Buddhists by birth are becoming interested in Buddhism.

The government of Sri Lanka, on its part, undertook numerous activities in commemoration of the Buddha Jayanti. A committee of leading Buddhist monks and laymen was appointed to advise the government on all matters relating to the Buddha Jayanti celebrations. Arrangements were made to translate the Tipiṭaka into Sinhalese and compile an Encyclopaedia of Buddhism in English and one in Sinhalese as well. It was also decided to compile other books dealing with the biography of the Buddha, his teachings and the history of Buddhism. The completion of the renovation of the Daladā Māligawa (the Temple of the Tooth) in Kandy, before the Buddha Jayanti and to aid the reconstruction of the Mahiyangana Thupa were among its other undertakings. A substantial grant was also given to the organisation which was handling the construction work of a Saṅghārāma for the Buddhist monks at the University of Ceylon, Peradeniya. Arrangements were made to hold a World Buddhist Conference in Colombo in the following year.

From the Buddha Jayanti year it was noticeable that the Buddhists in Lanka applied themselves more keenly to the practice of morality taught in Buddhism while showing interest in the celebration of Buddhist festivals. More and more people observe the eight precepts on the Poya days and young children are given a sound religious education. The government on its part has given the necessary encouragement for this religious re-establishment. In

January 1959 the Vidyodaya and the Vidyālankāra Pirivenas were made two universities. The private Buddhist and Christian schools were taken over in December 1960 and are now managed by the government. The four Poya days of the month (i.e., full and new moon, and the two quarter moon days) were made the weekend holidays in 1966, instead of Sundays as in previous times. It has also been planned to start a new Bhikkhu University in Anurādhapura.

Sri Lanka has today about 6.5 million Buddhists, which is about 65 percent of her total population. There are nearly 6,000 Buddhist monasteries all over the island with approximately 15,000 monks. Almost all the monasteries in the island have their Dhamma schools where Buddhist children are given religious instruction on the Poya days (previously on Sundays). The Colombo Young Men's Buddhist Association conducts an island-wide examination annually for the pupils of these Dhamma schools. The children are provided with free books, by the Ministry of Cultural Affairs and prizes are given to those who pass these examinations, including one on the Dhammapada, and this association spends annually a large sum of money on the religious education of children. In 1956–1957, 163,180 children sat for the Dhamma examination.

The foregoing account will tell the reader of the vicissitudes that this great religion, Buddhism, had to face during its history of over 2,000 years in this isle of Sri Lanka. It had its tidal ebb and flow. During the four centuries of foreign domination Buddhism withstood all the assaults that almost crushed it.

Since Sri Lanka gained its independence in 1948, there has been a revival of the Buddhist religion and culture in the country, and this reawakening was particularly noticeable when the Buddha Jayanti was celebrated in 1956.

The progress achieved since the eighties of the nineteenth century may well be called remarkable. Yet, to the Buddhists of Lanka, this should not be a cause of complacency, for which there is no room in a world of change. It remains the duty of the present generation and the coming ones to preserve and strengthen these achievements against the corrosive forces of a materialist age, and to work devotedly so that the Buddha's message of Wisdom and Compassion may grow still firmer and deeper roots in Lanka and also spread its beneficial influence over the world.

ABOUT PARIYATTI

Pariyatti is dedicated to providing affordable access to authentic teachings of the Buddha about the Dhamma theory (*pariyatti*) and practice (*paṭipatti*) of Vipassana meditation. A 501(c)(3) nonprofit charitable organization since 2002, Pariyatti is sustained by contributions from individuals who appreciate and want to share the incalculable value of the Dhamma teachings. We invite you to visit www.pariyatti.org to learn about our programs, services, and ways to support publishing and other undertakings.

Pariyatti Publishing Imprints

Vipassana Research Publications (focus on Vipassana as taught by S.N. Goenka in the tradition of Sayagyi U Ba Khin)

BPS Pariyatti Editions (selected titles from the Buddhist Publication Society, copublished by Pariyatti)

MPA Pariyatti Editions (selected titles from the Myanmar Pitaka Association, copublished by Pariyatti)

Pariyatti Digital Editions (audio and video titles, including discourses)

Pariyatti Press (classic titles returned to print and inspirational writing by contemporary authors)

Pariyatti enriches the world by

- disseminating the words of the Buddha,
- providing sustenance for the seeker's journey,
- illuminating the meditator's path.

www.ingramcontent.com/pod-product-compliance
Lightning Source LLC
Chambersburg PA
CBHW020349170426
43200CB00005B/106
* 9 7 8 1 6 8 1 7 2 1 4 8 4 *